CW01281468

Minto Jung Thapa received his B.Sc. Econ (International Relations) from the London School of Economics (1969) and his M.A. and Ph.D. (Government and Administration) from the Claremont Graduate School in California (1973 and 1976). As a journalist he was a Political Columnist and Editor with the Himali Bela English language daily in Nepal. He received a Diploma from the International Institute for Journalism in Berlin in 1971. He studied Human Rights as a Visiting Scholar at Columbia University in the City of New York (1994/95). He joined UNICEF (the United Nations Children's Fund) in 1978 and served in a variety of assignments in South and South East Asia, the Middle East and New York HQ. He is now retired.

Dedications

To my parents, Lt. Col. Lalit Jung Thapa and Mrs. Lalita Devi Bista Thapa, and to my brothers Pratap, Toren, and Mahabir Jung Thapa.

Minto Jung Thapa

PUBLIC ADMINISTRATION IN NEPAL

A Survey of Foreign Advisory Efforts
For the Development of Public Administration in
Nepal: 1951-74

AUSTIN MACAULEY PUBLISHERS™
LONDON • CAMBRIDGE • NEW YORK • SHARJAH

Copyright © Minto Jung Thapa 2021

The right of Minto Jung Thapa to be identified as author of this work has been asserted by the author in accordance with section 77 and 78 of the Copyright, Designs and Patents Act 1988.

All rights reserved. No part of this publication may be reproduced, stored in a retrieval system, or transmitted in any form or by any means, electronic, mechanical, photocopying, recording, or otherwise, without the prior permission of the publishers.

Any person who commits any unauthorised act in relation to this publication may be liable to criminal prosecution and civil claims for damages.

A CIP catalogue record for this title is available from the British Library.

ISBN 9781786930361 (Paperback)
ISBN 9781786930378 (Hardback)
ISBN 9781528951975 (ePub e-book)

www.austinmacauley.com

First Published 2021
Austin Macauley Publishers Ltd®
1 Canada Square
Canary Wharf
London
E14 5AA

Acknowledgements

This book is dedicated to all who have contributed to the development of public administration in Nepal. Thanks are due to all who helped with the original study effort, especially in the collection of information for it. Among Nepalis who deserve much credit for this are Shri Nepal Man Singh Pradhan, Chief of the Civil Personnel Records Centre (the *Nizamati Kitab Khana*); Shri Tej Prakash Malla, Under Secretary at the Administrative Management Department; Shri Bhakta Bahadur Rayamajhi, ex-Secretary to His Majesty's Government of Nepal, and subsequently an Advisor with USAID Nepal; and Shri Rishikesh Shah, who was witness to the developments of the period, as a politician and diplomat, and as a scholar of Nepali history and politics.

Among Americans special thanks are due to Professor Dr. Merrill R. Goodall (Government and Administration), who was several times a foreign advisor and Visiting Professor in Nepal, and who was my academic advisor and dissertation committee chairperson, for his constant kindness and encouragement; and also to Professors Dr. George S. Blair (Local Government) and Dr. Hans C. Ruyter (Asian Studies), who were the other members of my dissertation committee at the Claremont Graduate School in California. The original study was facilitated by a fellowship from the Foreign Area Fellowship Program of the Ford Foundation. Special thanks for their support.

CONTENTS

Preface	11
Introduction	12
CHAPTER 1: DEFINITION AND SCOPE	13
CHAPTER 2: BACKGROUND AND ADMINISTRATION	17
CHAPTER 3: POLITICS AND ADMINISTRATION	36
CHAPTER 4: THE INDIAN MISSIONS	53
CHAPTER 5: GENERAL ADMINISTRATION	64
CHAPTER 6: THE CENTRE FOR INVESTIGATION AND INQUIRY	78
CHAPTER 7: ORGANIZATION AND METHODS	82
CHAPTER 8: THE INSTITUTE OF PUBLIC ADMINISTRATION	101
CHAPTER 9: THE CENTRE FOR ECONOMIC DEVELOPMENT	112
CHAPTER 10: TRAINING IN ADMINISTRATION	132
CHAPTER 11: PERSONNEL SYSTEM AND ADMINISTRATION	150
CHAPTER 12: THE PERSONNEL ADMINISTRATION ADVISORS	170
CHAPTER 13: POSITION CLASSIFICATION	184
CHAPTER 14: PERSPECTIVES ON THE FOREIGN ADVISORY EFFORTS	199
Appendix 1: OBSERVATIONS OF A SENIOR CIVIL SERVANT	209
Appendix 2: OBSERVATIONS OF A SENIOR ARMY OFFICER	210
Appendix 3: LIST OF FOREIGN ADVISORS	211
Bibliography	212
Books and Articles	212
Reports and Documents	216
Sources and Note	220

List of Tables

Table 2.1. Prime Ministers of Nepal (1800-1951)	20
Table 3.1. Prime Ministers of Nepal (1951-74)	50
Table 3.2. Turnover of Ministers in Selected Portfolios (1951-74)	51
Table 5.1. Staff Assigned to the General Administration Function. (Gazetted Class Officers)	74
Table 9.1. Academic Background of CEDA Permanent Officers	123
Table 10.1 Administrative Training Centre: HMG Staff Trained (1956-74)	143
Table 11.1 Gazetted Class Officials in HMG Civil Service (July 1973)	152
Table 11.2 HMG Civil Service Personnel	168
Table 12.1 Proposed Unified Civil Service	181

List of Figures

Figure 2.1 Civil Hierarchy in Rana Administration (1935)	34
Figure 3.1. Panchayat Structure: Village to National Assembly	46

Preface

This is a shorter and edited version of the thesis that was presented to the Claremont Graduate School in California, USA in 1976. There have been some changes, adding and amending, to enhance interest and readability. Some details such as questionnaires and some charts and tables have also been omitted. But the integrity of the work is maintained in its time and tense and context, because the general insights and messages still have resonance. Things have changed but they have not changed!

There is resonance in the much paraphrased reminder of the philosopher George Santayana that those who do not remember the past, or who do not learn from history, are condemned to repeat it. The ideologically driven compulsion to equate progress and "enlightenment" with routine damnation of the past is the same thing.

Introduction

In February 1951 Nepal emerged from the century of family autocracy of the Rana Prime Ministers. It was a century when the country was kept largely isolated and remained very largely undeveloped. With the "revolution" that overthrew the Ranas came the hopes and urgency of change and reform over the entire spectrum of national life – social, political, and economic. These new needs and aspirations placed immense strain upon the administrative system of government, which previously had been oriented primarily to the traditional functions of control and revenue extraction. In short there was an obvious need for administrative development in the country, and outside assistance was soon forthcoming for this purpose.

This work is concerned with those foreign advisory efforts which in the years from 1951 to 1974 sought to enhance the administrative development capability of His Majesty's Government of Nepal (HMG). By administrative development capability is meant the ability to develop a public administration system so as to enhance its capacity to organize effectively to realize the public purposes of government. Such a capability is the key to the sustained development of public administration in Nepal.

It is the general conclusion of this study that the foreign advisory efforts did not measure up to their full potential, and to the manifest need for the enhancement of such a capability in Nepal. They were lacking in central design and institutional perspective, and in coherence, coordination and consistency. They seemed to have been too influenced by the perspectives of the donor nations, agencies and advisors, and not sufficiently informed by recipient system needs, realities and perspectives.

A key deficiency was the failure to develop an indigenous and institutional capability for the development of public administration in Nepal. This curtailed the ability of the recipient system to make optimal use of the foreign advisory efforts, and of related assistance, including foreign education and training opportunities. But the Nepali side, and its leadership, must also be primarily responsible for the failure to better utilize such assistance, and for the failure to create the proper and more optimal environment for it.

CHAPTER 1

DEFINITION AND SCOPE

Organization is the basic prerequisite of administration. Organizations are social units or human groupings that are deliberately constructed or reconstructed to seek specific goals.[1] The basics of any organization are personnel, policy, and processes. That is, organizations are characterized by interacting humans, ends or objectives, and some rational direction of behavior towards achieving them, within some formal (and informal) structure determining relationships between the interacting humans. Organizations must be given resources necessary for self-sustenance as well as for achievement of the purposes to which they are directed.

Administration is about the operation of an organization. It is concerned with organizations as human entities and its essence lies in the direction, coordination, and control of human interactions for the attainment of certain given objectives. It is a social art. It is basically a socio-political activity, as is indicated in the definition of administration as "the capacity of coordinating many and often conflicting social energies in a single organism, so adroitly that they shall operate as a unity."[2] Administration as a deliberate activity is common to all organizations that seek a modicum of uniformity and predictability in their operations.

Public administration is the administration of the public services of a country in the best interests of the public. It is essentially a socio-political activity revolving around the formulation and implementation of policies and the distribution of values in society. Its scope is as broad as that of the government it serves. It is intimately linked to the processes of communication, political socialization, interest articulation and aggregation, legislation, and adjudication.

In developing countries the socio-political aspect of public administration is also to be noted. In such countries what little there is of trained expertise tends to be concentrated in government, with a good deal at its strategic levels. Careers in government are prized not only for their status and relative security but also because they give access to mobilized national resources that are so heavily under

---

[1] Amitai Etzioni, Modern Organizations (Englewood Cliffs, New Jersey: Prentice Hall, Inc., 1964), p. 3.
[2] Brooks Adams, Theory of Social Revolutions (New York, 1913), p. 216.

government control, actual or potential. Quite often people and parties are more concerned with "infiltrating" the public administration system, and with "protecting" their own access to it, rather than in promoting it as an open, professional, qualified and capable service that is dedicated to public service and to national development. The classical values of public service based on administrative neutrality and the politics-administration dichotomy, and the rule of law, can then become more myth than reality.

Also, there can be the worst of all possible outcomes when the practice of "democracy" moves from the ideal of "government of the people, by the people, for the people" (*prajatantra* in Nepali), to the reality of "government of the parties, by the parties, for the parties" or what some call "partocracy" (*dalatantra* in Nepali). Some would say that the self-serving claims of "people's democracy" or *loktantra* are in essence the reality of "partocracy" or *dalatantra* operating under the guise or mantle of "democracy" or *prajatantra*.

Public bureaucracies can then become elitist in thinking and behavior towards the people (whose public servants they are supposed to be), and become compliant tools of the oligarchies that control the political parties. The shift is from subservience to the home-grown autocrat or foreign colonial master to subservience to the party oligarchies and political parties, to whose ideological imperatives and political convenience the bureaucrats will have surrendered the service-oriented professionalism of the ideal civil servant, as well as the core ethics, professionalism and practices of public administration that is truly public.

It might then be challenging to ask to what extent administration is a part of a government whose primary if unstated purpose is the enrichment of those who control the political process (perhaps now in their newer manifestation as political leaders and political parties) or of those who are comfortably ensconced bureaucrats?

To what extent is the system of administration free of a "casteist" cum exam-oriented elitism and the "closed-system" mentality that goes with it? To what extent has administration in Nepal moved away from its orientation of control (social and political) and revenue extraction?

To what extent is administration in Nepal inclusive at all levels of its composition, and particularly at its highest levels, of the wide variety of the Nepali peoples? So how truly "public" is public administration in Nepal?

One of the declared policies of governments in developing countries is that of "national development", with heavy economic connotations given the concept. Because of the significant concentration of mobilized national resources under government control, it is government that must not only facilitate national development, but also plan and implement a greater part of it. This has given rise to literature on the subject of "development administration".

Basically this is the administration of the national development process, and it calls for new perspectives in public administration. There is need for a more progressive social outlook; for a greater people-orientation; for greater "inclusiveness" in composition and mentality; for broader time horizons; and in general for a more rational, planned, productive and genuinely people-oriented (as opposed to personal, communal, or political party oriented) approach to the disposition of all manner of national resources. And there is usually need for administrative development too.

Administrative development is an inclusive term including both reform and change. Administrative reform might be viewed as change aimed at conversion of something basic in an existing administrative system. It will also tend to have a moral or valuational tinge about it. The replacement of a system of seniority-based promotion by one of merit-based promotion might be considered such a reform. By contrast administrative change might be something much more material and physical, such as improving the general facilities available to civil servants, or increasing their salaries and making service conditions more attractive. It is less liable to disturb basic values and processes in an administrative system. Administrative development ought to be aimed at enhancing the administrative capability of government.

Administrative capability is considered to be the quality or state of the public administration system of a country to be able to organize effectively and efficiently to realize the public purposes of government. Administrative development capability might then be considered as the ability to develop the public administration system of a country with a view to enhancing its administrative capability.

Administrative development is a matter of deliberate human choice and purposeful human activity. Such development involves change and especially reform in a vital and sensitive area of government – that of public administration. Such development calls for suitable and sufficient and sustained political will from the powers that be in a given country.

This work is an attempt at survey and analysis of those foreign advisory efforts which between the years 1951-74 have sought to enhance the administrative development capability of His Majesty's Government of Nepal (HMG). It is based primarily on field study and content analysis. The work is based mainly on the study of foreign advisory assistance as manifested in the reports and memos of the advisors as well as on the less public material available in the possession of various donor and recipient organizations. The views of people directly and indirectly concerned with the subject area were also sought, chiefly by the methods of direct interview and via specially formulated questionnaires. This general sample included the foreign advisors, as well as Nepali ministers, administrators, academics, and intellectuals. Reports, statutes, rules and regulations, and related pronouncements emanating from official Nepali sources have also been looked into. Last but not least were books and articles pertaining to this subject matter and written by both Nepali and foreign writers. With the aid of all this the attempt was made to identify problems and developments in public administration in Nepal, placing them in the context of past experience and political developments, and to relate them to the foreign advisory efforts, and develop ideas about their suitability and effectiveness.

Public administration covers a very broad area of activity. There are "line" organizations instituted to take services to the people in such areas as public health, public safety, or education. The public is the direct client. Then there are "auxiliary" units which service the line units in such areas as budgeting and planning, accounting, supply and transportation. And related to both, and at the core, are the "staff" units charged with the general direction, supervision, coordination, regulation, and development of the public administration system of government.

This work is directed at this core area of public administration. It is the area of personnel and training, organization and methods, direction and coordination, and research and development. Developments in this core area of public administration will have a crucial impact on the development of the public administration capability to meet both the regular operational requirements of a country as well as its more novel developmental needs. The concern of this study is with the efforts to enhance the administrative development capability of His Majesty's Government of Nepal, with the development of capability at this core area of administration.

CHAPTER 2

BACKGROUND AND ADMINISTRATION

Nepal is a Himalayan kingdom where China and India meet. It is a mostly mountainous east-west belt of land, about 500 miles long and from 90-150 miles wide, occupying a roughly central position on the southern side of the Himalayan mountain chain of South Asia. It had an area of about 56,800 square miles with a population of about 13 million people as of 1974. Geopolitically speaking Nepal is a small country landlocked by the colossi of China and India. Functional access to the outside world has been primarily via the territory and air space of India. Nepal became a member of the United Nations in December 1955. Among members of the UN in 1974 it had a roughly middle position regarding size of population and territory but ranked much lower in economic development.

In its cultural and ethnic content Nepal must be considered a mixture of the Aryan heritage which also covers India in the south, and the Tibeto-Burman heritage which also covers Tibet in the north. Nepal is the world's only Hindu Kingdom. Lord Buddha was born in Nepal, where Buddhism is a significant religion that has developed in a uniquely symbiotic relationship with Hinduism.

Nepal as a nation-state was established in 1769 by King Prithvi Narayan Shah, who was then a *Raja* (ruler) of the tiny hill-state of Gorkha in western Nepal. His Majesty King Mahendra Bir Bikram Shah, who was the ninth monarch of the Shah dynasty, in an unbroken line of succession from Prithvi Narayan Shah, was succeeded by his son Birendra in 1972. Prior to its unification Nepal consisted of a multitude of petty states living a rather balkanized existence. King Prithvi Narayan Shah unleashed a dormant national energy that took Nepal on a rapid path of expansion along the southern side of the Himalayas, until it had reached the rivers Sutlej in the west (near the India-Pakistan border) and the Tista in the east (near the Sikkim-Bhutan border).

This drive was checkmated by the parallel expansionism of the British in India. In the Britain-Nepal War of 1814-15 the country lost about one-third of its territory to the British in the west, east, and south. The trauma of the loss contributed to Nepal becoming largely isolationist and introspective. It remained independent, though isolated in the British imperial shadow, till the British quit India in 1947. Apart from some tiny strips in the south and west, which they returned in 1816 and 1860, the British did not return the considerable territories that they had seized from Nepal. The lost territories became part of British India and of the India that succeeded it in 1947.

The Century of Rana Autocracy

The Ranas were a *Bhardar* (noble) family of the Kunwar clan of *Chettris* (the Hindu warrior-caste of Nepal). In 1846 their leader Jung Bahadur Kunwar emerged successful from the byzantine maze of intrigue and murder centering on the Royal Palace. The King, his two Queens (it was the custom for Shah Kings to marry two wives), and the Crown Prince were often at the center of rival power factions. This was a time when much was troubled in the state of Nepal. Since 1777, the Kings were often minors when they ascended to the throne, and ineffectual and whimsical when they came of age. It was the age of petticoat politics of rival junior and senior Queens. It was rather unusual for Prime Ministers to die peacefully in bed. (See Table 2.1).

The unsettling politics of the period was also reflected in the unrelenting and often gruesome political vendettas of rival *Bhardar* (nobility) families, such as some Pandes and some Thapas, among others. Decline and fall often presaged confiscation and death. Jung Bahadur Kunwar emerged from the distaff side of one of the Thapa clans (that of Prime Ministers Bhimsen Thapa and his nephew Mathbar Singh Thapa). Prime Minister Mathbar Singh Thapa was assassinated by his own nephew (his sister's son) Jung Bahadur! On the King's orders?

Jung Bahadur was the superior of all in guile and mayhem. He killed many in the established *Bhardar* families, and reduced their survivors to a state of fear and subordination. He reduced the King to puppet status and usurped the sovereign power that was inherent in the monarchy. He established a family autocracy that lasted a century (1846-1951).

He initiated a symbiotic relationship with the British in India. This facilitated Rana autocracy and the isolation of Nepal, and it provided the British with a loyal ally, stable buffer, and the famed "Gurkha" mercenaries.

Jung Bahadur Kunwar took care to give his power the formal gloss of legal propriety. He secured from King Surendra Bikram Shah three important *Lal Mohars* (Royal Decrees)[3] upon which was based the formidable power of the Rana family autocracy. A *Lal Mohar* of 5 May 1849 granted to Jung Bahadur Kunwar and his brothers and family the exalted title-cum-caste of *Rana*, with an ostensible lineage traced back to high-caste Rana princes of Rajasthan in India. The family name Kunwar was then substituted by that of Rana. With the grant

---

[3] An English version of these *Lal Mohars* is printed in Satish Kumar, Rana Polity in Nepal (Bombay: Asia Publishing House, 1967), appendix 3, and pp. 158-60.

of Rana status came other privileges, such as the right to marry into the Shah royal family; and exemption from the death penalty for taking the life of others!

Subsequent marriages had the effect of turning the Shah Kings into Rana descendants as well. With this assumption of Rana status the Kunwars exalted themselves above their fellow *Bhardars*, imposing upon them a relative inferiority of socio-political status and caste. It was a clever use of caste and sub-caste designations in a "brahmanic" value system, in which caste was tied to socio-political status and power. It was a manifestation of cast-oriented presumption also termed as "sanskritization" by some.

A *Lal Mohar* of 6 August 1856 granted to Jung Bahadur Rana (former surname Kunwar) the title of *Maharaja* (ruler) of the principality of Kaski-Lamjung. The grant was hereditary. As Maharaja of Kaski-Lamjung, he was also given the unusual authority to restrain both the King and the Prime Minister in the interests of the country and people! A little earlier on 1 August 1856 he had resigned and passed on the post of Prime Minister to his younger brother Bam Bahadur Rana. But after his brother's death shortly thereafter Jung Bahadur once again took the post of Prime Minister, as per the *Lal Mohar* of 28 June 1857.

Jung Bahadur Rana was granted (or rather took) powers that can only be described as total and absolute. He assumed the power of life and death, of appointing and dismissing to and from office, and of declaring war and making peace. Those who disobeyed him he could kill or otherwise deal with as he thought proper. He assumed full military, civil, and judicial authority. These powers were conferred upon him for his lifetime. The office of Prime Minister became hereditary within the Rana family. Jung Bahadur Rana, the Maharaja Prime Minister, became the de facto ruler of Nepal. The Shah King was retained as a virtual puppet for purposes of religious and legal formalism.

The Ranas developed an ingenious system for keeping the absolute power within their family. The office of Prime Minister was combined with the Maharaja-ship of Kaski-Lamjung. The succession to the awesome position of Maharaja-Prime Minister went not from father to son, but rather from brother to brother by seniority of age, until a given generation was exhausted, when it would descend to the next generation in similar fashion. The succession was confined to Jung Bahadur Rana, his six brothers, and their male heirs of legitimate birth and direct lineal descent.

The Ranas were prolific and their assumption of power was followed by an expansion in numbers. Their progeny were divided into three classifications. "Class A" Ranas were fathered within marriage from wives of caste-equivalence to the Ranas. "Class B" Ranas were fathered within marriage but were excluded from the roll of succession to the post of Maharaja-Prime Minister. "Class C" Ranas were fathered outside of full formal marriage, or from lesser wives of lower-caste status.[4] They too were excluded. Those who were excluded resented this induced inferiority, and were a source of disaffection within the Rana ranks. Some "Class C" Ranas provided assistance to the movement that toppled the Rana family autocracy in 1951.

Table 2.1. Prime Ministers of Nepal (1800-1951)[1]

(A) Pre-Ranas (1800-46)	Tenure[2]	Comments
Damodar Pande	1800-4	Executed
Ran Bahadur Shah[3]	1804-6	Assassinated
Bhimsen Thapa	1806-37	Suicide in Prison
Ran Jung Pande	1837	Dismissed
Ranganath Pandit	1837-38	Dismissed
Puskar Shah Chautaria	1838-39	Dismissed
Ran Jung Pande	1839-40	Executed
Fateh Jung Chautaria	1840-43	Dismissed
Mathbar Singh Thapa	1843-45	Assassinated
Fateh Jung Chautaria	1845-46	Assassinated
(B) Ranas (1846-1951)		
Jung Bahadur Rana	1846-56	Resigned
Bam Bahadur Rana	1856-57	[4]
Jung Bahadur Rana	1857-77	[4]
Ranuddip Singh Rana	1877-85	Assassinated by nephews
Bir Shumsher Rana	1885-1901	[4]
Dev Shumsher Rana	1901	Deposed by his brother[5]
Chandra Shumsher Rana	1901-29	[4]
Bhim Shumsher Rana	1929-32	[4]
Juddha Shumsher Rana	1932-45	Abdicated
Padma Shumsher Rana	1945-48	Deposed by his cousin[5]
Mohan Shumsher Rana	1948-51	Deposed by Revolution[6]

1. Prime Ministers or their equivalent. 2. Approximate periods in office. 3. He was the Regent (on his return from exile); a former King himself, he had abdicated some years earlier and left the throne to his son the infant King. 4. They died while in office (presumably of natural causes).
5. They were induced to leave office by their own Rana brothers and cousins on the "Roll" (of succession to the position of Maharaja-Prime Minister). 6. End of the 105 year old Rana autocracy following the "Revolution" of 1951.

---

[4] Some Maharaja-Prime Ministers did attempt to include certain of their "Class C" progeny in the roll of succession. But their successors would throw them back out of the Roll.

There were "Class A" Ranas with expectations of the Maharaja-Premiership who became impatient. In 1885 the sons of Dhir Shumsher Rana (Jung's youngest brother) murdered Maharaja-Prime Minister Ranuddip Singh Rana (their own uncle and Jung's brother and successor), and usurped the roll of succession for themselves. The sons and heirs of Jung Bahadur (some were murdered), and those of his other brothers, were then excluded from the roll of succession, and reduced effectively to the status of "Class B" Ranas.

The overall system of succession ensured that only adults got to be Maharaja Prime Minister. But the men at the top were perpetually discomfited by the impatience of other "Class A" Ranas below them, and by the resentment of the "Class B" and "Class C" Ranas not on the roll of succession.

Administrative System under the Ranas[5]

What follows is a brief outline of the system of public administration that Nepal inherited in 1951 from the century of Rana autocracy. At the apex of the system was the Maharaja-Prime Minister, whose position had been made hereditary within the Rana family. The power of this individual was bolstered by sheer military might. His authority was based upon the transfer to him of the sovereign authority that was normally inherent in the Kings of Nepal, whom the Ranas held in virtual captivity.

What was the nature of the sovereign authority inherent in the Shah Kings? It was based upon the theory that the King was a living God, and that his authority was divine in origin, thus he could not be held accountable to any individual or group. So the King was responsible only to his own conscience as guided by Hindu scriptural values (often interpreted for him by high-caste Brahmins such as *Raj Gurus* or High Priests), and as informed by his perception of the public interest. His sovereign authority was not based upon any prior social contract with the people, as with the Leviathan of Thomas Hobbes. Nor was it balanced by any natural rights inherent in man, as postulated by John Locke. Thus the right to life, liberty, and property was held by the grace and favor of the King. This was the sovereign authority usurped by the Ranas. The Maharaja Prime Minister was Nepal, and Nepal was his.

---

[5] A useful and very detailed account of the structure of Rana administration can be seen in H.N. Agrawal, "The Administrative System of Nepal: 1901-60" (D. Litt. thesis, Patna University, India, 1969).

Orientation

The administrative system of the Ranas was informed by the basic motives of control and exploitation. Control meant the perpetuation of the Rana autocratic system and the maintenance of the total and absolute authority of the Maharaja Prime Minister. In practice this manifested itself in an administrative system geared to the maintenance of law and order and the preservation of static system stability. Since the Rana autocratic system was centered in the capital at Kathmandu, this also meant the concentration of power there and the domination of the centre over the field.

The field administration system was unified in structure and prefectural in tone. The primary concern was with law and order and revenue extraction. The *Bada Hakim* (district governor) was the local reflection of the might and majesty of the Maharaja-Prime Minister in Kathmandu, who appointed him, and who also decided the nature of the authority and the period of tenure of each *Bada Hakim*. The *Bada Hakim* was the chief executive in his district, with overall responsibility for all government functions within it. It should be noted that the districts in Rana times were much larger and fewer than the 75 under the *Panchayat* system of government beginning in the 1960s. The judicial function in the district was also sensitive to the attention of the *Bada Hakim*. He was often the superior magistrate of his district.

The basic units of district administration were a *Mal Adda* (district treasury cum-revenue office), an *Amini* or *Adalat* (district court), and a *Thana* (police station) or militia unit. The *Bada Hakim's* power was enhanced by two factors: local political culture was limited, and perhaps even non-existent institutionally, and the forbidding natural terrain and very poor facilities for communication often gave him something of a splendid isolation from Kathmandu. But the *Bada Hakim* was no feudal governor owing only nominal allegiance to the Centre. He was an extension in the field of Rana autocracy in Kathmandu, with emphasis on control and revenue extraction, and its phobia for any real national development. Quite often he was a Rana himself.

The state of the districts was not left entirely to the district governors. There was also the institution of the *Daudaha* (Tour Commissions). They were ad hoc commissions sent out from Kathmandu to tour specified areas of field administration. They were constituted and empowered at the discretion of the Maharaja-Prime Minister. They were a reminder to those in the field of the reality of the Centre, and in particular of the might and majesty of the Maharaja-Prime Minister. In general the functions of the *Daudaha* were to report upon the state of the areas toured; to inspect the district administration there; to receive petitions and dispose of the grievances of the people; to decide local cases; and to issue instructions and mete out punishment. The *Daudaha* could be very powerful.

There was one that is said to have returned to Kathmandu with a *Bada Hakim* (district governor) in chains!

The *Daudaha* might be seen as ad hoc machinery designed to provide the Maharaja Prime Minister with information and answers alternative to that available from the established administrative channels. They were an alternative means of communication between the power in Kathmandu and people in the field. Used properly and periodically, they could have great value for administration and system maintenance. They would be the sort of equivalent of the modern external audit cum ombudsperson.

Fiscal exploitation was a major orientation of the Rana system of administration. This meant the generation of net annual surpluses at the national treasury, by stressing the collection of revenues, while discouraging public expenditure by the government. The surpluses so assiduously induced usually went into the private coffers of the Rana family, according to the disposition of each individual Maharaja-Prime Minister.

The penchant for converting public revenue into private income was enhanced in each Maharaja-Prime Minister by the fact that succession went to the next oldest, often brother or cousin, rather than directly to one's own children. It has been estimated by one source that the public revenues diverted to Rana family coffers amounted to some twenty-five to thirty percent of total annual revenues.[6] In effect Nepal seems to have become one huge Rana estate.

The main source of revenue appears to have been the land-tax. This was collected by *Mal Addas*, which combined the functions of district treasury and land revenue office. They were subject to the supervision of the district governor in the field and the *Muluki Adda* (literally "Home Office") in Kathmandu. The *Mal Adda* did not itself collect the land-tax. This was done by private agents appointed by the State. These agents were called *Talukdars* in the hill regions (*Pahad*) and *Jamindars* in the subtropical lowlands of the south (*Terai*). They operated within revenue sub-divisions called *Mouja* or *Thum*, which in effect became administrative sub-units. The *Jamindars* and *Talukdars* became hereditary auxiliaries of the State. Initially the *Talukdars* were compensated with land grants and the *Jamindars* operated on a contract basis. The *Jamindars* were put on a commission basis in the early 20th century, and the *Talukdars* probably in the last decade of Rana rule. The *Mal Adda* received these revenues collected. It had also to survey all land in cultivation and grade and assess it for tax purposes. It had to record this, as well as land ownership, and liability to the land-tax. It had to maintain land records and to keep them current.

---

[6] Satish Kumar, Rana Polity, pp. 87-132. Among sources he claims for his estimation are the Auditor General of Nepal and his Deputy in 1959. Both of these officials had also served previously in Rana administration for long periods.

One qualified observer of the fiscal administration system of Nepal thought this land revenue system was a "unique feat of administration" and expressed surprise that such a well-developed system of direct taxation had been introduced in the country.[7] It seems to have been a system that was both economical and effective for its purpose.

The *Mal Addas* were district treasuries and therefore charged with the custody and disbursement of public funds. Surplus revenues were transferred either to the central treasury or to district treasuries in income deficit areas. These transfers were made on the express orders of the *Muluki Adda*. The treasury function at the centre was performed by the *Muluki Khana* (Central Treasury), which was usually run in tandem with the *Kausi Toshakhana* (Central Pay Office). It is interesting to note that disbursements were made not to an office but rather to that specific individual within it who was accredited as an accounting officer. It seems that each office had an accounting officer, who had the responsibility for receiving funds from the treasury, making payments, keeping accounts, and submitting them to the *Kumari Chowk* (Central Audit Office) for final audit. These officers signed a bond with the *Kumari Chowk* when appointed, promising to conduct their functions according to the relevant rules and regulations, and to submit the periodical accounts in a timely fashion.[8]

This pinpointing of individual responsibility may have generated a general reluctance to handle funds. But it probably also secured a greater element of integrity in the handling of funds. The Ranas were concerned with the extraction and conservation of funds. A general reluctance to handle funds would no doubt have been a severe handicap in any development-oriented system of administration. But it suited Rana fiscal parsimony to perfection. From that limited perspective it was probably better to fix responsibility on an individual rather than lose it within the bureaucratic abstractions of an office or committee; and from that more limited perspective it perhaps facilitated control, and integrity, efficiency and effectiveness.

The Ranas were very concerned with the fiscal integrity of their subordinates. They appear to have insisted upon, and generally secured, a higher degree of integrity in the handling of public funds than has perhaps been the case since the demise of their autocracy in 1951. To some extent this may have been due to a generally higher degree of ethics that informed Nepali society at the time. This set of ethics was convenient to the Rana autocrats in that it called for the strictest

---

[7] Eric Himsworth, Report on the Fiscal System of Nepal (Kathmandu, Nepal, 1959), p. 78. This is a very good and authoritative account of the fiscal administration system of Nepal.
[8] Bhubaneshwar Khatri, "Disbursement of His Majesty's Government Fund and Accountability," Kathmandu, Nepal, 1968, p.8. (Typewritten).

integrity from the administrators, while allowing a much greater degree of license to the Rana rulers. What "democracy" (*prajatantra*) may subsequently have done in Nepal is to loosen-up ethical restraints, rather than to secure more responsible conduct in the handling of public funds. Integrity in Rana administration was also facilitated by the fact that the Maharaja-Prime Minister considered the public monies to be as his own, and took a close interest in the handling of these funds.

But in the post-Rana era the concept of public property and the need for integrity in the handling of public funds may not have been adequately appreciated. So "democracy" can often boil down to the theory of the jungle, where what belongs to all belongs to none, and thereby constitutes a source of personal enrichment for the often rotating elites who dominate and operate the political, administrative, and economic processes of the State.

The concern for fiscal integrity in Rana administration was reflected in the work of the dreaded *Kumari Chowk* (Central Audit Office).[9] This office was located directly under the Prime Minister. It appears to have enjoyed his close attention and support. Its audit authority was substantially enhanced by its power to impose punishment upon those it had identified as defaulters. It appears that appeals from *Kumari Chowk* sanctions were heard by the *Shrestha* Appeal ("*Shrestha*" means accounts), and that the sanctions of the *Kumari Chowk* were enforced by the *Shrestha Adalat* (literally Accounts Court). Both offices were under the Prime Minister. The *Kumari Chowk* was very particular about the timely receipt of accounts from the various treasuries and accounts officers. It combed their accounts very minutely to ensure their accuracy and the legality of expenditures.

Punishment for default could be draconian, and appears to have run the whole gamut from fines to imprisonment and public humiliation. In theory at least, liability for default went beyond the errant officials up to their seventh generation! The system appears to have been effective, though negative in orientation. Perhaps it was at one end of the other extreme of scant respect for integrity in the handling of public funds.

The auditing function in Rana times was not generally concerned with efficiency of expenditure or accuracy of accounts. The Maharaja-Prime Minister did not want the people to know what the national revenues were or how they were spent. Expenditures were subject to his discretion. There was no budgetary system as such.

---

[9] An interesting and historical account of the Nepali audit and accounts system can be read in R.N. Chatterjee, Report on the Accounting System of Nepal (Kathmandu, Nepal, May 1967).

And yet in Old Nepal budgets were not unknown. Records are still extant of Bhim Thapa's (pre-Rana era Prime Minister Bhimsen Thapa, 1806-37) military estimates of the 1820s, and it may be that Nepal was much nearer a system of modern financial administration prior to 1847 (the pre-Rana era) than it has been since.[10]

A perhaps more positive institution of Rana administration was that of the receipt and disposal of petitions (*bintipatra*), and the processing of matters and grievances raised in them. At the apex of this system was the *Bintipatra Niksari Adda* (Petitions Office). It was located directly under the Maharaja-Prime Minister. It appears to have been something of a quasi-judicial agency, since it was also the Court of Appeal for civil and criminal cases. Petitions were received directly at this office, which then referred them to the appropriate agencies for comment prior to their final disposal; the other agencies receiving these petitions would process them for dispatch to the *Bintipatra Niksari Adda* and Maharaja Prime Minister for final disposal.

The Ranas appear to have taken some sincere interest in the grievances of the *duniya* (common people), if only from a sense of noblesse oblige, and provided the grievances were not against the Ranas themselves! In 1907 the Maharaja-Prime Minister issued two personal directives (*Khadga Nishana Sanad*). One expressed concern that delays in disposing of cases may put the *duniya* to inconvenience, and instructed the Senior Minister (*Mukhtiyar*) to see that such petitions were sent up promptly for disposal by the Maharaja-Prime Minister. The other directive stipulated that petitions must be disposed of within seven to thirty-five days of their receipt.[11]

This system for submitting petitions and addressing grievances is something that had potential for later adaptation and development. It was based upon a certain sense of obligation towards the people that came with the holding of power and privilege, and on awareness of the benefits of keeping the people content.

The post-Rana governments and political elites claim greater enlightenment and people-orientation. Yet there is no adequate system for the receipt of petitions and the airing and resolution of grievances. There is need for some public system designed to attend to the felt grievances of both the citizen and the administrator. Such matters do not always need legal or "higher" political resolution. In a well-functioning system they can more often than not be resolved without the disposition of the law courts, the vagaries of the political process and parties, or the discretion of officials in the Palace Secretariat. Many people may not care to get entangled in the above processes, or know how to. So their

---

[10] Himsworth, Fiscal System of Nepal, p. 78.
[11] Agrawal, "Administrative System of Nepal," p.63.

grievances may remain unaired and unresolved. The piling up of repressed frustrations cannot be healthy for government and administration.

The Ranas did not evince any distinctive political will for national development. Such development would hardly have been in conformity with the static system stability that they desired. Yet they could not remain totally oblivious to developments outside of Nepal. And with the ebb-tide of autocracy came the increasing need to pre-empt criticism and opposition by adopting at least the formal gloss of public altruism. In the last three decades or so of Rana autocracy the administrative system acquired a nucleus of offices designed to at least keep a fingertip on the development process. It seems there were councils for planning, agriculture and industry; agencies for mining, handicrafts, horticulture, and cadastral survey; and a few foreign personnel were hired to serve in the forestry service and electricity department. But the administrative system was not development oriented, because the autocratic system it served was not informed by any real belief in the necessity for national development, or in the people's right to improved life situations.

The reality of the autocratic superstructure could inculcate some negative bureaucratic attitudes. It discouraged initiative and innovation. It engendered a reluctance to wield meaningful decisional authority, which was matched by a parallel disinclination to delegate such authority in any consistent and institutionalized form. It may also have encouraged a sort of "jackal" mentality manifested in undue humility towards superiors, arrogance towards subordinates, and assumed superiority towards the people. The administrator might think himself to be the servant of the ruler and the superior of the people, and develop a habit of assumed paternalism towards the people.

He might tend to develop an aversion to the handling of funds, and ignorance of the fiscal processes in administration; and have a limited and fragmented perspective of the administrative system as a whole. Perhaps Rana administration was informed by a general atmosphere of distrust, which was manifested in undue elaboration and duplication of administrative processes for purposes of check and counter-check. Thus a single transaction may have required six to eight separate signatures before being expedited. This might be called administration by distrust.

Organization

The Rana system of administration was one of acute centralization of authority in Kathmandu, and of concentration there of all civil, judicial and military authority under the control of the Prime Minister. The top levels of the system were generally reserved for Rana family members. The topmost levels were calibrated to the roll of succession, with "Class A" Ranas moving up a hierarchy of civil and military positions until they succeeded to the position of

Maharaja Prime Minister. All Ranas, and many but not all *Bhardars* (notables) in service, tended to hold military ranks and pay, though they might be occupying such civilian positions as District Governor, Judge, Chief Engineer, or Postmaster General. This fused civil-military system may be traced to the fact that Rana autocracy was based on military might, and administration was less for public service and more to facilitate control and revenue extraction. But it may have made for effective coordination, perhaps because of the socio-political homogeneity of its participants and their expectations of the system.

In the Rana autocratic system the King was confined to the purely symbolic status of Head of State. It was the Maharaja-Prime Minister who was the Chief Executive, and in him was vested the effective sovereignty of Nepal. The effectiveness of Rana government and administration lay primarily in the powerful position of the Maharaja-Prime Minister. It could be argued that this individual wielded too fused and total an authority. It could hardly be healthy that he was responsible only to himself. But an attractive feature of his position, and one much missed in Nepal after the Ranas, is that this head of government possessed authority that was more than commensurate with his widespread government responsibilities.

Actually it was Bhimsen Thapa, a pre-Rana era Prime Minister (1806-37), who had done pioneering work in creating a unified system of government under a strong Prime Minister. He conducted the effective government of the country, though the Kings under whom he served had remained the ultimate source of sovereignty.

The Ranas revived and continued the strong-Prime Minister system of Bhimsen Thapa, which provided the basis for effective government. But they went further than him when they usurped the King's sovereignty, which led to absolute government that was responsible to no one (Jung Bahadur had effectively neutralized and subordinated the *Bhardar* nobility as a possible source of countervailing power).

The second man in the Rana hierarchy of government and administration appears to have been the *Mukhtiyar* (Senior Minister), who it seems was also the *Jangi Lath* (Commander-in-Chief). In effect he was deputy to the Maharaja Prime Minister in all civil and military affairs. Rana administration was characterized by a very limited delegation of decisional authority. Most matters had to be sent upward for ultimate clearance by the Prime Minister. These matters appear mainly to have been routed via the *Mukhtiyar*. This put him in a very strategic position. The *Mukhtiyar* could be a very powerful individual, since he was also a successor to the Maharaja-Prime Minister, who was usually his elder brother, cousin or uncle. Perhaps the *Mukhtiyar* had a strong impact upon the policies and preferences of Rana government and administration. In practice he appears to have functioned as the head of the administrative system of the government.

This was a noted feature of the Rana administrative system – that the person charged with its direction, coordination, and supervision should be so strategically located to the source of ultimate authority. It made for greater coherence, consistency, and effectiveness. Government and administration after the Ranas seemed often to lack such coherence and proximity to real power and authority, and the matching of responsibility with authority.

Another interesting feature of Rana government and administration were the strategically located offices which performed central staff functions for the Maharaja-Prime Minister and the *Mukhtiyar*.

The Maharaja-Prime Minister was assisted by a central executive office called the *Khadga Nishana Adda* (Office of the Prime Minister's Seal). This Seal had to be affixed to all documents requiring his clearance. This must have meant a lot of documents, which would have been subject to scrutiny and possible amendment by this office; and many major documents might have originated there. In it the Maharaja-Prime Minister had an executive office through which he had a directive and supervisory watch over the entire system of government.

The other centrally located office, and the one of major interest for administrative purposes, was the powerful *Muluki Adda* (Home Office). It was located directly under the *Mukhtiyar*, and functioned as the central office of administration. The functional sweep of the *Muluki Adda* might be indicated by a brief mention of some of its subordinate and satellite offices:

1. The *Ain-Sawal Phant* (Rules and Regulations Office) appears to have been responsible for the drafting, amendment, repeal, and codification of all laws, rules and regulations. It also determined the staff-strength of the various government offices and specified the amounts of money that they were to receive on account of recurring expenses like pay and stationery.

2. The *Purji Phant* (Authorization Office) appears to have been responsible for issuing authorization to the various offices of government, specifying their authority and functions.

3. The *Adda Janch* (Inspection Office) inspected work-performance at the various government offices in the Kathmandu Valley (containing the cities of Kathmandu, Patan, and Bhadgaon). It reported to the *Mukhtiyar*, who would decide on necessary improvements or what punishment to give to erring officials.

4. The *Haziri Goswara* (Personnel Attendance Office) checked on the attendance of officials at their places of work in the Kathmandu Valley. Even schools and the military were subject to check. It appears that the methods relied on were spot checks of actual attendance, and a regular check of the attendance

registers at the government offices. This *Goswara* recommended fines or other punishment (dismissal for habitual offenders) to the *Mukhtiyar*.

5. The Report *Niksari Phant* (Report Section) received reports from the field on various administrative matters and sent back instructions on the same. It was organized into separate sections for the Kathmandu Valley, the *Pahad* (hills), and the *Madhesh* (southern sub-tropical lowlands generally called the *Terai*). It seems the district governors (*Bada Hakim*) reported through this section to the *Muluki Adda* and thence to the *Mukhtiyar* and Maharaja-Prime Minister. This seems to have been the normal chain of command in field administration.

6. Revenue administration received the particular attention of two offices: the *Nepal-Pahad Bandobast Phant* for the Kathmandu Valley and Hills, and *Madhesh Bandobast Phant* for the south. The *Mal Addas* (district treasuries cum revenue offices) were subject to direction by these two sections.

7. The *Maskewari Janch Phant* (Central Accounts Section) appears to have been responsible for the proper functioning of the accounts and audit system of the government. It seems it also consolidated national revenues and expenditure for the personal information of the Maharaja-Prime Minister. The consolidation appears to have been done on the basis of monthly reports of income and disbursements received from the central and district treasuries.

8. The *Kitab Khana* (Personnel Records Office) was located directly under the *Mukhtiyar*, and may have operated as a satellite of the *Muluki Adda*. Its *Darshan Phant* (Audience Section) presented aspirants for government service to the Maharaja-Prime Minister for approval. In theory every position in government had to be filled with his approval. The *Darta Phant* (Registration Section) kept the personnel records of government servants, and also functioned as a placement section. The *Kitab Khana* also had to inspect and pass the monthly payroll of the government offices for release of salary by the Central Pay Office. It also administered the process of *Pajani* (annual evaluation of government personnel) for decision on their promotion, demotion, transfer, renewal or dismissal (*baduwa, ghatuwa, saruwa, thamauti* or *khosuwa*).

It appears that the *Muluki Adda* was responsible for the supervision of general administration, personnel administration, and revenue and field administration. In effect its supervisory scope covered the entire range of civil administration. As the central office of administration, it seems to have been well situated to do its job. It operated as the principal office of the *Mukhtiyar*, and it had the leadership, status and level of authority that was consonant with its administration-wide responsibility.

It has been claimed that Rana administration was run on the basis of the sudden flashes of intuition and wishes of the Maharaja-Prime Minister.[12] This may be a little bit dramatic. The Ranas had inherited, and had built up, a quite elaborate system of administration. This system had its structure, processes, and

---

[12] Anirudha Gupta, Politics in Nepal (Bombay: Allied Publishers Pvt. Ltd., 1964), p. 15.

norms. It was run on the basis of a detailed framework of laws (*Ain*) and rules and regulations (*Sawal*). It appears to have been the responsibility of the Rules and Regulations Section of the *Muluki Adda* to draft the *Ain Sawal,* and to periodically collect, consolidate, and codify them. The first consolidated code of Nepali laws, rules and regulations, was produced during the premiership of Jung Bahadur Rana (1846-77). The last Rana version was produced in 1935. It was called the *Muluki Panch Mahal Ain* (Consolidated National Code). It seems to have been quite detailed and elaborate, and in this respect it would have warmed the hearts of many bureaucrats.

Personnel Administration

The Ranas had a quite open, unified, and flexible civil service system (with regard to personnel administration). The minimum age for entry to government service was sixteen, and there seems to have been no maximum age restrictions on entry to government service, or on retirement from it. There were no particular grades at which entrants to government service must be inducted. This depended upon the discretion of the Maharaja-Prime Minister, who might be guided by such factors as need, the socio-political status of a person, and his academic and other qualifications.

It seems there were no specific levels of academic attainment that were required for entry to service. There does seem to have been an examination called the *Char Pass* (Four Passes). This referred to passes in the four subjects of accounting, arithmetic, handwriting, and administrative rules and regulations. The examinations, and the teaching leading up to them, were conducted by the *Shrestha Pathsala* (Accounts School), which was supervised by a *Raj Guru* (High Priest). The *Char Pass* facilitated, but did not restrict, entry to the lower clerical levels of service.[13]

Promotion was based upon three main criteria: the discretion of the Maharaja-Prime Minister; seniority or "roll-promotion", which was usually confined within a particular office or department; and merit, which was not precisely defined. There were fourteen grades within the civil service system, divided about equally between what might be differentiated as clerical and administrative levels. (See Fig. 2.1). This grade structure did provide ample room for promotion.

There were no rigid distinctions between clerical and administrative services, or generalist and specialist services. In effect it was a unified civil service system with scope for vertical and horizontal movement. But the super-structure of the system was reserved for Rana-family members. There was no clear distinction

---

[13]Pranchanda Pradhan, "Bureaucracy and Development in Nepal." (Ph. D dissertation, Claremont Graduate School, California, 1969), p. 93.

of civilian and military roles. It was common for officers with military ranks to be sitting in civilian posts. It was a relatively flexible system with much potential for adaptation and development.

In Rana administration there was no clear distinction between permanent and temporary posts. All posts were considered annually in a process called the *Pajani*, or the review of individual personnel records. These records were in the form of evaluation reports drawn along the lines of *Neki-Badhi* (pro-and-con). They were basically an evaluation by superiors of the strengths and weaknesses of their subordinates, with recommendations for action. Action might be in the form of *khosuwa* (dismissal), *thamauti* (retention), *baduwa* (promotion), *ghatuwa* (demotion) or *saruwa* (transfer). An official could be transferred to the administrative-limbo of the *Jagera* (Reserve), where he could be kept waiting pending subsequent posting. All posts were subject to *Pajani* (annual review), be they *Thulo* (senior, for Ranas and notables), *Nizamati* (civil), *Adalati* (judicial), or *Jangi* (military).

The *Pajani* was a denial of security of tenure or permanency, but in practice most civil servants could probably expect to enjoy a lifetime career in government. As the annual renewal of posts it did perhaps keep the bureaucrats on their toes. In Kathmandu the *Pajani* was carried out by the Maharaja-Prime Minister. It was a symbol of his absolute authority as previously it had symbolized the sovereignty of the King. The District Governors (*Bada Hakim*) conducted the annual *Pajani* in the districts.

The annual review of work performance is a normal function of many systems of administration. Perhaps the *Pajani*, with due changes for more open times, had potential for adaptation and development for the post-Rana period.

The personal style of Rana administration is highlighted by the institution of *chakari*. This was the practice of daily attendance by subordinates at the residence of their superiors, for whom they might also perform unofficial tasks. Related to *chakari* was the practice of bringing *koseli* (gifts) as *nazarana* (tribute) to the chief. There were gradations of *chakari*. There was *chakari* to the chiefs of offices and departments; there was *chakari* to Rana and *Bhardar* notables; and there were the grand *chakari* at the residences of the *Mukhtiyar* (Senior Minister) and the Maharaja-Prime Minister. *Chakari* played an important role in an official's career-development. Much ingenuity was involved in deciding which notable's patronage to cultivate.

Chakari facilitated access to superiors. It gave opportunity for airing grievances and transmitting information. It facilitated social and political control. But basically it involved a debasement of the individual. The Ranas perhaps looked to such obeisance as a confirmation of their own socio-political predominance. The particularity and the persistency with which the Ranas extracted deference may cause some to wonder just how secure they felt. Some would say that *chakari* has become an ingrained part of the social, political and administrative culture of the country.

Perspectives on Rana Administration

The administrative system of the Ranas was in effect one that was relatively unified, flexible, and also somewhat open in matters of personnel administration. These attributes were in some part due to the unchallenged authority of the Maharaja-Prime Minister. The resulting discretion was not necessarily manifested in sudden intuition or whimsy. But that it was based upon ultimately irresponsible authority was not healthy.

A noted feature of Rana administration was that the Maharaja-Prime Minister possessed the authority that was necessary to do his job. It looked to be a system with a strong Prime Minister who was clearly the Head of Government, and whose authority was commensurate with his responsibility or functions.

In the *Mukhtiyar* or Senior Minister he had a strategically located deputy, with a capability to facilitate unity in the administrative system. This was facilitated by the central office of administration (*Muluki Adda*), and by its satellite agencies like the *Kitab Khana*. Unity and coordination were facilitated by the clear chain of command going up through the *Mukhtiyar* to the Maharaja-Prime Minister, where the buck stopped.

At each level of administration there appears to have been a clear expectation as to roles played and individuals responsible. This appears to have been facilitated by the practice of granting documents of appointment and authorization to individual officials. These documents could be detailed, telling an official what his functions and authority were, how to conduct them, and what resources were given to him for the job. In effect they were a sort of job description against which subsequent performance could be checked. All this appears to have resulted in a unity and coordination that the civil service system seems to have lost in the post-Rana period. Some may say that there was also some loss of the flexibility and openness of the earlier time.

Figure 2.1 Civil Hierarchy in Rana Administration (1935).

Ministerial*	Reserved for Rana Family	

	Prime Minister (Supreme Commander-in-Chief)
	Senior Minister (Commander-in-Chief)
	War Minister (Senior Commanding General)
	Directors-General } Commanding Generals
	                          } Generals
	                          } Lieutenant Generals
	                          } Major Generals	

Administrative*	Open to non-Ranas	
	Bada Kaji *Kaji* *Sardar* *Mir Subba* *Subba* *Nayab Subba* *Kharidar-Ditha*	
Clerical*	*Nayab Ditha* *Mukhiya* Writer *Nayab Mukhiya* *Nayab* Writer *Bahidar* *Nausindha*	
Labour*	Peon *Tahalwa*	

* Illustrative categories only; there were no such strict distinctions in Rana times.
It should be noted that there were also officials holding civil or judicial posts but who had military rank.

The genius of the Ranas lay not in any capacity for invention and originality but rather in their sense of continuity, and their ability to adapt and elaborate upon that which they inherited. They knew what they wanted and fashioned an administrative system that was suited to achieve their purposes with economy and effectiveness. It should not be a surprise that the Rana century was rich in bureaucratic growth and elaboration. Autocrats are likely to value bureaucratic systems more than most. Such systems facilitate control and exploitation. But while condemning Rana politics, it might not be fully constructive to indulge in outright, blanket condemnation of the Rana administrative systems as well.

Administration is linked to politics, but it is also about structure, process and personnel. To damn and discard the latter, out of distaste for the politics, is a reaction that is not so productive or intelligent. What is inherited can be good and/or bad. The thing is to adapt and develop the positive, and to understand what was negative and why. That should have been the approach to perspectives on Rana administration.

It is interesting to note that there were eleven (11) Prime Ministers during the sometimes turbulent century of family autocracy of the Ranas (1846-1951). Jung Bahadur Rana held the post of Prime Minister twice. By contrast there were some sixteen (16) Prime Ministers or equivalents in the hardly twenty five years (1951-74) that followed the "revolution" of 1951! It might be observed from this that continuity of leadership and direction, and system stability, have not been hallmarks of the politics and *prajatantra* (democracy), and of the government and administration, of the "new" Nepal that followed the "revolution" of 1951.

CHAPTER 3

POLITICS AND ADMINISTRATION

The Rana Autocracy

The century of Rana autocracy (1846-1951) has been considered by some as something of a proverbial cave of darkness, out of which the Nepalis emerged with distressingly inadequate levels of political culture or social development. From the perspective of political development the Rana century has also been seen as a long dark age that did nothing to prepare Nepalis for the stresses and strains of the 20th century. The Rana family autocracy has been described by an observer as follows:

It was a blatantly unabashed military dictatorship run by and in favor of the Rana family. It was a system with no built-in correctives to absolute power. The Ranas were responsible neither to the King nor to the people. In fact to no one. In the interests of control and monopoly the borders were kept closed to (virtually all) outsiders coming in, and to most Nepalis seeking to leave. Education was not encouraged. Discussion of social problems (and any organization for this purpose) was strictly curtailed. The country was run for the benefit of the Ranas, with very few pretensions as to lofty motives.[14]

Nepal emerged from the century of Rana family autocracy with a literacy rate that was less than five percent. The same percentage appears to apply to the urban population, and to the people owing their living to sources other than agriculture. The people emerged substantially poor, rural, and illiterate. Their political culture was very limited. They had had no real experience of the processes of self-government. This limited political culture, and the associated lack of meaningful government experience, also applied to the relatively more privileged but subordinate elites under the Rana regime.

The Ranas had not cared to share their power with anyone. They had sealed off meaningful positions of authority for their own exclusive occupation. The others could only obey as subordinates, intrigue as favorites, and conspire as opponents. Such attributes are not the ideal basis for further political

---

[14] Betsy A. Goodall, "Tanka Prasad Acharya: A Political Biography" (Ph. D. dissertation, Claremont Graduate School, California, 1974), p. 37.

development. As for the Ranas themselves, it seems that a century of autocracy had had a negative effect on their political perspectives and adaptive capability.

A tendency to liberalism, however limited and relative, could be an occupational hazard in the time of the Rana autocracy. Dev Shumsher Rana lasted as the Maharaja-Prime Minister for hardly four months in 1901. He had relatively more liberal leanings, such as calling a public assembly at his palatial residence to discuss reforms; opening the country's first vernacular daily, the *Gorkhapatra*; and evincing an interest in establishing a network of vernacular schools throughout the country. He lasted in power for some 144 days, being deposed by his own younger brother and successor Chandra Shumsher Rana, whose son Mohan Shumsher Rana would do something of a repeat in 1948 when he pushed out his own relatively more liberal cousin Padma Shumsher Rana from the post of Maharaja-Prime Minister.

A few Ranas were a bit more sensitive to the realities of the 20th century and the needs of the Nepali people. But they could not succeed within the Rana autocratic framework. Padma Shumsher Rana was comparatively more liberal and was deposed by his cousin Mohan Shumsher Rana after less than three years (1945-48) as Maharaja-Prime Minister. To his cousins one of Padma's "dangerous" acts was to promulgate the Government of Nepal Act of 28 January 1948.

This Act was in effect Nepal's first "Constitution". It had been framed with the assistance of a panel of Indian legal experts led by Sri Prakash Gupta. This "Constitution" was a classic compromise between the principles and processes of parliamentary democracy, the reality of Rana autocracy, and the limited political culture of the Nepali people after a century of autocracy and isolation. It sought the best possible rather than the ideal best, to institute at least the form of parliamentary democracy and constitutional government. The substance was left to come later with practice and development.

Under the 1948 "Constitution" the Rana Maharaja-Prime Minister retained his "supreme authority". He was to remain the highest executive authority in the country. He was to govern via a Council of Ministers responsible to him, and whom he could select and dismiss at will. He had the power of absolute veto over Bills passed by the Central Legislature. He could decide "in the public interest" when or what questions, resolutions, or Bills should not to be put, moved, introduced or considered, by or in the Central Legislature. The Rana roll of succession to the position of Maharaja-Prime Minister was to remain inalienable and unalterable for all time. Which is a rather long time!

Some advances were envisaged. Fundamental rights were to be granted to the people, though "subject to the principles of public order and morality". Provision was made for limited-function, self-governing, local government bodies (*panchayats*) at the town and village levels. They were to be elected by eligible adult voters. The district bodies (District *Panchayats*) were to be elected from amongst the Village and Town *Panchayats*.

The 70-member Lower House of the Central Legislature was to consist of 60 percent members who were the chiefs of each District *Panchayat* plus some members elected by special interests (e.g. merchants and laborers), and 40 percent nominated by the Maharaja-Prime Minister. The Upper House members (about 30) were to be nominated by the Maharaja-Prime Minister to represent the major national interests and activities. Some ministers were to be selected from amongst the elected members of the Central Legislature. It would have Administrative Committees, of at least four members each, to keep an eye on the work of the various departments of government. There were to be an Office of the Auditor General, a Public Service Commission, and a High Court.

The Constitution did not give any power to the King, or restore his sovereignty. But it did raise him from the de facto status of puppet to the de jure status of a strictly constitutional monarch with a purely symbolic function as Head of State. But the 1948 Constitution was not implemented. The die-hard Ranas saw it as the thin-end of the wedge that would eventually finish off their absolute autocracy that had by then lasted for over a century.

The "Revolution" of 1951

The Rana autocracy was overthrown in 1951. Independent India played a very prominent role in this development. It provided a fertile and sympathetic soil for the Nepalis who organized to overthrow the Ranas. Leading Indian politicians such as the socialist Jai Prakash Narayan were intimately involved in the anti-Rana efforts.

India had already secured its special interests through the extraordinary "Treaty of Peace and Friendship between the Government of India and the Government of Nepal" that had been drafted in New Delhi and was signed in Kathmandu on 31 July 1950 by Ambassador C.P.N. Singh on behalf of India and the Maharajah-Prime Minister Mohan Shumsher Rana for Nepal. This was in itself unusual protocol! The extraordinary nature of the Treaty was highlighted by a separate and more confidential "Letter" signed by them on the same day that if anything reaffirmed the special status and the core interests of India.

Mohan Shumsher Rana had hoped that through his extraordinary "give" with the 1950 Treaty he could "take" or be guaranteed the continued support of the Government of India for himself and for the continuation of the family autocracy of the Ranas (as had been the case earlier when the British ruled India during the *British Raj*). He was wrong! Having secured its special interests through the extraordinary Treaty of 1950, the Indian Government proceeded to back the anti-

Rana coalition of the self-exiled King Tribhuvan and the Nepali Congress Party, which latter had been nurtured in India after it had gained independence from the British. The Indian embassy in Kathmandu had established surreptitious links with the then King Tribhuvan (a captive in his own palace), who on 6 November 1950 made a dramatic escape into the sanctuary of its grounds. He was flown to New Delhi by the Indian Air Force on 10 November 1950. The next day rebels of the Nepali Congress Party launched attacks into Nepali territory from the sanctuary of their Indian bases.[15]

The negotiations that followed were held in New Delhi between the Government of India and emissaries of the Rana regime. King Tribhuvan and the Nepali Congress Party were on the sidelines of the discussions. The "Delhi Compromise" that resulted from these talks could not have been achieved without the mediation and commanding arbitration of the Government of India.

Basically the compromise involved the return of King Tribhuvan as monarch; the election of a constituent assembly by 1952 to frame a constitution for Nepal; the formation of a coalition government for the interim period, composed equally of Ranas and members of the Nepali Congress Party; and Prime Minister Mohan Shumsher Rana was to stay on in his post for this interim period.

The India-brokered "compromise" signaled the end of the century of Rana autocracy. This end might be dated to 15 February 1951, the day King Tribhuvan returned to Kathmandu as the newly restored monarch.

It has been observed that the deciding factor in the struggle against the Ranas was the fullest Indian support given to the forces opposing them: [16]

Had the future of democracy in Nepal depended upon the decision on the battlefield, the cause would have been lost.......The decision was made in New Delhi, by the Indian government, though this was not admitted officially in quite such a crude manner. [17]

The looming reality of India in future developments in Nepal must be seen from this perspective. But how genuinely Nepali can such induced development ever get to be?

---

[15] The Nepali Congress Party that was formed in India in 1950 had its origin in the All India Nepali National Congress Party that had been created in India in 1946. Its leaders had been educated and nurtured there, and looked to Indian leaders for political tutorship, guidance, support and safe haven from which to launch activities in Nepal.
[16] Werner, Levi, "Government and Politics in Nepal: 1", Far Eastern Survey 21 (17 December 1952): p. 189.
[17] Ibid

The political change following the 1951 "revolution" constituted a reversion from Rana autocracy to Shah Rule. The King of Nepal regained the sovereign authority that his ancestor had been forced to surrender to the Ranas a century earlier. But the Ranas themselves remained a prominent force in the sociopolitical ecology of Nepal. They had forged intimate links with the Shah royal family through a century of matrimonial alliances. This gave them access to the Royal Palace and to the ear of the King. In the period 1951-60 three of eight Prime Ministers, or their equivalent, were Ranas, as were thirteen of the seventy four ministers of government. In the same period all of the four Commanders-in-Chief were Ranas. There were also the dissident "Class C" Ranas who had made common cause with the anti-government forces in India. They had contributed to the formation and financing of the Nepali Congress Party. After 1951 many "Class C" Ranas held important positions in government, administration, and the military. So 1951 was no catastrophe for the Ranas.

In the pre-Rana era the Kings of Nepal had shared effective political power with the powerful *Bhardar* (noble) clans, through whom they had conducted the business of government. But the Ranas had practically extirpated the *Bhardars* as an effective and operational factor in Nepali politics. In the post-Rana period there emerged some new political elites that might be characterized as being largely urban, middle-class, perhaps "professional" and "intellectual", with a greater penchant for party politics and associated political activity, and with a greater mastery of the rhetoric, if not the substance, of democracy (*prajatantra*).

Significant elements of these were upper-caste *Brahmins* (the Hindu priest caste), and to a lesser extent leaders from among the longtime *Newar* residents of the Kathmandu Valley who had had a long tradition of commercial activity and government service. A Nepali observer suggests that temperamentally, intellectually, and in lifestyle, these new elites were probably even further removed from the Nepali masses than were the *Bhardars*:

The educated class in Nepal belongs to the tiny upper crust of the privileged section of the society called the middle class as distinct from the majority of the people who live below the poverty line. But a large proportion of this middle class is itself subject to innumerable pressures because of its (relative) poverty. And the degradations of poverty can be resisted only with the help of a basic sense of integrity. Unfortunately for Nepal, the educated middle class in general has been found wanting in this regard. In recent years the gap between all of the educated modernizing elites – the political, the bureaucratic, and the military – and the masses has grown more rapidly and become much wider than between the traditional or feudal elites and the masses.[18]

---

[18] Rishikesh Shah, "The Political Development and Modernisation of Nepal: An Evaluation of the Prospect for Nation-Building", Kathmandu, 1974, p. 4. (Unpublished MSS)

The 1951 "revolution" might be said to have achieved some relaxation of the authoritarian temperament of government. It smashed the Rana monopoly of power and made for freer access by a relatively larger elite group to the top positions in politics, administration, and the military. But government and administration remained a largely elitist activity with a largely elitist temperament. In general the new elites did evince a much greater concern for the welfare and progress of the masses. While some were sincere, others were ineffective, lacking in comprehension, or merely calculating. The masses remained spoken for rather than speaking. In the decades to come the politics of Nepal consisted basically of the politics of interaction between and amongst the King and the new but relatively limited middle class elites.

The 1951 "revolution" was supposed to usher in a brave new world of parliamentary democracy in Nepal.[19] There was an "Interim Constitution" of March 1951 that was modeled after the Indian Constitution. It was supposed to provide the framework for future developments into the brave new world of "*prajatantra*" or democracy. It restored the sovereignty of the King, in whom was vested the executive power of the State. He was to govern via a Council of Ministers, and legislate with the assistance of an Advisory Assembly whose members were to be nominated by him. Two such Assemblies were convened by the King in July 1952 and June 1954, but they were both short-lived, ineffective, and a mirror of the inadequacies of the political groups. The stated purpose of the Interim Government was to create conditions as early as possible for holding elections for the Constituent Assembly that was to frame a constitution for Nepal.

It appears that King Tribhuvan had wanted to establish a system of parliamentary democracy and constitutional monarchy based on the British model. Perhaps the Nepali masses were not yet prepared for this alien and sophisticated system. It seems that the new Nepali elites were not much better prepared!

The unity of the political groups during their struggle against the Ranas broke down after the achievement of victory. Factionalism and civil unrest disturbed the country. Some 35 political groups vied for position and power. Disunity prevailed even within the major parties, particularly the Nepali Congress, the two most prominent leaders of which, the half-brothers M.P. and B. P. Koirala, could not cooperate.[20]

---

[19] From 1951-59 Nepal was governed in accordance with the Interim Government of Nepal Act (30 March 1951), also commonly called the Interim Constitution.
[20] Levi. "Political Rivalries in Nepal", Far Eastern Survey 23 (July 1954): 103.

The situation of Nepali politics in the 1951-60 decade has been put as follows:

Political parties were appendices of leading individuals rather than the representatives of fundamental principles and issue. The struggle for power among the various factions and individuals continued unabated, absorbing their strength and causing a paralyzing sense of insecurity throughout the country. On various occasions, usually when their rivalries forced the King to ignore them and govern without their participation, they formed a "united front" in opposition to the government. But these unions always fell apart quickly when the lure of office enticed one or the other group into the government camp. Neither the King nor important Indian friends were able to overcome the eternal rivalry between B.P. Koirala (Chief of the Nepali Congress Party) and his half-brother, the Prime Minister (M. P. Koirala), which was one of the fundamental disturbing factors in Nepali politics.[21]

During this generally unstable period the one center of reference for all was the monarchy, with its strength based upon accumulated tradition, the devotion of the people, and the loyalty of the Army. The monarchy was the prime force for stability and continuity in the country.[22] But the political leaders and political parties could not work with each other and with the monarchy to provide good governance and move smoothly towards a functioning system of "democracy".

The Parliamentary Interlude

Both the "Delhi Compromise" and the 1951 Interim Constitution had provided for elections by adult franchise to a constituent assembly, which was to frame a constitution. The elections were never held. B. G. Murdeswar, the Indian Legal and Constitutional Advisor to His Majesty's Government, pointed out in 1956 that there could not be two sovereigns in Nepal. It was the function of a sovereign to grant a constitution to the country. In Nepal this sovereign was indisputably the King. So King Mahendra caused to be framed, and subsequently promulgated, the Constitution of the Kingdom of Nepal (12 February 1959). It provided for the institution of parliamentary democracy.

---

[21] Levi, "Politics in Nepal", Eastern World (Nov. 1954), p. 11.

[22] Two Advisory Assemblies were convened by the King – one in July 1952 and the other in June 1954. The members were nominated by the His Majesty, with the aim of giving representation to the various political parties/factions being a major consideration. It seems that neither Assembly had any significant impact on government and legislation. It appears that neither the Governments of the time nor their Opposition were keen about the Assemblies. The first was dissolved in September 1952; and the second in June 1955.

There was to be a 109-member House of Representatives elected on the basis of direct adult franchise, and a Senate of 36 members, half of whom were to be elected by the House of Representatives on the basis of proportional representation, and half nominated by the King. The Prime Minister and Cabinet were to be responsible to the House of Representatives. The sovereignty of the King was left intact. He remained the supreme executive authority in the country.[23]

The subsequent elections of 1959 saw the Nepali Congress Party sweep into power. This party secured 74 of the 109 seats in the House of Representatives. The composition of the elected House of Representatives showed some of the vagaries of the 'winner takes all' system of parliamentary elections. The Nepali Congress Party had secured only some 37 percent of the total votes cast. Yet it secured some 68 percent of the total seats in the House – an overwhelming two-thirds plus majority with which it could virtually steamroller its preferences in that House. Also, only some 44 percent of the total electorate had cast their votes. This meant that the overwhelming majority of the Nepali Congress Party in the Parliament, and its capture of power, was based upon a favorable vote of hardly 16 percent of the total national electorate.

Such was the basis upon which the Nepali Congress Government of Prime Minister B.P. Koirala swept into office in May 1959. The Party had won by the superiority of its organization and resources, and the vagaries of the 'winner takes all' and 'first past the post' system of elections. It is a moot point whether this makes for "popular" government, given the limited political culture of the country at that time.

While B. P. Koirala had won, many of the prominent leaders of the other parties had been defeated, even humiliated, at the polls. Some may have thought that this taught them a well-deserved lesson. But it cannot have done much to secure their commitment to the parliamentary experiment. In fact it was soon politics as usual for the opposition factions. Some indication has been given here of how generally inadequate and chaotic that "usual" was.

Soon the validity and integrity of the general elections was challenged by some of the losers, perhaps with some justification. The Nepali Congress Government was also described as "anti-national and reactionary" by some opposition factions.[24]

---

[23] The 1959 Constitution was drafted by a four-man Constitution Drafting Committee appointed by the King on 6 March 1958. Two members of the Committee were leaders of the Nepali Congress Party. The Committee had the advice of Sir W. Ivor-Jennings, the noted British constitutional expert.

[24] Anirudha Gupta, Politics in Nepal (Bombay: Asia Publishers Private Ltd., 1964), p. 151. His source is "Resolution of the National Democratic Front", Kathmandu, Nepal, 1959.

The perennial feud of the Koirala half-brothers flared-up again when M. P. Koirala led a rival faction of the Nepali Congress Party into the opposition, asking that the King save the country from Nepali Congress "dictatorship." [25]

Prime Minister B. P. Koirala was seen by his rivals, and by others at the time, as a controversial and egotistical person with a basically autocratic temperament. Perhaps he moved too far and too fast, at least by Nepali standards and in the light of his limited electoral mandate. Perhaps he forgot that parliamentary government was still more a novel experiment than a well-established reality. He may also have taken the political opposition inside and outside Parliament less seriously than was wise.

Perhaps he could have done more to secure the confidence of the one solid and indigenous political institution in Nepal – that of the monarchy. The King himself may not have felt very comfortable with this Prime Minister with a seemingly overwhelming ego and passion for power. King Mahendra was himself a powerful personality. The politics of Nepal would have been very different if there had been understanding between these two leading figures. But sadly it was not to be!

It did not take long for Nepal to drift once again towards chaos and political uncertainty. The opposition factions were doing their usual to undermine the political situation. Riots and revolts flared up in several parts of Nepal. Rumors were rife in a Kathmandu that had perhaps become more than usually neurotic. The Government appears to have succeeded in alienating a broad segment of the people, including rather ominously, both the landlords and the peasants.

On 15 December 1960, King Mahendra dismissed the B. P. Koirala Government and dissolved Parliament. He had had enough of divisive party politics. A Nepali scholar, diplomat and observer noted:

The Nepali people hardly shed any tears for this sudden demise of the experiment in Parliamentary democracy. Their attitudes partly stemmed from the failure of the political elites in Nepal to adapt a modern western form of Government to a social milieu which lacked the necessary economic and political infrastructure.[26]

---

[25] Gupta, p. 159. His source is Naya Samaj, (Kathmandu) 9 September, 1960.

[26] Rishikesh Shah, "Nepal and India-Friends and Strangers", Nepal Council of World Affairs, (12 July 1968), p. 11.

The *Panchayat* System

The "parliamentary" Constitution of 1959 was replaced by the "*panchayat*" Constitution of 16 December 1962 (amended 27 January 1967). The *panchayat* aspect seems to have some resonance with the Constitution of 1948. The term "*panchayat*" appears to be of ancient origin and steeped in the Hindu cultural ethos of South Asia. Broadly speaking it would seem to denote the running of community affairs by a council of elders, and by consultation, and in this sense it might also be considered to be the equivalent of local and community self-government as it is understood today.

The traditional *panchayats* did not have the powers, scope, development roles and functions, or democratic establishment of more modern local self-government. Nor were they the electoral basis for a hierarchical pyramid of governing bodies culminating in a national assembly at the center. The system was perhaps capable of adaptation and innovation. Some thought that an adapted *panchayat* system might provide the basis for establishing a modern but indigenous system of government that would be suited to the developing needs of the country, while maintaining political and cultural continuity. But it would have required imagination, statesmanship, real devolution and sharing of power, and an innate dynamic for change and evolution.

The *Panchayat* System was established by King Mahendra as an alternative to British-style parliamentary democracy. It was supposed to be a "partyless" system of democracy with the political initiatives and energy coming from local communities rather than from centrally organized parties. The system was hierarchical in that every layer of government was based on the one below, with the foundation being the village and urban "*panchayat* councils" elected on the basis of direct adult franchise.

Originally, in order to be elected as a member of the National Assembly (*Rastriya Panchayat*) one had to be first elected to the primary units of the system – the Village and Town *Panchayat* Councils. Then one had to be successively elected by one's peers to the District *Panchayat* Assembly; the District Executive Council; the Zonal *Panchayat* Assembly; and finally to the National Assembly. This system of elections was supposed to put more political stress on the grass roots and local units of government than would be the case with the parliamentary system, since in the latter the members of parliament may be elected from constituencies in which they may have no genuine residential background or "roots", and which may also have little correlation to local units of government. Figure 3.1 below gives an illustration of the classic hierarchical structure of the new *panchayat* system of government.

Figure 3.1. *Panchayat* Structure: Village to National Assembly.

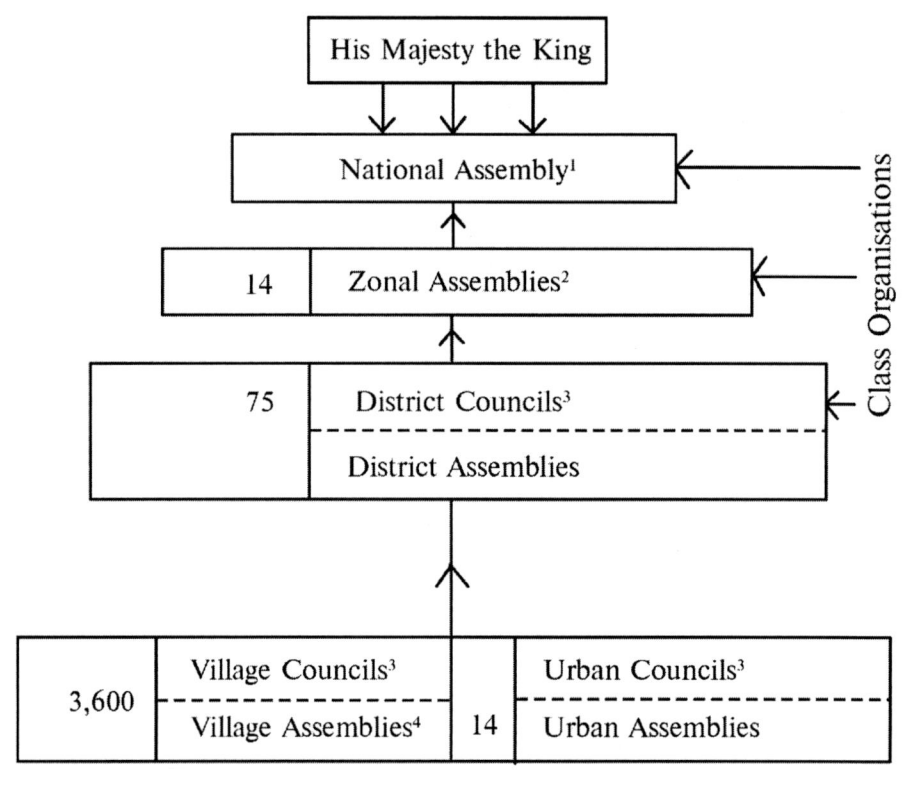

```
                    ┌─────────────────────────┐
                    │   His Majesty the King  │
                    └─────────────────────────┘
                          ↓   ↓   ↓
        ┌───────────────────────────────────────────┐
        │         National Assembly[1]              │ ←────────┐
        └───────────────────────────────────────────┘          │
                              ↑                                │
        ┌──────┬────────────────────────────────────┐          │
        │  14  │      Zonal Assemblies[2]           │ ←────────┤  Class Organisations
        └──────┴────────────────────────────────────┘          │
                              ↑                                │
        ┌──────┬────────────────────────────────────┐          │
        │      │      District Councils[3]          │          │
        │  75  │- - - - - - - - - - - - - - - - - - │ ←────────┘
        │      │      District Assemblies           │
        └──────┴────────────────────────────────────┘
                              ↑
        ┌──────┬──────────────────┬─────┬──────────────────┐
        │      │ Village Councils[3]│     │ Urban Councils[3]│
        │3,600 │- - - - - - - - - -│ 14  │- - - - - - - - - │
        │      │ Village Assemblies[4]│   │ Urban Assemblies │
        └──────┴──────────────────┴─────┴──────────────────┘
```

Note: (1). The National Assembly consists of 90 Members coming up through the constituency elections, and 19 Members elected from the Class Organizations representing Women, Youth, Peasants, Labor, ex-Servicemen, and University Graduates. The King nominates up to 15 percent of the total elected membership of 109 (90+19). This brings the total membership of the National Assembly to 125 (90+19+16) Members. (The Class Organizations are also supposed to input to the District and Zonal Assemblies). (2). The Zonal Assemblies are not governing bodies. (3). The Village and Town Councils are the executive governing bodies of the Assemblies, by and from amongst whose membership they are elected. (4). The Village Assemblies consist of the entire electoral body of a village.

In its current form and practice the National Assembly (*Rastriya Panchayat*) appears to be largely a consultative body to which the Government comes for debate and legitimation. It functions as a legislative body, but it appears to be primarily a body for debating and ratifying the legislation proposed by Government. The Prime Minister and Council of Ministers are members of the National Assembly. They are individually and collectively responsible to the King, who appoints and dismisses them; their function is to advise and assist the King in the exercise of His functions.

The Sovereignty of Nepal is vested in His Majesty and all power, executive, legislative, and judicial emanate from Him. These powers are exercised by His Majesty through the organs established by or under this Constitution and other laws for the time being in force keeping in view the interests and wishes of the subjects according to the highest traditions of the Shah dynasty.[27]

The *Panchayat* System may perhaps provide a promising basis for the political development of the country. It may have scope for innovation and development. Its basic premises appear to fit well with the local political culture. In its essence it is a system that is consensual rather than conflictual. It seeks to avoid the divisions of party factions and ideology that had made a mockery of the Nepali political process.

In theory at least it seeks to call forth representatives of the localities and the people, rather than fit them into the structure of party politics and ideologies. Its "grass roots to the top" structure of elections from village, town, district and zonal assemblies to the national assembly was supposed to ensure that people vote for leaders and issues that are closest to their level of reality. This might facilitate the comprehension of issues and problems, and the continued (as opposed to periodic) responsibility of elected leaders.

The *Panchayat System* was supposed to involve more people more directly in the processes of government than the parliamentary system it replaced. It drew inspiration from traditions of community self-government and consultation, and it had monarchy as a force for unity, stability, and continuity.

There is need for improvement in this *panchayat* system of government. The elites who run it could certainly do with more political maturity and personal integrity, and a broader socio-political vision and will for reform and political accommodation. Factionalism and consumptive drive for power have hampered political development. The "partyless" system and a stabilizing monarchy may have blunted some negatives, but more is needed to move to the positives.

It has been noted by some observers that the "partyless" system seems to be developing into a sort of one-party system with a reluctance to tolerate different perspectives, and with a loss of opportunity for participation for people outside of it and at the various levels of the hierarchy. There is also scope for making devolution and local self-government more of a reality.

There is also need to delegate more authority over the entire spectrum of public institutions, both political and administrative – whether it is to the Prime Minister and Council of Ministers; the National Assembly; the Village, Town, and District *Panchayats*; or to the organs and individuals of the administrative

---

[27] Constitution of Nepal, 16 December 1962, Article 20 (2).

system. There is need to give more substance to the form of these bodies. Some feel that the seeming tendency for effective authority to be gravitating towards the Palace Secretariat cannot be healthy; it tended to fuzz lines of authority and responsibility. This can result in a disconnect between power and public responsibility; those with public responsibility often do not have the meaningful authority to do what they must.

There also appears to be a tendency towards increased "governmentalism" – or the arrogation by the Government of more and more resources and activities of the nation and the people. This ought to be seriously considered and debated, less from the angle of ideology and more from that of scope and practicality. It would be naïve to assume that more government (and taxation) will per se bring more and better services to the people. Is there in Nepal the organization and discipline, dedication and integrity, will and vision, and quality of leadership that such *ipso facto* assumptions require? Perhaps No. So too much of "governmentalism" will benefit the elites, who control, influence and operate the government and administrative processes; it will be less likely to do the people themselves much good.

The sort of negative "governmentalism" indicated above, as well as an autocratic temperament in government, and impatience with the slow pace of development, could lead to the associated danger of technocracy in the political development process ….. the tendency to take the short cut and to have the skill-derived elites (technocrats) supplant and subordinate the community-derived elites at the effective levels of policy-making and government. The community-derived elites then tend to be used to ratify and do propaganda for issues decided elsewhere, by those other elites whose virtue lies in their possession of "professional" qualifications, but not in any ability to relate to the people, or to articulate and aggregate their needs and interests. This sort of development can widen the gap between the people and the processes of government, and present the Government with problems of legitimacy. It is worth noting that the administrative system might itself become more distant from the people, if its decisional levels are directed and dominated by technocrat elements.

Some observers see a tendency towards increased concentration of effective authority in the Palace Secretariat and feel that this tends to fuzz lines of authority and responsibility. Those with power often do not have public responsibility, and those with public responsibility do not possess meaningful and effective authority. Civil servants appear to sense a general inability of the Prime Minister and Council of Ministers to give them effective leadership. They feel that for leadership they must look to the Palace Secretariat, which to some observers appears to have established a clear predominance over both the Civil Secretariat and the Council of Ministers, and perhaps become the third and predominant institution of government.

Perspectives on Politics and Administration

The political development of Nepal has left much to be desired when it comes to the encouragement of administrative development in the country after the end of the century of Rana autocracy in 1951. The country had at the time a quite elaborate structure of administration that could have been the basis for innovation and development. It was a Nepali system whose elements went back to before the Ranas.

In the anti-Rana reaction after the "revolution" of 1951 much was discarded that might have been useful. The office of the Prime Minister was one such casualty. As one observer noted:

On its pinnacle of visibility, the prime ministership then became to the public mind a symbol and embodiment of Rana tyranny and oppression. When the Ranas were overthrown, the office of prime minister became a prime target of vengeance, and its deliberate erosion and diminution as a focus of authority became a game all could play. The approach did not at the outset follow the lines of adding to the responsiveness of that office, but rather to cut away at its significance, here and there, more in answer to emotional repugnance than to any logical theory of organization.[28]

Post-Rana Prime Ministers have not had the prestige and authority commensurate with their responsibilities. Their tenure in office has also tended to be much too short for them to hope to give effective leadership to government. (See Table 3.1). This has very seriously impaired the capability of government to operate in a coherent and effective manner. It has also deprived the administrative system of that strong executive leadership and support that is so badly needed.

The very high rate of political turnover in the Council of Ministers makes it very difficult for political superiors to give the requisite leadership and support to their administrative subordinates, or indeed to the administrative and national development processes. In the period 1951-60 there were eight Prime Ministers or equivalent, and nine Cabinets (plus three Cabinet reshuffles), with a total of 74 separate Ministers (some held office in several different Cabinets). In the years from 1960-74 there were five different Prime Ministers or equivalent, and seven Councils of Ministers (with nine Council reshuffles) with a total of 96 Ministers (some holding office in several different Councils). The total of Ministers for the period 1951-74 was 163. There were 13 different Prime Ministers in the less than 24 year period from 1951-1974!

---

[28] Betsy Goodall, "Tanka Prasad Acharya", p. 89.

Table 3.1. Prime Ministers of Nepal (1951-74)

(1951-60)	Tenure From	To	Months	Major Cabinet Reshuffles
Mohan Shumsher Rana	18 Feb 51	16 Nov 51	9	1
Matrika Prasad Koirala	16 Nov 51	14 Aug 52	9	
Kesar Shumsher Rana[1]	14 Aug 52	14 Jun 53	10	
Matrika Prasad Koirala	14 June 53	2 Mar 55	21	1
Gunja Man Singh[2]	14 Apr 55	27 Jan 56	9	
Tanka Prasad Acharya	27 Jan 56	15 Jul 57	18	
Kunwar Inderjit Singh	26 July 57	14 Nov 57	4	
Subarna Shumsher Rana[3]	15 May 58	27 May 59	12	
Biseswar Prasad Koirala	27 May 59	15 Dec 60	19	1
(1960-75)				
H. M. King Mahendra[4]	26 Dec 60	2 Apr 63	27	1
Tulsi Giri[3]	2 Apr 63	26 Jan 65	22	1
Surje Bahadur Thapa[5]	26 Jan 65	7 Apr 69	50	3
Kirti Nidhi Bista	7 Apr 69	12 Apr 70	12	
H. M. King Mahendra[4]	12 Apr 70	14 Apr 71	12	
Kirti Nidhi Bista	14 Apr 71	16 Jul 73	27	2
Nagendra Prasad Rijal	16 July 73	1 Dec 75		2

[1] He was designated Chief Advisor in the Royal Advisory Government.
[2] He was designated Principal Royal Advisor in the Council of Royal Advisors.
[3] They had the designation of Chairman of the Council of Ministers.
[4] At this time H.M. the King himself was Chairman of the Council of Ministers.
[5] Chairman of the Council of Ministers; then Prime Minister from 29 May 1967.

In the light of these very high turnover rates (see above and below) it may be too much to expect that senior ministers and administrators can or will give the administrative development process the sort of serious and sustained attention that it deserves. It may be too much to expect that the government process as a whole will get the sort of responsible and innovative leadership that it needs.

Table 3.2. Turnover of Ministers in Selected Portfolios (1951-74)

Portfolio	1951-60	1960-74	1951-74
Foreign	9(10)[1]	5(7)[1]	14(17)[1]
Defense	6(7)	4(6)	10(13)
Home	8(9)	14(15)	22(24)
Finance	5(6)	7(8)	12(14)
Transport	8(9)	9(10)	17(19)
Agriculture	10(10)	12(13)	22(23)
Forest	9(9)	14(16)	23(25)
Industry & Commerce	9(9)	8(9)	17(18)
Education	10(10)	9(9)	19(19)
Health	10(10)	14(16)	24(26)
Administration[2]	10(10)	11(12)	21(22)
Planning[3]	4(4)	5(6)	9(10)

Note: 1. Figures in brackets indicate the number of times the portfolios have changed hands. Figures outside indicate the total number of Ministers who had charge of the portfolio in the periods indicated. 2. The Home Minister is counted when Administration was not a separate portfolio.
3. After 1968, the Prime Minister was also Chairman of the Planning Commission.

The turnover of Ministers in charge of individual portfolios has been quite remarkable. See Table 3.2. above for the turnover in selected portfolios: the total number of Ministers who have been in charge, and in brackets the number of times that each portfolio has changed hands, between 1951-74. Where two or more Ministers have held the portfolio at one time, only the seniormost of the Ministers has been counted.

Table 3.2. indicates that in the 24-years period from 1951 to 1974 the Home Ministry has been led by 22 different Ministers, among whom the portfolio rotated 24 times; Finance was led by 12 different Ministers with 14 changes in the portfolio; Health has had 24 Ministers with a total of 26 changes in portfolio; and Education had 19 Ministers.

In the 24-years from 1951-1974 the General Administration portfolio was held by 21 different Ministers, between whom it was rotated a total of 22 times!

In this same 24-year period (1951-74) there were 13 Prime Ministers leading a total of 16 different Governments!

Public administration has suffered in the post-Rana years because there has not been the requisite capability to give the government and administration of the country the leadership that it has deserved, from the positions that have counted. Administrative development involves deliberate choice and activity, and vision and perspective. It calls for suitable, sufficient and sustained political will by the leadership of the country. Such a will appears to have been sadly lacking.

The frequent changes at the leadership levels of government have concentrated the minds of the Prime Ministers and the other Ministers on the basic problem of their own survival. They have therefore tended to possess neither the tenure nor the authority, nor the commitment and inclination, to concentrate their minds on and to give leadership to the national need for change and reform; and for the need for administrative development in particular.

There appears to be a general distrust against endowing officials with meaningful authority. The Rana autocrats had symbolized authority without responsibility. The reaction to their system appears to have turned this defect the other way around. Officials now tend to bear responsibility without consonant authority. This appears to arise from the negative expedient of securing responsibility and control by denying any meaningful authority. One reason may be that those who are in power are generally not willing to delegate authority when they themselves feel inadequate and insecure in what little of it they possess. It is not surprising that these and other problems in the system of administration are themselves a reflection of challenges in the larger system of politics of which public administration is a part.

It may also be noted that in the absence of a culture of constitutionalism in the country there have been, and will continue to be, problems with the rooting and relevance of "Constitutions" and with their durability and life spans. This lack of constitutional culture is all the more telling and unfortunate within the political leadership and political parties, and also within the individuals and collectivity of the "intellectual classes" and "professional groups" that are associated with one or other of these "leaders" and political parties. There have been several "Constitutions" in the past few decades of politics in Nepal.

CHAPTER 4

THE INDIAN MISSIONS

Independent India's attitude to Nepal was indicated in some speeches given by Prime Minister Jawaharlal Nehru at the Indian Parliament on 17 March and 6 December 1950.[29] He acknowledged the independence of Nepal, but asserted India's right to a special and exclusive relationship with it. This claim was an inheritance from British India, and was primarily geo-political in nature, though ethnic and cultural ties were also alluded to. The primary consideration was security directed against the actual or potential threat imagined to emanate from Communist China.

Like his British predecessors, Nehru considered Nepal to be at best an independent buffer within the framework of security and sphere of influence of India. The Indian Government tried to safeguard its perceived special stake in Nepal by encouraging the growth of political and administrative systems based upon Indian models and looking to India for advice and assistance. The idea was that India was both necessary and sufficient for Nepal, and what was good for India was good for Nepal; India would provide and development should imitate and follow the Indian example.

With the Rana autocracy gone, the Government of India felt some concern about the need for system and stability in Nepal. The struggle against the Ranas had had the effect of shattering the district administration structure in many areas, where some "freedom-fighters" had, among other things, looted district treasuries, burned and destroyed land revenue offices and records, and degenerated to the level of banditry. Things were a bit better in Kathmandu; but the administrative system and personnel there were quite often damned for their association with the Ranas and hence distrusted by the new leadership. The general political uncertainty and instability that followed the Rana downfall tended to have a paralyzing effect on administration.

In general the new leaders had little real experience of government and administration. They had been bred in the ideological ferment and conspiratorial politics of pre-independence India. They had been educated and nurtured in

---

[29] Jawaharlal Nehru's Speeches: 1949-1953, 2nd ed. (New Delhi: Publications Division, Ministry of Information and Broadcasting, Government of India, June 1957), pp. 145-46 and 176-77.

India, and looked to Indians for tutorship and guidance. They were not likely to sympathize with or to understand Nepali systems. These new leaders of the "new" Nepal did want some "modernization", but to them this invariably meant following Indian models as faithfully as possible. Their image of reality was strongly bound by their Indian inspiration and experience.

The First Indian Mission (1951)

In early 1951 the Government of India dispatched three senior civil servants to Nepal to render administrative technical assistance. Two were from the famous Indian Civil Service (ICS). These Indian officials were loaned to the Government of Nepal, which was to provide them with remuneration and other facilities as determined by the Government of India. Their initial appointment was for one year. They were to work from within the Nepali machinery of government, and as an integral part of it.

One was named Advisor to the Home Minister and one Advisor to the Finance Minister (both Ministers were Nepali Congress leaders); and one was appointed Secretary to the King. This appointment was formalized in the Nepal Gazette of 28 October 1951, which stated that all official communication with the King must pass through this very strategically placed Secretary on delegation from the Indian Civil Service!

In effect this Indian official functioned as Chief of the Royal Palace Secretariat, in a relatively novel post-Rana political scenario in which the tendency was for the King to both reign and rule. The intimate association of the Indian officials with the top political levels of the Nepali Government gave rise to discomfort and widespread anti-Indian sentiment in Kathmandu. Many Nepalis saw this as an unwarranted intrusion in the internal politics of their country, and as assistance to their opponents in Government (whenever they themselves were out of it). It was a time when Prime Minister Nehru took a personal interest in who should or should not be Prime Minister in Nepal and so advised King Tribhuvan. The discomfort was not improved when in 1952 Nehru sent an Indian Military Mission to do to the Nepal Army what the three civilian Advisors were to do for the government and administration.

It would not be inaccurate to say that these Indian officials functioned as de facto political advisors to their Principals. The late King Tribhuvan appears to have had the fullest confidence in his Indian Secretary, whom he consulted on a wide range of issues, including the formation of Governments and choice of Ministers. Some observers might argue that the emergence of the Royal Palace Secretariat as a key and proactive player in future developments in Nepal owed much to these initial post-Rana years, when the Senior Advisor from the Indian Mission was also effectively the Chief of the Royal Palace Secretariat and the Principal Advisor to King Tribhuvan.

The Indian Advisors sat at Cabinet meetings, apparently to initiate the Nepali Ministers and administrators into the mysteries of Cabinet procedure; and the Indian Secretary to King Tribhuvan appears even to have taken down the minutes of the Cabinet deliberations of the Royal Advisory Government (August 1952 to June 1953). The Indian Advisors also functioned as de facto legislators. Some of the legislation they drafted sailed through to the Royal Assent, without any adequate Nepali deliberation and debate. Two key pieces of legislation were the Emergency Powers Act of April 1951 and the Interim Government of Nepal Act of 30 March 1951.

This latter Act, also called the Interim Constitution, was drafted by the King's own Indian Advisor-cum-Secretary in less than three weeks. He had a M.Sc. in Physics, and had had administrative experience in the regulatory type of field administration for which the Indian Civil Service was renowned. This was an unusual background for writing Constitutions! The Interim Constitution appears to have been modeled on the Indian Constitution, and reflected the defects of undue haste and faithful imitation. It was not so very "interim" after all! It was the basis for government from 1951-1959.

The Indian Advisors did not understand the Nepali system of administration. It is not clear that they seriously attempted to. They tried instead to convert what existed into the Indian model and frame of reference that they were familiar with. The offices of Rana administration were converted into Indian-type ministries, departments and sections, with designations to match. This may have caused some confusion.

The huge Singha Durbar Palace of the former Rana Maharaja-Prime Ministers was converted into Civil Secretariat premises, housing almost all the principal government offices in Kathmandu. Some symbolism! Associations with this Rana Palace may have given what should be public administration a more grandiose air than was wise!

A series of rules and regulations were drafted to cover the entire scope of administration, including organization and procedure, personnel, finance and district administration. These were modeled on Indian manuals, and rules and regulations. A useful innovation was the Nepal Gazette, which was first published on 9 July 1951.[30] Government laws, rules and regulations, proclamations, personnel appointments and other announcements were henceforth to be published in the Gazette, to become official. All concerned were to follow what was printed therein.

---

[30] Nanda Lall Joshi, Evolution of Public Administration in Nepal (Kathmandu, Nepal: Centre for Economic Development and Administration, 1973), p. 19.

The Advisors were laboring in a difficult environment. One of them wrote to the writer, in a letter dated 19 September 1974, that:

Our biggest disappointment came from the political groups largely concerned with their own existence and with the maneuvering during the evolution of the democratic political system – I felt that the political climate which required many changes in the political set-up, did not furnish the correct time or the stability necessary for the introduction, the evolution, and the establishment of administrative change.

The work of these Advisors is a compendium of things that a critic might expect to find in attempts at transnational inducement of administrative development. The advisors seem not to have made any serious efforts to study the system of administration inherited from the Ranas. Rather there was a tendency toward wholesale replacement of existing organization, practices, and designations with those of the Indian type. This created some confusion and an unnecessary sense of discontinuity. The Advisors made no real effort to collect, codify, consolidate, and circulate the existing *Ain-Sawal* (rules and regulations), and to amend or repeal those that were unsuitable. They circulated substitute instructions which clashed with what existed, without however amending or replacing them. This appears to have caused confusion, and possibly some disregard for rules and regulations.

The methods and procedures introduced were lifted from the Indian Secretariat Manual and were not entirely suited to Nepali needs and conditions.[31] The resulting and rather incongruous mixture of the inherited and the imitated cannot have done much for coherence and consistency in administration. Take the changes in the filing system. The local system of *missils* (roll files) was replaced by hard-cover files. But the result was somewhat superficial. The new filing system was not fully understood. It was taken to mean the placing of paper one on top of the other, between two hard covers called a file. The precise arrangement of the papers and files via a suitable classification scheme was not understood; nor was the importance of matters like access, storage, retrieval and retirement fully appreciated. The filing job was often given to one of the more junior clerks in the office. Only he knew where a file or paper might be; only he could advise on the metaphysical questions about its existence!

In some cases the changes introduced may have been a retrograde step. The 14 (fourteen) grades of Rana administration, divided equally between the equivalent of administrative and clerical levels, were reduced to seven (three administrative and four clerical). Later, with the addition of one more grade at the administrative level, the structure remained substantially the same. It has been inadequate for purposes of career development. It has hampered the upward

---

[31] Ibid., pp. 13-14

mobility of deserving people and has given rise to some terrible personnel frustrations and debilitation of morale. Also, the more familiar Nepali personnel designations were substituted by Indian (British) ones.

Imitation is not always good, and this has proven to be the case with the Nepal Public Service Commission (PSC). This constitutional body was created in June 1951, pursuant to the relevant enabling sections of the 1951 Interim Constitution. It seems that the PSC was created and assigned its duties more in imitation of the Indian model rather than with any independent analysis of what would best serve Nepali needs. The section on the PSC in the Interim Constitution was lifted almost bodily from the parallel sections of the Indian Constitution. The PSC seems to have been designed with a primarily protectionist and regulatory set of functions. It seems to have been a quite inadequate instrument for locating and recruiting the best talent according to need and availability. The PSC, with its "constitutional" grip on the process of recruitment and appointment, had the effect of discouraging more timely and effective personnel administration, and the development of a central personnel agency capable of operating a coherent, coordinated, and a flexible system of personnel administration.

A critic points out that no agency of government was created to handle management improvement responsibilities.[32] The work of the advisors suffered from there being no central agency charged with coordinating technical assistance efforts in public administration, and developing perspectives on local needs and resources. No attempt was made to institutionalize an indigenous capability in the area of administrative reform. There were a set of offices within or allied to the powerful *Muluki Adda* (Home Office) of Rana administration that if suitably adapted (towards a more developmental orientation), and consolidated, might have made for an effective central executive office of government, to facilitate coordination and development in public administration. But this potential seems to have gone unrecognized.

There were also problems of communication. The materials circulated by the Advisors were written in English. They cannot have reached more than a limited audience in the Civil Secretariat. There were also complaints about the superior manner of the Indian advisors. Some felt that they had a style of operation that stressed imposition rather than consultation. One local observer felt that they treated higher civil servants like "cogs in a machine" rather than as "personalities".[33]

---

[32] Merrill R. Goodall, "Administrative Change in Nepal, " in Asian Bureaucratic Systems Emergent from the British Imperial Tradition, ed. Ralph Braibanti (Durham, N.C.: Duke University Press, 1966), p. 619.
[33] Joshi, Evolution of Public Administration in Nepal, p. 13.

On most occasions, they limited their consultations to the ministerial levels of government. Several Instructions prepared by the Indian officials did not even bear the signature of the Nepali Secretary concerned.[34] Some officials did express reservations as to the relevance of Indian models to the Nepali situation. But it seems that the Advisors tended to silence them with the rejoinder that these were policy questions – presumably to be decided at higher political levels. (See Appendix 1). Such attitudes and problems must have hampered the success of the Indian technical assistance efforts, and given them an air of elitism, and of transnational imposition.

When the senior Nepali Congress leader M.P. Koirala, newly appointed as Prime Minister, visited New Delhi in late 1951, he made two seemingly contradictory requests to the Indian Government. He asked that the three Indian Advisors be recalled to their country. It appears that he did not appreciate the political associations and influence they had established in Nepal. Two of the Indian Advisors were recalled in early 1952. But the Advisor-cum-Secretary in the Royal Palace was too strongly placed in King Tribhuvan's trust and favor to be budged. He stayed on till April 1954.

The other request made by Prime Minister Koirala was for the loan of some 300 Indian officials to work at various levels of Nepali administration![35] Prime Minister Nehru seems to have been quite startled by the request. He asked how the Nepal Government could expect to handle so large an influx of Indian officials, when the three Advisors alone had been the apparent cause of much discontent, and of anti-Indian sentiment. But he offered to send a three-man observation mission to identify Nepal's needs in the matter of administrative development and assistance. They arrived in late May 1952.

In April and May of 1952 Prime Minister Koirala hired the services of Dr. Merrill R. Goodall as his Consultant on Public Administration. Goodall was a Fulbright Research Scholar and Visiting Professor at Delhi University (1951-52). He was hired on the recommendation of Chester Bowles, then United States Ambassador to India and Nepal, stationed in New Delhi. Little could be done in

---

[34] Ibid.
[35] Nepal Administrative Reorganization Committee ("Buch Committee") Report. New Delhi: Ministry of External Affairs, Government of India, 1952, p.1 The figure of 300 is an estimate based upon the size of request indicated on page one:
The request was: for the Cabinet Secretariat 7 Officers of Under or Deputy Secretary status, 27 Assistants, and 5 Stenographers; for the districts 3 Commissioners, 16 District Officers, 16 Head Clerks, 16 Superintendents of Police, and 16 Inspectors; for the judiciary 2 District and Sessions Judges and a Registrar or Deputy Registrar. In addition teams of officials were requested for the departments of Jails, Forests, Posts and Telegraph, Supplies, Wireless and Telephones. (The Report says that the requests were formalized in an April 1952 letter to Indian Prime Minister Nehru by Prime Minister M.P. Koirala of Nepal).

two months, though Goodall did give the Prime Minister a Report on Administration in Nepal.[36]

Goodall argued that prospective technical assistance in public administration should be international in character; that no country had a monopoly of technology in administration; and that it would be prudent for Nepal to receive assistance in this sensitive field from a wide variety of sources. Goodall urged the Nepal Government to conduct an inventory of its administrative resources, particularly at the district level. He urged the development of a central executive office, so that the Prime Minister's responsibility could be matched by his capability in government and administration.

The urge for diversification of the sources of technical assistance in public administration was hardly likely to please the Indians, who at the time enjoyed a monopoly in Nepal. They felt this area was much too sensitive for any but themselves. This feeling may have contributed to Goodall's very short tenure in Nepal! The Government was very susceptible to Indian sensitivity and pressure.

But Goodall's brief appointment did perhaps contribute to thinking on diversifying technical assistance in public administration. It may have contributed to developing an awareness that besides India (and the experiences that had been gained from the many years of British Rule or *British Raj* in India) there were indeed other sources of excellence in the teaching and practice of government and administration. It might take some time for the realization of this to be grounded in the collective consciousness of the "elites" who dominated the political and administrative and "intellectual" landscape of the "new" Nepal, but the groundwork was at least being laid.

The Buch Committee (Nepal Administrative Reorganization Committee)

In late May 1952 the three-man Nepal Administrative Reorganization Committee or "Buch Committee" arrived from India. Its terms of reference were:

To study the organization of the civil administration in Nepal in the various departments at the centre and in the districts and make recommendations for its reorganization, and to assess the requirements of the Nepal Government of Indian officers to help them, the qualification of the officers required, and the period for which their services will be needed. [37]

---

[36] Merrill R. Goodall, Report on Administration in Nepal to the Prime Minister (Kathmandu: Government of Nepal, 1952).
[37] Nepal Administrative Reorganization Committee, Report, p.1

The team leader, N.M. Buch, ICS, was known personally by Prime Minister Nehru. He had been a principal administrative lieutenant to his Deputy Prime Minister Sardar Patel in his successful drive to absorb the former princely states of British India into the new Indian Union. Another member, K.P. Mathrani, ICS, had experience with the administrative integration of former princely states into the Saurastra and Bombay States of the new Indian Union. The third member, S.K. Anand, was a Deputy Inspector General of Police in Uttar Pradesh State, with which Nepal had a long border. Nehru met personally with the Buch Committee members. He advised them on the importance of their task and the need for system stability in Nepal. As with some other advisors, he appears to have alluded to the danger of communism gaining ground in Nepal!

The Buch Committee was given one month to do its job! Most of this time was spent in Kathmandu, with two brief forays into two nearby districts. It then returned to India to do its write-up. The Report that followed was marked "Confidential" and only one or two copies were given to the Government of Nepal. A Nepali observer said that there was no cooperation and coordination between the reporting and operating groups; even those who were supposed to implement the recommendations did not have access to the report. "The Report looked like superimposition," he added. [38]

A major recommendation in the Buch Report was for the deputation to Nepal of some 43 Administrative (Gazetted Class) officials and some 175 clerical level (Non-Gazetted) officials for periods ranging from six months to two years.[39]

The posts to be filled included such strategic ones as: 1. Chief Secretary of the Nepal Civil Service; 2. Superintendents in the Ministries of Defense, Foreign Affairs, Finance, and General Administration; 3. Secretary of the Nepal Public Services Commission; 4. Member of the proposed Screening Committee to screen all administrative personnel and decide who should be retained and who separated from the Civil Service; 5. The senior, and possibly both, Members of a two man Board of Revenue, which was to have administrative, appellate, and punitive authority over the entire structure of district administration, revenue collection, and customs; 6. A judge each in the Law Commission and the High Court; and 7. A number of the *Bada Hakims* (district governors), presumably for the districts bordering India.

Obviously this was to be a broad-based inducement of administrative change and retrenchment from within the machinery of government. It would also have given the Indian Government a firm grip on the administrative system of its sovereign neighbor. It would seem that the Buch Committee members were not

---

[38] Joshi, Evolution of Public Administration in Nepal, p. 16.
[39] Nepal Administration Reorganization Committee, Report, pp. 123-27.

very caring of, or were perhaps sublimely oblivious to, the growing anti-Indian sentiment in Nepal.[40]

They seemed not to have appreciated the sensitivity of the public administration function because of its intimate links with the political processes of government. The Nepali Government could hardly be expected to accept such a large influx of Indian officials, whatever Prime Minister Matrika Prasad Koirala might himself think, and the Buch Report suffered in credibility for having recommended it. It is small wonder that the Report was given an extremely restricted circulation in Nepal!

The major part of the Buch Committee recommendations dealt with regrouping or redistribution of functions among the various ministries and departments. This sort of thing can be quite glamorous, and is often a substitution of form over meaningful action. It is not easy to see any coherent rationale in the Buch Committee recommendations for reorganization. There is a spirit of retrenchment, and perhaps a desire for organizational neatness, and administrative convenience, as perceived by the Committee. But retrenchment in itself can seriously hinder the capabilities of an administrative system for its own development, and for development administration. It seems that the Buch Committee wanted to reduce the administrative organization to what it felt were the limited and necessary functions of the Nepal Government. But by doing so it might have actually had the effect of limiting the necessary functional scope of Nepali government and administration.

To this limited organizational perspective was added an inadequate development perspective. The potential of civil aviation in Nepal was hardly recognized in the quaint recommendation that the Civil Aviation Department be downgraded into a section of the Posts and Telegraphs Department![41] Nor can political development have been served by the curious recommendation that the Ministry of Parliamentary Affairs be abolished and its functions transferred to the Law Ministry.[42] Also, the Committee said that "There is no need for a Planning Commission."[43] The central planning function was to be handled by a Planning and Development Ministry, which was also to handle agriculture, mines and natural resources.[44] Planning was seen as the bureaucratic process of

---

[40] This sentiment was further inflamed by the arrival of a 150-man Indian Military Mission to reorganize, and presumably to Indianize, the Nepal Army. The mission came originally for one year, but continued in Nepal in various forms till about 1969. The presence of this Mission became a hot political issue in Nepal. (See Appendix 2 for the sort of disillusionment and sense of distrust that this generated within the Army itself).

[41] Ibid. pp. 134 and 45.

[42] Ibid. pp. 133 and 27-28.

[43] Ibid. pp. 135 and 47.

[44] Ibid. pp. 48.

aggregating the various development schemes of the ministries and departments. Agriculture did not even rate a separate ministry! In Nepal! The Agriculture and Irrigation Ministry was to be dissolved, with Agriculture going to the proposed Planning and Development Ministry, and Irrigation to go into a Works and Communications Ministry.[45]

A major defect of the Buch Committee Report was its failure to encourage or provide for such functional units as might constitute the nuclei around which future developmental capabilities might grow. There seems to be no recommendation for building up an institutional capability in the administrative development area.

The Buch Committee did recommend that a Chief Secretary or Secretary General be appointed in place of a Cabinet Secretary, and that the Cabinet Secretariat be amalgamated with the Ministry of General Administration.[46] This merger took place in 1952 and it resulted in this Ministry being reduced effectively to the rank of a Department! The disbandment of the Ministry of General Administration was possibly a setback and a missed opportunity for the development of a core capacity for the reform and development of the system of public administration in the country.

It may also be noted that, in Nepal at least, the merger of the political staff functions of a Cabinet Secretariat with the administrative staff functions of a General Administration Department does not seem to work very well. The political side tends to take on a prominence of its own, and the administrative side suffers, especially in areas like training, and research and development and capacity building.

The Chief Secretary at the helm of such an amalgamated General Administration Department tends to lapse into the role of a glorified Cabinet Secretary. He is unable to do justice to his other role of Chief of the Nepal Civil Service, and the key official giving direction and continuity to the development of public administration in the country.

As noted above, in 1952 the General Administration Ministry was merged with the Cabinet Secretariat, to become the Prime Minister's General Administration Department. But this Department was dissolved four years later, and its administrative functions went to the Home Affairs Ministry. The Chief Secretary post itself appears not to have been filled till 1955. The Buch Committee recommendations in this area may have enhanced administrative control, which appears to have been their main orientation, but they did little for administrative development.

---

[45] Ibid. pp. 133 and 135, 33 and 48.
[46] Ibid. pp. 19 and 24.

It seems that a useful part of the Buch Report was the section on Police and Jails, covering 24 pages out of its total of 168 pages. The Nepal Government asked Inspector General S.K. Anand (Buch Committee member) to stay behind for at least a year, to help with the reorganization and training of the Nepal Police Force. This he seems to have done well. This gave rise to the wry comment that the Buch Report was a "police report"!

Parts of the Buch Report were adopted over the years. But these appear mostly to have been confined to the perhaps more superficial areas of reorganization of the superstructure of administration – of the ministries and departments. The Buch Report cannot be said to have had any noticeably positive effect from the viewpoint of enhancing the administrative development capability within the country. It was too restrictive in spirit, and too imitative of Indian models. The recommendations that hint of any change, in personnel, financial or field administration, were faithfully modeled on Indian examples.

The Report was impolitic in its proposal for the deputation of some 200 Indian officials to work in Nepali administration. The Committee appears to have viewed Nepal like a former princely state of British India that was to be amalgamated conceptually, if not politically, into the political and administrative system of India. But Nepal had inherited its own quite elaborate system of administration from the Ranas, and from before the century of Rana autocracy. It had not experienced two centuries of rule by a metropolitan British power. Its needs and realities were somewhat different from that of the India that had emerged from the *British Raj*.

Some Observations

In the early days following the end of Rana autocracy the Indian technical assistance efforts may have helped to prevent a sense of general confusion from getting worse. But these efforts appear to have had no very noted success in enhancing the administrative capability of the Government of Nepal.

Whether this was a missed opportunity for development in this important field, or whether it was something that was not the basic intention anyway, is something that can be debated. The efforts to transplant Indian models to Nepal, and the general disregard for the indigenous system of administration, contributed to confusion in Nepali administration. Overall the Indian technical assistance efforts in public administration contributed a mostly Indianized system and form to government and administration, without contributing to any noted forward orientation, or to developing an indigenous capability for the development of public administration in Nepal.

CHAPTER 5

GENERAL ADMINISTRATION

In the first post-Rana Government of 18 February 1951 there was a General Administration Ministry charged with functions somewhat reminiscent of the *Muluki Adda* (Home Office) of Rana Administration. Its functions were varied: coordination of the work of different ministries; supervision of district work; appointments, promotions, posting and transfer of all *Bada Hakims* (district governors) and Heads of Departments; receiving general references from the Public Service Commission; overseeing general terms and conditions of service; dealing with matters of conduct and discipline of Government servants; coordination of internal security measures; *Adda Janch* (work inspection); and control of Guest Houses (not their maintenance).[47]

The General Administration Ministry had limited central personnel functions and was also responsible for Civil Service rules and regulations. It was also responsible for the supervision of district administration. But this Ministry did not have the strong executive support or strategic location of its Rana-era predecessor; it was put under one of the less influential Cabinet Ministers. Shortly thereafter in 1952 it was merged with the Cabinet Secretariat into a General Administration Department. This disbandment of the Ministry of General Administration, also recommended in the Nepal Administration Reorganization Committee (Buch Committee) Report of 1952, was possibly a missed opportunity, and a setback, for the development of a core capacity for reform and development of public administration.

Situating the General Administration Function

From 1951 the staff function of providing general direction, supervision, coordination, study and development of Organization and Methods, oversight of civil service rules and regulations, and development of the system of public administration in Nepal went through a bewildering array of locations and designations. The General Administration Department (that was created in 1952 through the merger of the General Administration Ministry and the Cabinet Secretariat) was also supposed to function as the executive office of the Prime Minister. It was put under the charge of a Secretary to HMG (after October 1955

---

[47] Nepal Administration Reorganization Committee (Buch Committee) Report (New Delhi, Ministry of External Affairs, Government of India, 1952,), p.147.

this person was designated the Chief Secretary and was thus effectively also the Head of the Nepal Civil Service).

But in May 1957 the General Administration Department was disbanded! Its personnel and general administration functions went to the Home Ministry, and the Cabinet Secretariat regained its separate identity. The Organization and Methods (O&M) Office that had been established in the Finance Ministry in August 1957 was also transferred to the Home Ministry in September 1958.

Then in February 1961 an Administrative Board was established by combining the O&M Office of the Home Ministry with an Administrative Training Centre (*Prashasan Prashiksan Kendra*) that was set up in 1959. This Board had the status of a separate entity outside any ministry; it was led by a Secretary, who reported to the seniormost Cabinet Minister. But in September 1961 this Board was sent to the Finance Ministry, where it became the Public Administration Department (PAD) under a Joint Secretary (one rank below a full Secretary). In May 1962 this PAD was transferred back to the Home Ministry!

In July 1962 this Department was given the status of a separate entity with the senior most Secretary of HMG as its Head, and he reported directly to the Vice-Chairman of the Council of Ministers (at this time the King was the Chairman). In April 1966 this Department (PAD) was disbanded! Its O&M function went to an Administrative Reforms Division, and the personnel function went into a Management Improvement Division, both within a reorganized Cabinet Secretariat. But the PAD's training function went to the Economic Planning Ministry as its Central Training Department. The Secretary of the disbanded Public Administration Department became Chief Secretary, and Head of the Cabinet Secretariat. Two years later, in April 1968, the Administrative Management Department (AMD) was set up. Into it went the Administrative Reform Division (including the O&M function) and Management Improvement Division of the Cabinet Secretariat, and the Central Training Department of the Economic Planning Ministry. This AMD had a separate status equivalent to a ministry, with its own full Secretary as its Head.

Foreign Advisory Inputs for General Administration

In its Report of 1952 the Buch Committee had recommended that a Chief Secretary or Secretary General should be appointed in place of the Cabinet Secretary; that this Chief Secretary should coordinate the work of all Secretaries; and that he should be Head of the Nepal Civil Service, while also functioning as Cabinet Secretary.[48]

---

[48] Ibid. p. 19.

It also recommended that the General Administration Ministry should be divested of responsibility for district administration and internal security, which should go to the Home Ministry, and that its other functions should be amalgamated with the work of the Cabinet Secretariat within a new Department to be headed by a Chief Secretary. So the Cabinet Secretariat and General Administration Ministry were merged into a Prime Minister's General Administration Department in 1952. But the Chief Secretary post appears not to have been filled till 1955.

District administration and internal security coordination went to the Home Ministry. The new location under the Prime Minister may have enhanced the status of the General Administration Department. But from the perspective of administrative development the value of the change was less certain. The amalgamation of the political staff functions of a Cabinet Secretariat with the administrative staff functions of a General Administration Department does not seem to have worked very well. The political side of the work that is normally handled by a Cabinet Secretariat takes on a prominence of its own. The administrative development aspect suffers, especially in areas like O&M, research and development, and capacity building.

The Chief Secretary heading such a composite Department tends to lapse into the role of a glorified Cabinet Secretary. He is generally unable to do justice to his role as Head of the Civil Service, and principal reform agent in administration. There has been a general distrust against endowing public officials with meaningful authority. Were the Chief Secretary to be given such authority then his post would be a very strategic one in the context of the coordination, reform and development of public administration. But the political leadership is not likely to give such authority.

It is interesting to note that the first Chief Secretary, Chandra Bahadur Thapa (1955-58), was actually accused of being "tyrannical" by one of the Prime Ministers whom he had served under (K.I. Singh, July-November of 1957)![49] No Chief Secretary was appointed during the parliamentary government of Prime Minister B.P. Koirala (May 1959-December 1960). An observer says that the position itself was abolished by it.[50] A successor to Chandra Bahadur Thapa was not appointed till April 1966, and some feel that they have since lapsed into the role of a glorified Cabinet Secretary.

As noted above, the composite General Administration Department that was created in 1952 as a result of the Buch Committee Report was itself disbanded in

---

[49] Bhuwan Lall Joshi and Leo E. Rose, Democratic Innovations in Nepal (Berkeley: University of California Press, 1966), pp. 220-21.
[50] Nanda Lall Joshi, Evolution of Public Administration in Nepal (Kathmandu, Nepal: Centre for Economic Development and Administration, 1973), p. 23.

May 1957. The Cabinet and ministerial coordination functions went into a Cabinet Secretariat under the Chief Secretary. Other functions, such as civil service rules and regulations, and personnel administration, went into the Home Ministry. The Home Ministry was a multi-functional organization oriented towards law and order, control, security, and regulations. It was unlikely to be able to give the personnel administration function the specialist attention it deserved. Nor was it a promising source of inspiration for administrative development in HMG. With this new arrangement the responsibility for administrative coordination and development was fragmented: the Home and Finance Ministries; Cabinet Secretariat; Public Service Commission; and so on.

Why precisely these various stabs at reorganization took place is hard to say. One possible answer is that administrative improvement was seen primarily as the task of improving the "integrity" of the Civil Service system, and the models looked to were mainly Indian, with a mentality that was perhaps unduly protectionist and inadequately developmental.

A casualty of this limiting and confusing perspective was the Chief Secretary post. It was vacated in June 1958, and not filled till March 1966. This did not enhance leadership and coherence in the administrative system. This lack of coherence in perspectives and leadership was manifested when, as noted above, an Administrative Board was created in February 1961 by combining the Organization and Methods (O&M) Office and the Administrative Training Centre (at the time both were within the Home Ministry). The Board had a full Secretary of HMG at its Head, and he reported to one of the senior most Cabinet Ministers. But in September 1961 the Board was demoted into the Finance Ministry, as the new Public Administration Department, under a Joint Secretary (one rank below a full Secretary).

This move seems to have been motivated by the belief that the Administrative Board was primarily an O&M unit with position creation responsibilities. Its job was thought to be that of processing the requests for additional posts, and changes in the level of existing posts, coming from the ministries and departments, and of advising the Finance Ministry on their validity, and on the number and level of the posts. It was a limiting perspective of the O&M function, and the role of the Administrative Board.

S.T. Divers (UK) was the then Senior Public Administration Advisor to His Majesty's Government from the United Nations Technical Assistance Program (UNTA). He seems to have been sometimes taken by surprise by the various and frequent stabs at reorganization. On 29 January 1962, he noted in his ninth progress report that:

A most hopeful stage has been reached. Public administration is now accepted fully as the keystone to progress. The Public Administration Department is in being and anxious to start active work.

This proved to be an unduly optimistic assessment of the situation. A month later, on 21 February 1962, he noted in an annex to his final progress report that:

The Department had been destroyed for all practical purposes. There is now but one Under Secretary and one Section Officer left serving (both part-time); all the remaining Gazetted officers have been posted away or are on leave. The organization through which the public services of Nepal might have become more efficient has been destroyed.

Divers had succeeded Hartvig Nissen as the UNTA Public Administration Advisor in early 1960. While in Nepal (September 1959- February 1962), he was also the local UN Correspondent (Head of the UNTA Program). He had been a Brigadier General in the British Army, and had then gone into the U.K. Civil Service, where he had reached the rank of Permanent Secretary. His mixed civilian-military background and senior status seem to have impressed many of his Nepali counterparts.

He seems to have enjoyed access to senior levels of government and administration. But he seems to have played an unclear role in the reorganization of the machinery of government. He left behind no formal reports. The various manifestations and migrations of the general administration function in government indicate that he had no great success in contributing to the institutionalizing of this function, or in establishing a core agency for administrative development in HMG.

Dr. Merrill R. Goodall (United States) succeeded S.T. Divers as the UNTA Senior Public Administration Advisor to His Majesty's Government of Nepal. Earlier, in April and May of 1952, he had served as Consultant on Public Administration to the then Prime Minister of Nepal. This time he stayed much longer, from March 1962 to August 1963. Goodall was Professor of Government and Asian Studies at an American university. The Public Administration Department, to which he was attached as Advisor, had had some reservations about his primarily academic background. The bureaucrats would have preferred someone more in their own image. But Goodall was a healthy influence. He brought an emphasis on institutionalization that was badly needed in the administrative development process in Nepal.

Goodall found that the advisory efforts had been piecemeal, uncoordinated, and even competitive. On the Nepali side, he saw no agency capable of giving these efforts coordination and continuity in accordance with a central design.

In his 30 April 1962 memo to the National Planning Council he urged that the Government appoint a specific committee to make an assessment of proposals in the administrative field. On 15 May 1962, the Government did appoint a Committee on Administration, with some senior Secretaries and Goodall as members. But the Council of Ministers did not give the Committee written terms of reference. It seems the Committee met only five times to discuss and consider revisions to a draft report prepared by Goodall, and its final report of 23 July 1962 was very substantially his own work.[51] It was not a very wide-ranging document. Goodall had felt that the fairly modest recommendations might at least gain worthwhile support.

The main recommendation concerned the Public Administration Department (PAD). A draft report of the Committee, dated 26 June 1962, had urged that the PAD be organized independent of any one ministry and that it be designed to serve all ministries and departments of government. On 8 July 1962, the PAD was taken out of the Home Ministry (to where it had only recently been transferred from the Finance Ministry in May 1962) and placed directly under the Vice-Chairman of the Council of Ministers (at this time the King himself was the Chairman). The PAD was also put under the full-time charge of the senior most Secretary of His Majesty's Government.

The final report of July 1952 recommended that the Public Administration Department be built into an effectively functioning organization to promote the quality of administrative operations in HMG. It stated that this Department needed assurances of greater continuity than it had so far enjoyed; that its junior staff members needed relief from the assignment of duty outside the jurisdiction of the PAD; that they needed the sort of professional training that comes from day-to-day practical work; and that young staff trained in public administration should be assigned to the PAD.[52]

A broad ranging program was outlined for the PAD, including: O&M surveys and production of a descriptive Manual of Government; conduct of pre-service and post-entry training in administration; development of an Institute of Public Administration with functions including internal consultancy, research, documentation, administrative training, and clearing-house activities; and coordination of foreign assistance covering administrative improvement programs.

Goodall felt that the Public Administration Department should be developed into an instrument for administrative improvement in HMG. Commendable progress was made in this regard during his tenure. The Department was given

---

[51] His Majesty's Government of Nepal, Committee on Administration, Report (Kathmandu, Nepal, July 1962).
[52] Ibid. pp. 9-10.

an enhanced status and location. Its Secretary was the senior most Secretary in HMG, with access to the King. Its strength had been built up from two part-time officials in February 1962 to fourteen full-time administrative class (Gazetted) officials, with a supporting staff of about twenty-four, by April 1963. Four of the officers had had administrative training abroad on UN fellowships. The fourteen officers constituted a promising collection of professional skill and dedication to improvement in administration.

The Department had developed an increasingly active role in the conduct of administration. It received copies of decisions from the Council of Ministers, and reported back to the Council on what departmental action, if any, had been taken in support of these decisions. The Public Administration Department (PAD) also had the functions of: Organization and Methods; administrative training; coordination of technical assistance efforts in public administration; and recommendation of approval or rejection of staff-increase proposals submitted by ministries and departments. Also, the Secretaries of HMG began to meet in weekly conference at the PAD to discuss administrative matters. But the Government balked at a key step that it might logically have taken – that of making the PAD Secretary the Chief Secretary of HMG, and therefore the Head of the Civil Service.

There were problems. It was not clear that the Government was fully conscious of the need for sustained and purposeful administrative development, or of the full value and potential of the Public Administration Department, which also did not receive the active and interested support of the country's leadership.[53] The Department was operating within a highly factional civil service. It attracted the opposition of those jealous of its status and functions, and not wanting them to be enhanced. Its Secretary had difficulty in mobilizing the trust and goodwill of some colleagues, and his strained relations with the then Economic Planning Secretary, who was also the Chief Foreign Aid Coordinator, cannot have helped. The Department also continued to suffer from general uncertainties of leadership and policy orientation.

Goodall did try to enhance the status of the Public Administration Department. In a 13 February 1963 memo to the Secretary of the PAD he urged that the Department be elevated and attached to the Chief Executive (at that time the King), as his Executive Office. He felt that such an Office should be directed by a Secretary General and become the main link between the Chief Executive and the country's growing administrative organization, and that the Office should assist His Majesty to see that His purposes were carried into effect. It would interpret authoritatively the objectives of Government to administration, and pull

---

[53] Merrill R. Goodall, "Administrative Change in Nepal" in Asian Bureaucratic Systems Emergent from the British Imperial Tradition, ed. Ralph Braibanti (Durham, N.C. Duke University Press, 1996), p. 624.

the diverse sections of administration into line with these objectives. It would "light a fire" under the administration! Goodall sent his memo to the King on 18 February 1963 after due consultations with senior Secretaries of HMG and National Planning Council members. There was no response!

The emphasis on His Majesty reflected the fact that at that time the King was concurrently the Chairman of the Council of Ministers, or Head of Government, as well as the Head of State. It might have been wiser if Goodall had specified that the proposed Executive Office should be under the Council of Ministers, as a diplomatic way of indicating that it should not be with the Royal Palace Secretariat. This was not clear. It caused some unease in the Civil Service Secretariat and in the Council of Ministers.

In his final report Goodall urged that the Public Administration Department be developed into a Central Executive Office of HMG.[54] The functions suggested were: to be the Secretariat of the Council of Ministers and of its Chairman; and to be the instrument for administrative improvement of HMG, capable of administration-wide initiative, stimulation, and coordination. But some in the Civil Service Secretariat may have worried that the grant of the proposed new and administration-wide authority and responsibilities to such a Central Executive Office of the Council of Ministers might divert the Public Administration Department from its proper role and function regarding the improvement of public administration in Nepal.

Sir Eric Franklin (U.K.) succeeded Goodall as the UNTA Senior Advisor in Public Administration (May 1964 to December 1966). Sir Eric (some say that he insisted on the Sir) was the sort of advisor that the Public Administration Department had been looking for. He had served with the Burma Cadre of the Indian Civil Service (1935-47), and later in Pakistan (1949-57) where he had been Chief of the Establishment Division of the Cabinet Secretariat. In that capacity he had also been principal advisor to the Prime Minister on all establishment matters, including Organization and Methods, training, and personnel administration. Given this background there was some apprehension in Nepali and UN circles as to whether he would adjust to the more modest role of an UNTA expert. He did! His status and background were an advantage in that he had access to the senior levels of government and administration, and he was listened to with some respect.

Sir Eric continued the support and advocacy for the Public Administration Department that his predecessor had begun. He was concerned with its status. He noted that: it had originated as an O&M Office and was still looked upon as such by other ministries and departments; that it was not thought to be, and was not

---

[54] Goodall, Development of Public Administration in Nepal. Kathmandu, Nepal, August 1963), p. 40.

yet, a Department with overall responsibility for the improvement of public administration; and that if the Department did not soon widen the scope of its interests and activities, it would disintegrate, suffer raids upon its staff, and revert to being a mere O&M unit.

In his Report on the Development of the Public Administration Department (September 1964), Sir Eric supported Goodall's recommendation for developing the Department into a Central Executive Office. He felt that this Office should have administration-wide supervisory roles and responsibilities. He proposed that it should be given the administrative leadership of the Head of the Civil Service, in effect by a Chief Secretary, who would report to the Chairman of the Council of Ministers. Sir Eric also wanted its functions and status as a ministry to be clearly specified by statute.[55]

But it is not clear that Sir Eric wanted the Public Administration Department to be merged with the Cabinet Secretariat into an Office of the Council of Ministers, as Goodall had recommended. It is not clear that he wanted such an enhanced entity for administrative improvement to be also given responsibilities for servicing the Cabinet.

Sir Eric also urged the transfer of the central personnel function from the Home Ministry to the Public Administration Department.[56] He pointed out that in recent years the personnel administration function was becoming increasingly a subject for specialists, and there was no reason why it should not receive the same specialized treatment that it was receiving in other countries.

He thought that the Home Ministry was a general and regulatory entity with a primarily law and order function. It was not likely to give the personnel administration function the specialist attention it deserved. It would be more logical to attach this function to a central office charged with O&M responsibilities, training, and coordination functions. In this respect Sir Eric was lending his advocacy to a felt desire of the Public Administration Department, and one that it had not been able to realize because of the opposition of the Home Ministry. In this, as with the Public Administration Department, he was a good advocate and catalyst for change.

In April 1966 the Public Administration Department became part of a newly established Cabinet Secretariat. The Department lost its separate status. Its Secretary became Chief Secretary and Head of the Cabinet Secretariat. This Cabinet Secretariat was given the following functions: to function as the Office of the Council of Ministers; to function as the Office of the Prime Minister; to

---

[55] Sir Eric Franklin, Report on the Development of the Public Administration Department (September 1964) p.p. 32-34.
[56] Ibid. pp. 25-26.

coordinate the policies and programs of His Majesty's Government (HMG); to deal with the personnel administration matters of HMG; to conduct the central Organization and Methods function of HMG: and to deal with matters relating to administrative reform in general.

But the administrative training function of the Public Administration Department was transferred to the Economic Planning Ministry, where it became the Central Training Department with its own Secretary. This looked to be a retrogressive step to Sir Eric. In his final Report he urged that the Central Training Department be brought back into the central office charged with administrative improvement in HMG.[57] He said that the administrative training function was related functionally to the central personnel function, and that it should be run in conjunction with it.

The Administrative Management Department

The composite Cabinet Secretariat set-up of April 1966 proved not to be a very good idea. The staff functions to the Council of Ministers did not fit in well with the focal administrative improvement functions of the former Public Administration Department. The Cabinet side of its work began to take on a glamour, insistence and prominence of its own, and the control function began to be stressed at the expense of the administrative improvement function. The Chief Secretary tended to lapse into the role of a Cabinet Secretary, unable to do justice to his other role as the principal agent for reform and development of the system of public administration in the country.

In April 1968 the former Public Administration Department was resurrected in the form of the Administrative Management Department (AMD). This AMD was separated from the Cabinet Secretariat and given the equivalence, though not formally, of a separate ministry, with the full- time leadership of a Secretary. Into it went the Administrative Reform (Organization and Methods) and Management Improvement Divisions of the Cabinet Secretariat, and the Central Training Department of the Economic Planning Ministry.

The AMD became HMG's designated instrument for administrative improvement. Its functions were:

1. Personnel Administration: functions relating to the Public Service Commission; administration of the law relating to the Nepal Civil Service; administration of the Nepal Administrative and Miscellaneous Services; and administration of the Civil Personnel Records Centre (*Nizamati Kitab Khana*).

---

[57] Sir Eric Franklin, Development of Public Administration in Nepal (Kathmandu, Nepal, December 1966), pp. 62-63.

2. Administrative Training: formulation of His Majesty's Government policy on training; survey and formulation of the training requirements of His Majesty's Government; coordination and evaluation of the different training programs conducted by His Majesty's Government; approval of the training plans and programs of different departments inside the country and abroad; and management of administrative training programs.

3. Administrative Reform: including Organization and Methods; and coordination of foreign technical assistance in public administration.

4. Miscellaneous: such as participation in international conferences on administration.

5. Publication and Library: publication of *Prashasan* (the Nepali Journal of Public Administration); and maintaining a public administration library.[58]

The Administrative Management Department had some 38 full-time administrative class (Gazetted) officers in 1974. This was a huge increase from two part-timers that the former Public Administration Department had in February 1962, or the 14 officers that it had as of April 1963. (See Table 5.1).

Table 5.1. Staff Assigned to the General Administration Function. (Gazetted Class Officers).

Date / Rank	1 Feb 1962	1 Apr 1963	1 Sep 1964	2 Jul 1968	2 Jul 1969	2 Jul 1970	2 Jul 1971	2 Jul 1972	2 Jul 1973	2 Sep 1974
Secretary		1	1	1	1	1	1	1	1	1
Joint Sec		1	1	2	3	3	2	3	3	3
Under Sec	1	6	6	9	6	6	7	7	7	9
Section Officer	1	6	6	23	19	20	23	23	23	25
TOTAL	2*	14	14	35	29	30	33	34	34	38

1. The Public Administration Department. At this time the personnel administration function was with the Home Ministry. 2. The Administration Management Department. It now also had the personnel administration function. * Both were working part-time only in the Department. (Note: Sec = Secretary)

---

[58] Nepal Gazette, Vol. 18, No. 23, 16 September 1968. Amendment, His Majesty's Government (Allocation of Functions) Rules.

But all has not been well with the Department (AMD). Some of its problems are familiar. The Department is not getting the sort of top executive leadership consonant with its administration-wide functions, and that are essential for its work on administrative improvement. This is especially essential if major administrative reforms are to be carried out. Support for the AMD has been erratic, as is indicated in the changes in the status of the General Administration portfolio in the Government.

Turnover in the General Administration portfolio has also been very high. Between April 1968 and April 1975 the portfolio (and therefore the political charge of the AMD) had changed hands some ten times, between eight different Ministers! Between April 1968 and April 1970 the General Administration portfolio was put under the Prime Minister, assisted successively by an Assistant Minister and then a State Minister for General Administration. It was then put under the sole charge of a Minister (there was no Prime Minister) until April 1971, after which it reverted to the charge of the Prime Minister but without the assistance of a junior minister. From April 1972 to February 1974 it was placed under the charge of a Minister assisted by a State Minister for General Administration, and then under two successive Ministers without the assistance of a junior colleague. In the year following February 1974 the portfolio rotated from the charge of the Prime Minister, to a State Minister for Administration and Communications, and back in April 1975 to the Prime Minister.

To put things in the overall perspective of post-Rana Nepal, the political charge of the General Administration portfolio (or equivalent) had from 1951 to 1960 changed some ten times between as many Ministers, and from 1960 to 1974 it changed eleven times between twelve Ministers. In the 24 years from 1951-74 the charge of the portfolio changed 21 times between 22 Ministers! In this same period the function had been in the administrative charge of some 15 different Secretaries, and seems to have experienced nine separate identities and locations!

There was high turnover of leadership on the administrative side too. Between 1968 and 1974 the Administrative Management Department (AMD) was led by five different Secretaries, one of whom led it twice. It seems that vigorous, purposeful administrators would find it hard to survive as AMD Secretary. The central personnel function of the AMD was linked to patronage and power, thus exposing the Secretary to often unhealthy pressures.

Also, efforts at administrative improvement would inevitably annoy many in the other ministries and departments of HMG, thus attracting negative attitudes towards the AMD and its Secretary. The temptation to have a pliant Secretary in the AMD hot-spot must have been great. The Secretary may have felt constantly pressured by the prospect of an abrupt transfer out, and so to have had an incentive to concentrate on the relatively more routine matters of administration.

Turnover of personnel was also rather high. Of an estimated 35 Gazetted Class officials with the AMD in 1968 (when it was set up), only some 7-10 remained by September 1974. The Secretary, both Joint Secretaries, 4 of 9 Under Secretaries, and most of the Section Officers who were with the AMD in 1968 were not there in 1974.

Attaching the central personnel function to the AMD presented challenges. The personnel function has tended to take the lion's share of the attention of the Department, including some 80 percent of the time of the Secretary, with attention given to mostly routine matters of personnel administration.

A Report of September 1974 on the management survey of the Department (AMD) observed:

The (Department) is not fulfilling the role that it should in His Majesty's Government. Whereas it should be taking the lead in introducing improvements in the civil service system and in proposing and implementing basic administrative reforms, it has been content to assume a more modest role. Instead of focusing its attention on significant problem areas and policy issues, it has concentrated on performing routine functions, such as handling transactions related to employees in the Administrative service, conducting repetitive training, collecting promotion forms, etc. [59]

Some Observations and Recommendations

An important recommendation from this mixed experience would be that the Administrative Management Department should be developed into a strong and effective central office of administration, with the formal status of a ministry. Some advisors and other observers have suggested that it should be located under the Chairman of the Council of Ministers, with the full-time leadership of the Chief Secretary. But it should not be amalgamated with the Cabinet Secretariat.

The Administrative Management Department should be the principal agency of HMG that is responsible for supervising the personnel administration system of the Nepal Civil Service in a coherent and coordinated manner. It should be responsible for the coordination and development of the public administration system of HMG. It should determine the needs of the civil service in matters of training, survey and research, and consultancy, and it should formulate policies

---

[59] Administrative Management Department, HMG/Nepal, Management Survey of the Administrative Management Department of His Majesty's Government of Nepal (Draft Report, Kathmandu, Nepal, September 1974). Lee D. Bomberger was Survey Team Leader. Some of the observations here are similar to an earlier report by Bomberger, Proposed Organization of the Administration Management Department (Kathmandu, Nepal, 4 November 1971).

and evaluate services in this regard. But the conduct of training and related research should be left to a separate Institute of Public Administration.

Such a division of responsibilities for training is also reflected in the recommendations of the survey team that looked at the organization and functions of the Administrative Management Department (AMD) in 1974. It recommended that the Training Division of the AMD should be separated from its Administrative Training Centre, and that both should report directly to the Secretary of the AMD.[60]

There is need for an Institute of Public Administration to provide support and technical services to the civil service in such areas as training, research and development, and consultancy. There should be two distinct but linked entities like an Administrative Management Department (or Ministry of General Administration) as the central office of administration, and a separate and autonomous Institute of Public Administration, in order to facilitate this.

---

[60] Ibid. p. 66.

CHAPTER 6

THE CENTRE FOR INVESTIGATION AND INQUIRY

The *Janch Bujh Kendra*

The civil service system of Nepal remained unduly factional and fragmented with no central agency capable of giving it coherent and consistent leadership and direction. The location of effective authority in government and administration was indicated by the establishment in January 1971 of the *Janch Bujh Kendra*, or Centre for Investigation and Inquiry (henceforth referred to mostly as the JBK).

The then Crown Prince Birendra (who became King some months later in January 1972) played a key role in its creation. The JBK is responsible to His Majesty the King. It is in effect a part of the Palace Secretariat and operates under the general supervision of one of the Principal Secretaries to the King. The location of the JBK highlights two key realities of the current system of government and administration:

1. The theoretical and practical sovereignty of the nation resides in the King, more colloquially in the Royal Palace. So, for practical purposes, it is from there that effective and sustained influence and inspiration for administrative and national reform and development will (or will have to) come.
2. The Royal Palace Secretariat has become a major entity in terms of the formulation and implementation of policy, and the reform and development of the system of public administration in Nepal. It is the executive office of the King, who is effectively both the Head of State as well as the Chief Executive.

It seems that the young and reform-minded Crown Prince and soon-to-be King Birendra saw the *Janch Bujh Kendra* as a major instrument in the effort to reform and develop the administrative system and practices of the country. It was to mix youthfulness and expertise, while taking an empowered and task force oriented approach to the job. The functions of the JBK might be put as follows:

1. Vigilance: to locate and inquire into malfeasance and nonfeasance in administration, and to submit to His Majesty any scheme or set of recommendations to combat these evils.

2. Rewards and Punishment: to recommend punishment for offenders and rewards for work well done, as identified in the course of its inquiries.

3. Grievances: to contribute to remove any injury suffered by the public as a result of administrative shortcomings.

4. Supervision: to function in such a manner as to bring effective coordination for the purpose of execution and enforcement of government policy, and to assist His Majesty by observing whether His purposes are being carried into effect.

5. Reform: to conduct studies on administrative system and practices with a view to removing their faults and weaknesses, and making them more capable of carrying out the functions of government.

This is a unique mix of functional responsibilities. It is doubtful that it would have been practical in any agency that did not enjoy the intimate attention and support of the Royal Palace. Because of this the JBK commands tremendous prestige and authority. Due to this strategic location, and its ability to borrow talented staff from anywhere in government, the JBK has had considerable success in implementing and seeing through its projects, and in getting its proposals adopted and implemented.

The power of the *Janch Bujh Kendra* (JBK) is enhanced also by its:

1. Function of recommending punishment and rewards. This is not theoretical. In the course of its work the JBK has had officials sacked or fined, and others promoted, decorated, or awarded sums of money.[61]

2. Penchant for secrecy. It has the option whether or not to publicize its activities. Officials of the JBK are personally bound to maintain secrecy regarding the work that they do while they are posted or seconded there.

3. Access to documents relevant to its work. All offices of civil administration in the country are bound to provide to the JBK, within a prescribed period during the course of an inquiry, all documents, files, ledgers, equipment, appropriate answers, and any other information together with other relevant materials.

The JBK has a very large recruiting base. All Nepali nationals are eligible for appointment. It can recruit staff on an ad hoc basis depending upon the nature of a particular assignment and the time necessary for its completion. Appointments to the JBK seem to be very much sought after. The remuneration is good, with a monthly allowance added to the salary that the individual continues to draw from the position in which his lien remains. Service in the JBK can be beneficial to an official's career, because it can facilitate promotion prospects, and brings officials to the attention of seniors in administration. There is also the learning

---

[61] Nanda Lall Joshi, Evolution of Public Administration in Nepal, p. 55.

experience of the JBK emphasis on disciplined inquiry and analysis, and its task force and problem-solving approach.

The JBK has been very effective from the point of view of securing the resources (including information) necessary for its work and in getting its reports adopted and implemented. It has been instrumental in producing a shower of plans and schemes (often with the prefix "New" attached to the title) which have impacted on the issues and systems they applied to. There have been "New" plans or schemes for Education, Industry, Communications, Agriculture, and Civil Service Promotions. There have also been schemes for the reorganization of the National Planning Commission, Public Service Commission, and district and regional administration. The general impact seems to have been beneficial. It would take a brave soul to evaluate the work of the *Janch Bujh Kendra*!

There are problems. In the context of the *Panchayat* System of government, royal patronage for administrative improvement is absolutely vital and must be sustained. But it is questionable whether the JBK ought to be located within the Royal Palace set-up. The particular location of the JBK, its penchant for secrecy, and its power to recommend reward and punishment, may not be a healthy combination for the administrative development function and process. As one knowledgeable administrator and local observer put it:

When a member of the Kendra (JBK) approaches an individual for interview, whether a government official or private citizen, it is doubtful whether the interviewee speaks his mind, since he feels very insignificant or suffers from an inferiority complex, or thinks of the risk involved, unfounded as this may be. [62]

The JBK penchant for secrecy tends to mean that its schemes for improvement in government do not get the circulation and debate they deserve, prior to adoption and implementation. This, together with its strategic location and the resulting image of power and infallibility, tends to inhibit outside critical input into JBK efforts. There is also the possibility of uncritical acceptance of JBK sponsored programs and policies. What emanates from the JBK is usually accepted because few wish to seem to oppose it (or the power behind it).

The JBK efforts may perhaps give the task of reform and development an unduly elitist and esoteric air, and make it seem to be a secretive and power-oriented activity. There is also the possibility that the JBK might be used by skill-derived elites (technocrats) to supplant or subordinate community-derived elites, who might be reduced to ratifying and propagating issues decided elsewhere.

The JBK might also reduce motivation for reform in the civil service system. It could inhibit initiative and innovation there, where it is already less than

---

[62] Ibid.

widespread and spontaneous. Reform then tends to become a matter on which officials act only when a specific push to this effect comes from "higher" levels. When the push stops or slackens, the efforts tend to peter out too.

The JBK seems to be duplicating the administrative improvement functions of the Administrative Management Department (AMD), particularly of its Organization and Methods work. In this respect it may have further contributed to the inadequacies of the AMD. It may also have contributed to the fragmentation of authority and responsibility for the coordination and development of the process of administration.

On a more philosophical level, the *Janch Bujh Kendra* may be seen as another manifestation of a deeper psyche that sees the Nepali go outwards and upwards and beyond the self and the existing institutions to the "higher authority" for validation and inspiration. The "higher authority" is associated with power and with access to the internal and external resources that comes with it.

The perception of who or what and where is this "higher authority" may change with changes in the political system (Rana autocracy; or forays into the party mediated and basically indirect "democracy" that is the "*prajatantra*" or "*loktantra*" of the parliamentary system, often manifested as "*dalatantra*" or "partocracy"; or the presumably more tradition-based, community participation oriented system of "*panchayat*" democracy). But the underlying psyche is there, despite claims of moral superiority by the political system that is in power.

This psyche is thought to be based on an extraneous and overlying culture of what some observers have termed variously as "sanskritization" or "brahmanism", and they feel that this has eroded a more natural and pre-existing habit of self-reliance and self-confidence that was a natural corollary to living in a rugged and demanding sort of environment. This underlying psyche is there to be exploited by the political elites and parties in power in an unstable political landscape; and through them also by the foreign donors and associated tutors of political, social and institutional correctness. This induced psyche of dependence is also quite contrary to the essence of institutionalization of the capabilities for administrative development in the country.

Yet there is something to be learned from the experience of the *Janch Bujh Kendra*. It has been effective in the conduct of its functions; has attracted respect and attention; and has had an educative influence on the civil servants who have worked in its task forces. It has secured effective executive support for its administrative improvement activities.

It would be wise to transfer these positive features to entities outside the setup of the Royal Palace Secretariat, attached to but not necessarily within the civil service system, and enjoying the personal and sustained support of the King. One such entity, among others, might be an Institute of Public Administration.

CHAPTER 7

ORGANIZATION AND METHODS

Organization and Methods (O&M) is about the study and analysis of organizational structure, relationships, and procedures with a view to making an organization more effective in achieving its goals and more efficient in the use of resources available to it. Procedures are the "how" of an organization, the body of rules and practices comprising the methods by which given tasks are performed. Organization and Methods is not unique to the West or to the modernization it typifies. But it is in the West that O&M seems to have acquired its present distinction and discipline as an area of study and as a staff function of administration.

The first O&M Office in Nepal was established in August 1957. This was recommended by the Administrative Reorganisation Planning Commission of the government of Prime Minister Tanks Prasad Acharya (January 1956-July 1957). The O&M Office was located initially in the Finance Ministry. The principal reason for this location appears to have been the belief that the O&M function was related primarily to the budget work of the Finance Ministry, in particular with the function of filling positions in the civil service and determining their grade level – or to the position creation function. This was a rather limiting perspective of the O&M function in His Majesty's Government. The normally conservative Finance Ministry was also unlikely to be able to give this vital function the specialist attention and administration-wide perspective that it deserved.

Within the Finance Ministry the O&M Office was given the leadership of a Deputy Secretary who was also the Head of the Revenue and Taxation Division. This official had been to the U.S. on a Fulbright Scholarship and had returned in 1954 with a Master's Degree in Public Administration. He was a natural choice to lead the O&M Office – since he had urged the establishment of this office while serving as "Secretary" of the Administrative Reorganisation Planning Commission. But he could not give the O&M function the full-time leadership it deserved.

Some have suggested that the O&M function went to Finance because this gentleman was there at the time. This is possible. It also reflects the general superficiality of organizational perspective in the Government. So the O&M

Office was given a less than full-time leadership, in an inadequate location, informed by an inadequate perspective.

When in September 1958 the O&M function was transferred to the Home Ministry:

The justification given for this change was that the Ministry was responsible for a number of central personnel activities and that it would be advantageous to locate the O&M Office in the same agency, where the work could be coordinated more easily. [63]

The many changes in location that followed tend to reflect the inadequacies in perspective behind the O&M function in His Majesty's Government. It became something of a shuttlecock! Between 1957 and 1975 it had had nine changes in location. The Finance and Home Ministries had held it twice each – they had each captured it once, recaptured it once, and lost it twice. The position creation function seems to have been the attraction.

United Nations Technical Assistance Program (UNTA) Advisors

Hartvig Nissen (Norway) was the first UNTA Public Administration Advisor in Nepal (January 1957 to January 1960). In his native Norway he had worked in banking, where he appears to have acquired some O&M expertise. Later he had helped to establish a central O&M Directorate for the Norwegian Government and had served as director of this agency for six years. He had then gone to Egypt as an UNTA expert. There he had advised the Government on O&M matters and had been involved in the establishment and teaching programs of the Cairo Institute of Public Administration. Then he had come to Nepal.

Nissen had been a principal advisor to the Administrative Reorganisation Planning Commission, and he subsequently advised the O&M Office that was established as a result of its recommendation. He trained a team of three technicians for this office, and also designed an O&M training course and produced material for this purpose. He assisted the O&M team to develop work measurement standards and to estimate the staff requirements of government – work related to the position creation function. But he seems to have been unable to correct the limiting perspective that largely confined O&M efforts to this kind of work. Nissen had no success in institutionalizing the O&M function in HMG. His successor S.T. Divers noted in early 1960 that the O&M Office was no longer a really effective unit. Divers said this was due to the many changes in personnel.

---

[63] Lee D. Bomberger, The O&M Function in HMG: Past, Present and Future. Draft Report (Kathmandu, Nepal, 15 January 1974), p. 2.

But it was due also to the limiting O&M perspective within HMG, and the lack of comprehension of, and appreciation for, the O&M function.

Nissen advised and assisted in the preparation of the Secretariat Manual of 1958. It was primarily the work of that Deputy Secretary of the Finance Ministry who also had charge of the O&M Office, and who retained this charge even after its transfer to the Home Ministry in 1958. The work was preceded by a survey of work of conditions and office procedures.

The scope of this (Secretariat) Manual was limited to the general work procedures to be followed with reference to receipt and dispatch, filing, letter writing, typing and performance reporting. Most of these functions were placed under the control of a Superintendent of a non-gazetted (clerical) level whose general duties and responsibilities were outlined therein. This original manual was later revised but this revised manual was never formally adopted or put into practice. [64]

The Secretariat Manual of 1958 governed administrative procedures in HMG. Some 500 civil servants were given special training in the use of this Secretariat Manual; this was done at the Administrative Training Centre that was established in February 1959.

S.T. Divers (UK) succeeded Nissen as the UNTA Public Administration Advisor in early 1960. While in Nepal (September 1959-February 1962), he was also the local UN Correspondent (Head of the UNTA Program). What precisely Divers did as a Public Administration expert is hard to locate. He appears not to have left any formal report. He wrote to this writer to say that his greatest contribution was: "To make Nepalese think for themselves". It was perhaps a too generous self-assessment of his success and effectiveness!

Divers has been variously credited with: 1. A report on the machinery of government in Nepal; 2. A survey of administration in Pokhara district; 3. A survey of the Customs Administration; and 4. A study of two ministries (which?). This was presumably done in tandem with the O&M Office.

The short-lived Administrative Board (February-September, 1961) in which this office was located is credited by one local observer as follows:

---

[64] Organisation and Methods Section, Administrative Reform Division, Secretariat of the Council of Ministers, His Majesty's Government of Nepal (with assistance of the Public Administration Service) A Survey Report on Internal Administration and General Office Practices (Kathmandu, Nepal, February 1968), p. 1.

It made a study of all the Secretariat Departments, including their subordinate offices, and determined the number of positions required at all levels. The Board also collected all the department Acts and Rules (Sawals) and consolidated them......The Administrative Board also developed a pattern for delegating authority from the Heads of Departments to their subordinates, since the decision-making process was still centralized and as the more complex nature of government problems demanded more delegation. [65]

It appears that Divers also reported that job descriptions had been prepared for all administrative class officials (Gazetted Class) in HMG. This presumably was done either by the Administrative Board or by its successor, the Public Administration Department. This indicates some stupendous efforts by the Administrative Board, the Public Administration Department, and by Divers as Advisor. But Divers' successor Merrill R. Goodall could find no formal records of these efforts. Nor could this writer locate this fugitive material.

Divers was working at a rather difficult time in Nepal. King Mahendra had dissolved Parliament on 15 December 1960 in a Royal Coup, and he had dismissed the elected government of Prime Minister B.P. Koirala. This was followed by a purge of civil servants in February 1961. This purge claimed the heads (figuratively) of some 200 administrative class (Gazetted) officials, 600 clerical (Non-Gazetted) officials, and about 400 peons and equivalent (labor-messenger group). A little later there followed the introduction of the *Panchayat* system of government to replace the discarded parliamentary system.

Divers was involved with the reorganization of the machinery of government that followed the events of December 1960. It is not clear that this reorganization was based upon systematic administrative analysis at the departmental and sub-departmental levels. There seems to be no evidence of any kind that such administrative studies were completed by either Divers or his Nepali counterparts. It appears that the reorganization consisted primarily of the usual regrouping of functions among the various ministries. One interesting change at the time was the full integration into their parent ministries of the previously autonomous executive departments. Perhaps the intention was to avoid a lot of unnecessary duplication of administrative effort and to hasten the pace of work. Though they were deprived of autonomy, the relocated departments may perhaps have secured greater access to the political and material resources of the parent ministries into which they were reintegrated.

It seems fair to say that Divers was an administrative generalist who was perhaps involved in a general and undefined way in the reorganization of the machinery of government. He was not the sort who could give the O&M function

---

[65] Nanda Lall Joshi, Evolution of Public Administration in Nepal (Kathmandu, Nepal: Centre for Economic Development and Administration, 1973), p. 25.

the specialist attention it deserved. As a generalist, he did not also succeed in institutionalizing this function in HMG. This was not for lack of access to the upper levels of government and administration. But when he completed his term in Nepal in February 1962 there was but one junior administrative official (Section Officer) left serving in the O&M Section (which was itself within an almost defunct Public Administration Department), and he was there part-time!

Dr. Merrill R. Goodall (USA) succeeded Divers as the Senior UNTA Public Administration Advisor to His Majesty's Government of Nepal. He stayed in Nepal from March 1962 to August 1963. Goodall was surprised to find that up to then no descriptive analysis of the Nepali administrative system had been prepared. There was no valid information on the allocation of functions and operations carried out by the ministries; the manner in which subordinate units were grouped within the ministries; what functions they undertook; what goals they pursued; and how these were advanced and with what resources. He could not find even a rudimentary organization chart of His Majesty's Government!

Goodall felt that the fact that the top-most Civil Service levels were unusually fluid (to put it delicately!) attached greater than normal importance to the appropriate structural arrangements of the subordinate units of the ministries of government. He felt that if external consultants were to be employed usefully, and if HMG was to make an informed judgment on their recommendations, then some common understanding had to be gained of the system of administration, its structure and its process. It was his contention that one could not presume to speak of management improvement in Nepal until basic data was developed on the structure and functioning of public administration in the country. He felt that sound, phased schemes for structural change or training could not be made in the absence of such basic data.

In the Report of the Committee on Administration (23 July 1962) Goodall and his Nepali colleagues (three Secretaries of HMG) recommended O&M as a major area of concentration for a greatly strengthened Public Administration Department. They urged HMG to acquire data on such things as: 1. Organizational Structure of ministries and subordinate units; 2. Allocation of Functions to them; 3. Legal Authority to carry out these functions; and 4. Resources, human and material, to carry out the functions. Necessary changes could then be determined to match functional responsibility with the necessary authority, organization and resources.[66]

The Committee urged that the highest priority should be given to the preparation of a descriptive Manual of Government, and that such a manual

---

[66] His Majesty's Government of Nepal, Committee on Administration, Report (Kathmandu, July 1962), pp. 2-3.

should be issued annually by the Public Administration Department (PAD).[67] It commended the survey of district administration being undertaken by the PAD, and felt that the eventual aims of the survey should include the issuance of a handbook for the use of the district officers.[68] The Committee also recommended that the Public Administration Department undertake the following sort of specialized surveys as it gained in experience: [69]

1. Assessment of alternative methods of organization for the conduct of development activities; 2. Study of methods of securing public participation in the work of administration, particularly in development administration; 3. Evaluation, in specific terms, of the requirements in Nepal of a modern system of personnel administration, including criteria for entry and promotion, classification, compensation and tenure; 4. Examination of the tools available for an independent, periodic evaluation of administrative performance; 5. Space-planning studies, especially with respect to the better utilization of the Singha Durbar (Civil Secretariat) complex; 6. Study of the method of handling papers, of forms design, and of record keeping; 7. Continuing study of the conditions underlying good supervision in the career service; and 8. Consideration, with the government Accounting Committee, of the ways of adopting the recently approved accounting system in the development budget.

Goodall assisted the O&M staff of the PAD in a comprehensive survey of the organization of HMG. The survey produced much data and helped bring this Department to the notice of the civil service generally. The survey resulted in the production of a descriptive manual of HMG in April 1963. [70] This manual gave a brief description of the organization of HMG, and the functions and responsibilities of its constituent parts. Its detail tended to be at the ministerial level only. Still, it was a commendable effort – one worth building upon.

In addition, charts were prepared of the various ministries and departments of His Majesty's Government. A single large chart of His Majesty's Government offered for the first time a comprehensive overview of the country's administration. The project had the strong cooperation of the US Agency for International Development (USAID) in Nepal, which traced and reproduced the charts in their various revisions. The organization charts were in much demand by Ministers, Secretaries, and by the officials of the Royal Palace Secretariat.

While the charts indicated the formal structure of government organization and relations, they did not necessarily reflect the reality of such relationship

---

[67] Ibid. p. 3.
[68] Ibid. p. 4.
[69] Ibid. p. 4.
[70] Organization of His Majesty's Government of Nepal (Kathmandu, Nepal: Department of Publicity, Ministry of Panchayat Affairs, HMG/Nepal, April 1963).

patterns. Nevertheless they could educate the concerned individuals and broaden their organizational perspectives, and they could constitute a first step towards narrowing the gap between the formal and informal relationship patterns. Whether this did happen or not is another matter. There is perhaps still room for improvement in this respect. But in the meantime the charts do serve an affirmative function – like the country flags that are displayed as affirmation of country identity, they can be prominently displayed as an affirmation of organizational entity.

Goodall was also assisted by an O&M official in the establishment of a system of classification and maintenance of historical documents in the Foreign Ministry archives. It seems that prior to this effort there had been thousands of these documents lying piled up in unprotected rooms.

In perspective one can say that Goodall helped to preserve, and even enhance, the O&M function in HMG. He mentioned the function repeatedly in his memos and reports and urged its further development. He played a prominent part in the production of the Manual of Government, and the organization charts. Above all, he helped enhance the Public Administration Department as the instrument for administrative improvement in HMG. When he left Nepal in August 1963, there were two capable and qualified Gazetted Class officials (an Under Secretary and a Section Officer) working full-time in the O&M Section of the Public Administration Department.[71] This was an improvement on the one part-time Section Officer left when S.T. Divers had completed his tour in Nepal in February 1962.

Sir Eric Franklin (U.K.) succeeded Goodall as the Senior UNTA Public Administration Advisor. He stayed from May 1964 to December 1966. His main contribution to the O&M Section was the indirect and institutional one of helping to enhance the functions and status of the Public Administration Department (PAD) as the principal instrument for administrative improvement in HMG. In this respect his efforts constituted a commendable continuity with those of his predecessor. In April 1966 the PAD was converted into the Cabinet Secretariat under the leadership of the Chief Secretary to HMG.

Sir Eric did a survey and report on the administrative machinery of the Tourism Department.[72] He conducted a survey of the relationship between His

---

[71] In 1965 the Under Secretary, Mangal Krishna Shresta, produced a Handbook of Public Administration in Nepal (Kathmandu, Nepal: Department of Publicity, Ministry of Panchayat Affairs). It was a very useful book for purposes of information and orientation.

[72] Sir Eric Franklin, *Preliminary Report on the Administrative Machinery of the Tourism Department* (Kathmandu, Nepal, February 1965)

Majesty's Government and the public enterprises in Nepal.[73] In addition he conducted organization surveys of several public corporations: the Royal Nepal Airlines Corporation, the National Trading Limited, the National Transport Organisation, and the Nepal Electricity Corporation.[74] He may have involved the O&M Section in these studies, but they seem to be largely his efforts.

The resulting reports were sound without being unnecessarily technical. They contributed to an enhanced awareness in government of the organizational problems of public enterprises in Nepal. Where the recommendations in these reports were implemented, and some were over a period of time, there were some tangible improvements in those organizations. Sir Eric recommended that the public corporations should be given greater autonomy from the control of government and the bureaucracy.[75] A recommendation honored mostly in the breach! The public corporations are sources of patronage, positions, and perquisites, including in their Boards of Directors; hence the disinclination of those at the top levels of government and administration to loosen their grip on them. There is also the disinclination to empower individuals and entities with necessary and meaningful authority to do the job given to them.

United States AID/Nepal Advisors

To the United States Agency for International Development in Nepal (AID/Nepal) must go the credit for giving any really concentrated and specialist attention to the area of O&M in HMG. This assistance had been recommended by the Kroeger Report (March 1962),[76] which felt that the improvement of the administrative system and practices of HMG was an essential step to achieve accelerated overall development of the country.[77]

---

[73] Sir Eric Franklin, Report on the Relationship between His Majesty's Government and Public Enterprises in Nepal (Kathmandu, Nepal, September 1966).

[74] Ibid., Report on the Administrative Machinery of the Royal Nepal Airlines Corporation (Kathmandu, Nepal, March 1966); Special Report on the National Transport Organisation (Kathmandu, Nepal 1966); Report on the Administrative Machinery of National Trading Limited (Kathmandu, Nepal 1966); and Report on the Organisation of the Nepal Electricity Corporation (Kathmandu, Nepal 1966).

[75] The need for a favorable balance between the autonomy of the public Corporations and Government control was also urged in Rune Tersman, Supervision of Public Enterprises in Nepal (Kathmandu, Nepal: United Nations, June 1963).

[76] Louis J. Kroeger, A Public Administration Program for His Majesty's Government of Nepal (San Francisco; Griffenhagen Kroeger Inc., March 1962),

[77] The report was based on a four-week survey made by Louis Kroeger of the public administration needs of His Majesty's Government. The survey and report were the result of a contract funded by AID/Nepal and entered into between HMG and the management consultancy firm of Griffenhagen-Kroeger Inc. of San Francisco, California.

Regarding O&M the report recommended that AID/Nepal provide three "Exemplars" to HMG to render technical assistance in the areas of procedures, internal organization, communications, management of records, and in forms design and control. This was to be part of a comprehensive program for improvement of the administrative system of HMG within a five year period. It was to include 11 U.S. "Exemplars" aided by 77 local technicians and 112 local clerks. The subsequent technical assistance in public administration that was provided by AID/Nepal was informed by this Kroeger Report, though not *in toto*.

The Government had not been keen to let a major cold-war power like the U.S. into the sensitive area of public administration. But AID/Nepal felt that its assistance efforts would continue to be seriously hampered without major improvement in public administration, and it seems that further overall assistance was made contingent upon AID/Nepal technical assistance in public administration. The Government gave in.

Harold L. Smock (U.S.) was AID/Nepal's first O&M Advisor to His Majesty's Government. He was in Nepal from June 1963 to June 1965. For much of that time he also acted as Chief of the Public Administration Division of AID/Nepal. The Division was responsible for promoting and supporting the development and improvement of public administration in the country, in cooperation with HMG. This other role involved Smock in much paperwork, and thus reduced the time available to him for project accomplishments.

Smock had worked in the U.S. Postal Service, where he had acquired much experience in management and research. He assisted in laying the foundation for a modern postal service in Nepal by: helping to establish a national organization capable of developing and administering such a service, and of starting a formal parcel post service; sending Nepalis to the U.S. for training; and advising in the signing of a bilateral agreement between Nepal and India, which provided for formal postal channels between Nepal and other postal administrations of the world. He collaborated in a survey of the postal organization in Nepal, which resulted in the development of a five-year plan of action for the postal service.[78]

Smock also helped the Public Administration Department to plan and conduct a six-month study of field administration in Nepal. This resulted in a 105 page report of findings and recommendations.[79] This report may have had some influence on subsequent developments in this area, but it was never formally

---

[78] Five Year Plan of the Postal Services Department of His Majesty's Government of Nepal (Kathmandu, Nepal, February 1965).

[79] Public Administration Department, His Majesty's Government of Nepal, A Survey of Field Administration of His Majesty's Government of Nepal (Kathmandu, Nepal, August 1964).

adopted by HMG. Smock had involved the O&M Section of the Public Administration Department in these efforts.

AID/Nepal next contracted with the Public Administration Service (PAS) in Chicago to secure the services of two O&M experts, and one administrative training expert. This team of three American advisors was known collectively as the PAS team. The training expert was Howard L. Grigsby (September 1966 to September 1968), and the O&M experts were John H. Hettler (October 1966 to February 1969) and Robert W. Ferrell (December 1966 to February 1969). Hettler was Team Leader. He had acquired experience in city management in the U.S., particularly in finance and budgeting. Later he had worked as consultant to some foreign governments and cities (Ghana, Istanbul, Addis Ababa, and Abidjan) in the establishment of water and sewer systems. Prior to the Nepal assignment he had served as management consultant to the Government of Thailand in the area of budgeting, accounting, and revenue administration. Robert W. Ferrell had since 1957 been a management consultant with the PAS group in Chicago. He had served in that capacity in both Liberia and Afghanistan.

When they started work in Nepal, the O&M advisors found that the O&M Section (then located in the Administrative Reforms Division of the Cabinet Secretariat) had but two technicians, of whom only one was qualified. Five untrained recruits were added in January 1967. The two PAS Advisors (Hettler and Ferrell) conducted a short pre-service training program for the untrained technicians, and provided practical training by involving them in two administrative studies. But the team of six O&M technicians that was thus formed did not last long. Most of the technicians were "development" personnel in the temporary employ of HMG. They were therefore ineligible for the service tenure and pension benefits granted to "regular" civil service personnel. The result was low morale, which did not benefit the pace or quality of work done.

There was also a very high turnover rate. When the PAS project terminated in February 1969, only one technician remained in the O&M Section. Of the other five, two had been dismissed (for protests related to their insecure "development" status); one had resigned; one was transferred out as a district administrator; and one was sent to the U.S. for training in management analysis. He was not posted back to the O&M Section on return!

Two documents had been prepared as a result of the practical training in administrative survey and analysis given to the O&M technicians. One was the Manual of Internal Administration and General Office Practices of His Majesty's Government (July 1968).[80] This Manual was intended to replace the 1958

---

[80] O&M Section, Administrative Reform Division, Administrative Management Department, HMG/Nepal (With assistance of Public Administration Service), Manual of Internal Administration and General Office Practices (Kathmandu, Nepal, July 1968)

Secretariat Manual. The 1958 Manual had only dealt with general office procedures, and these had become outworn with time. The 1968 Manual updated these procedures. It also covered the internal administration function of the ministries and departments – areas such as general services and personnel and financial administration. Some twelve months of effort were involved in the preparation of the 1968 Manual. It was a commendable exercise. But the Government did not officially adopt this Manual. Yet it was not all a wasted effort. The 1968 Manual was to provide the basis for a similar one adopted three years later. It also provided useful material for training purposes.

A related work was the Survey Report on Internal Administration and General Office Practices (February 1968). This report recommended that "internal administration divisions" should be established in each ministry and department to perform auxiliary and staff functions. These divisions were to be headed by Under Secretaries (Gazetted Class II), who would each be assisted by a Personnel Officer, a Fiscal Officer, and a General Services Officer, all at the level of Section Officers (Gazetted Class III). This was aimed at enhancing the status and quality of the internal administration function of the various ministries and departments; work that had usually been assigned to a superintendent of clerical status. This recommendation was accepted in spirit. But implementation in fact has not been uniform.

There is still a rather inadequate appreciation among administrators and politicians of the staff function in organization. The distinction between line and staff roles and functions is not clearly understood. There is a tendency to view the staff function as a sort of wasteful and officious activity conducted by backseat drivers. It might be said that some in staff roles do perhaps have a tendency to turn staff work into the direction of control. It is this sort of attitude that could, for instance, turn planning into a "policing" function. Ideally, of course, the proper staff role in administration is to facilitate rather than to control.

Another document resulting from the on-the-job training effort was the Report on the Organisation and Administration of the Civil Personnel Records Centre (July 1968).[81] It was a comprehensive review of the organization and work of the Centre, with recommendations for improvement. These recommendations were partially implemented over the years. More staff and space was provided to the Centre; its organization was improved; a card-index system was adopted to facilitate the location of employee files; a system of individual employee files was initiated; and the files were kept in steel cabinets.

---

[81] O&M Section, Administrative Reform Division, Administrative Management Department, HMG/Nepal, (with assistance of the Public Administration Service), Memorandum Report on the Organization and Administration of the Civil Personnel Records Centre (Kathmandu, Nepal, July 1968).

In general, attention was drawn to an agency that was not normally the object of administrative improvement efforts in HMG.

The PAS advisors worked with the O&M Section in conducting administrative studies of other organizations of government. The work was hampered by the loss of the trained O&M technicians. Still, reports were produced on the National Planning Commission; the District Administration; the Ministry of Agriculture; the Departments of Public Works, Land Administration, Food, Land Reform, Water Resources and Meteorology, Irrigation and Drinking Water; the Civil Aviation Department; and the Nepal Engineering School. The reports were in draft form, partially in Nepali and partially in English.

At the time the PAS team left (February 1969) only the report on the Land Administration Department had been accepted, and was in the process of implementation. The possibility of implementation of the reports was no doubt hampered by the virtual withering away of the O&M Section.

The PAS advisors did not quite succeed in institutionalizing the O&M function in HMG. At this stage the primary problem was not so much the level of technical competence available but rather the inadequate degree of its institutionalization. This brings into question the wisdom of the April 1966 conversion of the Public Administration Department into the Cabinet Secretariat. The aim of this had been to give the administrative improvement processes close top-level executive support. But the administrative reform function did not mix well with the Cabinet function, and inadequate attention was given to this vital area. It seems that the Chief Secretary had been too busy with the Cabinet side of his work to be able to give any adequate support and sustained attention to the administrative reform and development side of his responsibilities. Among other things this also reminds us of the missed opportunities due to disbandment of the Ministry of General Administration in 1952. The inadequate attention and support given to the O&M Section at this time is a sad commentary on the administrative development capability of the Cabinet Secretariat.

The PAS advisors appear to have been quite technically capable, though perhaps lacking in institutional perspective, at least in the Nepali context. They perhaps concentrated too much on survey and report work, and too little on the institutionalization of the O&M function in HMG. The six O&M technicians they had trained seem to have acquired an encouraging degree of technical competence. But they did not get the necessary institutional support from HMG and the Cabinet Secretariat where they were located.

The PAS team of O&M advisors wanted two more years in Nepal. In their final report they urged the need for continued O&M assistance to help train technicians and build up local capability in the field. They felt their program was just beginning to gain impetus.[82] But AID/Nepal thought that 56 man-months was too much time and effort to merely indicate the beginning of an impetus. AID/Nepal wanted tangible results and it felt that the PAS team could not show much in this regard. So their services were terminated in February 1969.

Lee D. Bomberger (U.S.) succeeded the PAS advisors. He served as the AID/Nepal Advisor in Public Administration (O&M) from August 1970 to September 1974. AID/Nepal acquired his services on contract from the Development and Resources Corporation of New York. Bomberger had had extensive experience as a management and fiscal policy analyst in the California State Government. He had been in Nepal before (September 1963 - December 1965) as Associate Director of the Peace Corps. Unlike his PAS predecessors, Bomberger seems to have gotten on very well with the AID/ Nepal establishment. He was cautious, quiet, industrious, and knew his way around. He seems to have been a suitable person to help promote institutionalization of the O&M function in HMG. During his tenure in Nepal some commendable progress was made with regard to the O&M function in government.

The 1968 Manual of Internal Administration and General Office Practices had not been adopted by Government. Bomberger led the effort to revise this Manual and to reset it in a more suitable format. It was converted from a hardbound to a loose-leaf volume to facilitate revision. It took over a year of effort before the Manual was printed and ready for distribution. On 16 December 1971 the new Manual came into effect in the thirteen ministries of HMG, the Administrative Management Department, the Secretariat of the Council of Ministers, and the National Planning Commission.[83] It replaced the 1958 Secretariat Manual.

The subsequent fate of the Manual is interesting. An analyst within the O&M Section had been designated manual coordinator and charged with its maintenance. Staff from the ministries and departments had been instructed in the use of the Manual. But in his subsequent surveys the coordinator found that the Manual was largely occupying desk-space in the various government offices – its forms and procedures were generally ignored.

The O&M Section revised the 1971 Internal Administration Manual in 1974, with a view to making it more acceptable, and to improve the chances of its implementation. This revised version came into force in April 1974 in all

---

[82] Public Administration Service, Project for Improving Government Organization and Method and Management Training, Government of Nepal; Final Report (Chicago: Publication Administration Service, 29 May 1969), pp. 13-14.
[83] His Majesty's Government of Nepal, Internal Administration Manual Rules, 23 November 1971, and Nepal Gazette, 16 December 1971.

ministries and departments of HMG.[84] Success of this revised version was a work in progress; experience indicates that formal official sanction alone will not secure compliance. It is the old adage about how form alone will not guarantee substance, or action; or create the culture and the comprehension of it.

Bomberger tried to follow-up on another PAS legacy – the 1968 Report on the Civil Personnel Records Centre. In mid-1971 a committee was formed within the Administrative Management Department (AMD) to study the report and to recommend how it might still be applied to develop the organization and procedures of the Centre. It seems little was achieved, because by mid-1974 yet another committee was formed within the AMD for precisely the same purpose!

The problem was apparently one of both tactics and personality. The Chief (*Hakim*) of the Centre was an old hand who had served in administration for thirty years, and had been heading the Centre for fifteen (as of 1971). Under him some considerable improvements had been made at the Centre. The Centre had become synonymous with the Chief. With such an individual, personal contact might have been better than communication by committee, and cooptation better than inducement from outside and above. The Chief was not opposed to change – but a very good case would have had to be made for it. Perhaps Bomberger made the mistake of trying to induce "reform by committee". It did not work.

The first Organization Manual of His Majesty's Government had been produced by the O&M Section in April 1963. The Report of the Committee on Administration (July 1962) had recommended that the Manual should be issued annually by the Public Administration Department. The O&M Section issued the next Manual ten years later (April 1973)! The 1973 Manual contained the organization chart and information on staff complement of each of the ministries and departments of HMG. The earlier manual did not have this. But, unlike the earlier manual, the new one did not contain information on the functions and responsibilities of the ministries and departments. A newer version of September 1974 did contain all of the above information and the relevant organization charts, but it was immediately put under wraps for further editing. This Organization Manual is expected to be revised annually. Whether this will be done remains to be seen. The 1974 Manual had had heavy input by AID/Nepal staff. Whether the O&M Section of the Administrative Management Department can produce the Manual on its own is to be seen.

Bomberger himself compiled an O&M Analyst's Handbook in late 1972. It combined within a single document, in a readily usable form, much information that the O&M analyst would need to do his job. It was a very useful document for reference and training purposes. In 1974 this O&M Analyst's Handbook was

---

[84] Nepal Gazette, 12 May 1975.

revised and translated into Nepali. He also prepared some twenty O&M seminar lesson plans, and assembled back-up materials as well.

During Bomberger's contract period some twenty administrative studies were completed by the O&M Section. Three of these studies produced concrete results: I.D. cards were issued to all civil servants; standards of office furniture were developed; and a central messenger service was established for HMG offices in and around Kathmandu. Two reports on the Mint Department and Tourism Department were also adopted and recommendations implemented. But the fire that gutted the Civil Secretariat building in July 1973 incinerated the reports and working-papers on at least seven other studies of ministries and departments. The work on two studies (delegation of authority and field administration) was abandoned because of parallel efforts by the Investigation and Inquiry Centre (*Janch Bujh Kendra*) of the Palace Secretariat. The other studies were being discussed, resisted, or simply pigeon-holed.

The batting average on the O&M studies has not been too bad by Nepali standards, especially if the vaporizing effects of the Civil Secretariat fire of 1973 are taken into account. Perhaps the *Janch Bujh Kendra* (Investigation and Inquiry Centre) attached to the Royal Palace Secretariat had a much higher degree of implementation of studies completed under its own aegis. But the Administrative Management Department, where the O&M Section is located, cannot compare in influence and authority with the Palace Secretariat. The duplication of functions cannot be very helpful either.

Bomberger did not actually participate in the O&M studies as the PAS Advisors had done before him. He concentrated on the role of resource person to whom the O&M analysts could come for guidance and advice. This created some misgivings amongst the analysts. They felt that his training and counsel would have been more valuable had he had a more hands on role. His backseat role may also have limited his ability to give on-the-job training to the O&M analysts. They may have felt that the seminars and training material that he had developed had a general and introductory value – but that they did not go much further.

It is interesting to note that in early 1974 the O&M analysts balked at Bomberger's suggestion that they conduct a workshop on O&M techniques for officials from the ministries and departments and the public corporations. The idea was to establish an O&M capability in these agencies. But the analysts felt that they had not been prepared for this kind of effort. They felt that they did not possess the capability for such training responsibilities. It appears that during his contract period the O&M Section did develop a general survey capability, but what was still lacking was an indigenous all-round O&M functional capability.

Bomberger did make some useful contributions to the institutionalization of the O&M function in HMG.[85] He conducted seminars and developed material for training purposes, and he helped to develop procedures to improve the overall management of the O&M Section, and to facilitate the work of its analysts in a planned, coordinated, standardized manner. When he left in September 1974, the O&M Section had eight analysts – two Under Secretaries and six Section Officers; and another team of one Under Secretary and three Section Officers had been approved in the budget for fiscal year 1974-75. This build-up owed much to his advocacy, and to the support given to him by AID/ Nepal.

Many problems still remained. This was reflected in some of the recommendations that he made in his January 1974 draft report on the O&M function in HMG. Such as: 1. The O&M Section of the Administrative Management Department should strive to develop a cooperative working relationship with other HMG agencies;[86] 2. The O&M staff should place increasing emphasis on the implementation of approved recommendations resulting from their studies;[87] 3. There should be a well-planned staff development program for the O&M Section;[88] 4. The O&M Section should begin building centers of expertise around its staff.[89] 5. A central O&M Section should be maintained in the Administrative Management Department, and individual staff members should be deputed to work with the ministries, departments, government corporations, and CEDA (the Centre for Economic Development and Administration);[90] and 6. The O&M staff should play an active part in identifying major management and administrative problems in HMG.[91]

The first recommendation highlighted the situation that there was still a tendency for the ministries and departments to lean towards an adversarial stance towards the O&M Section. It seems that many viewed it as at best a necessary evil, and at worst a potentially threatening and disruptive force. Bomberger observed that some top officials were unaware of the existence of the O&M Section, and were not well informed of its work and function.

The O&M analysts were themselves not sure about the suggestion that they put increasing emphasis on the implementation of the recommendations resulting

---

[85] He might have contributed more had he been able to concentrate on O&M. He spent some 25 percent of his time on other areas – such as on personnel administration, management training, and as a resource person to the Centre for Economic Development and Administration.
[86] Bomberger, The O&M Function in HMG, p. 16.
[87] Ibid. p. 18.
[88] Ibid. p. 23.
[89] Ibid. p. 24.
[90] Ibid. p. 19.
[91] Ibid. p. 19.

from their studies. They felt that such an emphasis could involve them in deep-ended, long drawn out affairs that would suck up all of their relatively limited resources of manpower and expertise, and they feared that this would impair their survey and research function.

The O&M analysts felt that the stress on implementation should be contingent upon further institutionalization of the O&M function within HMG. They agreed with the call for well-planned staff development of the O&M Section, but they felt that their involvement in implementation would be best after there was more certainty and comprehension of the value and role of the O&M function in the overall system of administration of HMG.

The O&M analysts felt that only after progress on this, and on staff development, could there be effective work done and development achieved towards meeting the need for greater in-depth capability in such areas as records management, forms design, and work measurement. They also felt that such enhanced expertise would be better maintained for the time being in a strengthened O&M Section, instead of dispersing it within various ministries and departments. Also, there was the feeling that in the light of the generalist mentality in HMG it was likely that the O&M expertise located in such dispersed cells would be wasted on unrelated functions, and dissipated through transfers.

Observations on the O&M Function in HMG

The O&M analysts tended to favor an emphasis on the study of methods rather than of organizations. They thought that the former involved problems of techniques, procedures, and matters common to a generality of administrative entities. So it would excite less hostility and suspicion, and implementation was likely to face less resistance, and to have a greater impact upon administrative improvement. They felt that emphasis on organization studies was likely to produce opposition to the O&M function, as it would be seen as threatening existing patterns of organizational and personal relationships. It is an interesting view, based on a desire to minimize conflict, by concentrating on techniques rather than on people.

There is also the problem of leadership and status. In a generally hierarchical society the O&M Section has been troubled by inadequacy of leadership and the relatively low rank of its analysts. Most of them are Section Officers, and a few are Under Secretaries. But in the ministries and departments, the decisions as to the fate of the O&M studies are made by more senior Joint Secretaries and Secretaries. Something must be done to rectify this situation if the leadership of the Administrative Management Department (AMD) wishes to give the O&M Section the requisite degree of support and status to more effectively do its work. But this appears not to have been the case. The AMD appears to concentrate most of its work on routine matters of administration – about 80 percent of the Secretary's time seems to go to routine matters of personnel administration.

It would help if the O&M Section were given the undivided attention of a Joint Secretary. During Bomberger's four-year tenure there were five different Joint Secretaries in charge of the O&M Section. Of these only one was engaged full-time with the Section, and he was an "acting" Joint Secretary who lasted about a year in that position. Of these five Joint Secretaries only this "acting" Joint Secretary was an O&M analyst. He was sent back to his lower rank of Under Secretary! The Section was then put under the part-time leadership of four transient Joint Secretaries with no O&M expertise, or the time to develop any. In December 1974 the O&M Section got its sixth Joint Secretary in four years!

The institutionalization of the O&M function in His Majesty's Government has been rather poor indeed. Since its inception in August 1957, the O&M Section has been located and relocated some nine times in various HMG ministries and departments. Staff turnover has been high, and staff strength unstable. The O&M Section has suffered from the lack of a stable, properly trained staff complement of adequate numbers. The Section has been subjected to frequent raids on its staff – more recently for the position creation function and the Position Classification Project.

The number of Gazetted Class officers in the O&M Section has fluctuated widely, as follows: 1958-3; February 1962-1; March 1963-2; December 1966-2; February 1967-7; February 1969-2; December 1970-10; September 1974-8. Some of the officers were working part time, and some were deputed to the O&M Section on a temporary basis.

Between March 1964 and September 1971 a total of thirteen officers received training in management analysis in the U.S., on AID/Nepal sponsorship. Another two received training in paperwork management. Yet as of September 1973 only two of these fifteen were working in the O&M Section of the Administrative Management Department. Others were employed in such activities as auditing, personnel administration, district administration, election administration, general administration, and (private and personal) business administration!

A contributing factor to this rather poor utilization of trained expertise (and of the training opportunities to develop such expertise) has been the "distributive" attitude regarding the selection of people for foreign "training". Training "opportunities" are often seen as just that; as opportunities to travel abroad for those next in line in the "queue", and as reward to favorites or others.

It is too often the case that little emphasis has been given in this regard to using these foreign training opportunities for the purposeful development, optimal utilization, and sustaining of expertise; and on institution building in areas of need in administration and development.

After seventeen years of technical assistance, the O&M function continues to suffer many disabilities. It has not been given adequate leadership and support, be it executive or administrative; and it has had an inadequate status and location. It lacks an adequate and stable complement of well-trained analysts. There is incomplete understanding within HMG of the nature of the O&M function. O&M capability appears to be confined largely to general organizational survey work. There is need to develop a broader range of expertise; and to build an indigenous capability for the regeneration and development of the O&M function.

CHAPTER 8

THE INSTITUTE OF PUBLIC ADMINISTRATION

The Idea and the Advocacy

Hartvig Nissen (Norway) was the first United Nations Technical Assistance (UNTA) Advisor in Public Administration to His Majesty's Government. He was in Nepal for a three year period from January 1957 to January 1960. While on a previous UNTA assignment in Egypt he had helped to establish, and taught at, the Institute of Public Administration in Cairo. Nissen brought with him a deep belief in the value of such institutions for administrative development efforts. He felt that the establishment of such institutions should take priority in technical assistance efforts in public administration.

He believed in the Nepal case also that direct advice on administrative practices and organizational structures should be postponed pending the institutionalization of an administrative development capability in an Institute of Public Administration. He felt that such an institution would help relate the foreign experts to the ecology of the host country; that technical assistance should be channeled via such an Institute; and that in its absence the foreign experts would be tempted to plagiarize systems and organizational structures of the developed countries.

Nissen put a lot of effort on advocacy for an Institute of Public Administration. He was principal advisor to two sub-committees of the Administrative Reorganization Planning Commission (1956-57) that recommended that an Institute of Public Administration be established, and that drew up plans for it.[92] The plans resembled the objectives and activities of the Cairo Institute to which Nissen had been affiliated. The Institute was to be attached to the Ministry of Home Affairs. It was to have a Board of Directors and an Advisory Committee; an Academic Council; and to have its own budget. A Clerical Secretarial Training Centre was to be located within the Institute. The Institute was conceived essentially as an in-service training institution for all levels of government employees. A fairly elaborate prospectus was prepared. It was modeled on work being done in large, well-financed, inter-country Institutes.

---

[92] Ad Hoc Advisory Committee Regarding an Institute of Public Administration in Nepal, Report (Kathmandu, Nepal, 1957), and Committee on the Institute of Public Administration in Nepal, Report (Kathmandu, Nepal, 1957).

Unfortunately, the Administrative Reorganization Planning Commission, that had recommended the establishment of an Institute of Public Administration, did not long survive the Government that had created it – that of Prime Minister Tanka Prasad Acharya (January 1956 to July 1957).

It appears that an "institute" was established notionally in early 1958 when a number of in-service training courses were commenced in some rooms of the Civil Secretariat (*Singha Durbar*) building. There were courses on elementary bookkeeping, the use of the new Secretariat Manual, and a popular course called Training within Industry (TWI), among others. Nissen and other foreign experts from the aid missions were involved in these training efforts. The status of this "institute" was formalized somewhat in February 1959, when King Mahendra declared open the *Prashasan Prashiksan Kendra* (Administrative Training Centre). Thus Nissen's recommendation for an Institute of Public Administration was adopted in the much more watered-down form of a Centre.

What really appears to have happened is that some existing in-service courses that were being conducted in a few rooms of the Civil Secretariat building were brought under the largely declaratory framework of a Centre. It had no full-time director, or full-time instructors. Lectures were given on an ad hoc basis by senior civil-servants and experts from the aid missions. The Government gave little encouragement to the Centre. Nissen's rationale for the Institute may have moved some Nepalis, but there seems to have been little comprehension of the idea, or appreciation of its value for administrative development, at higher levels. His recommendations for a robust Institute of Public Administration required perspectives and values that did not exist in the context of administration.

It seems that the government did not value the idea sufficiently to be willing to divert enough of its own scarce resources to it. In March 1959 blueprints and plans for an Institute structure had been submitted to the Home Ministry, and a site had been allotted for the Institute within the Civil Secretariat grounds. The United States Operations Mission in Nepal had made available some $106,000 (in fiscal year 1959-60) for construction of the Institute building, but nothing was constructed. There the matter stopped. The hopes of massive external support did not materialize – perhaps because the Government had itself shown no great commitment to the Institute project.

S. T. Divers (U. K.) succeeded Hartvig Nissen as the Senior UNTA Advisor in Public Administration in January 1960. He was also the local UN Correspondent (Head of the UNTA Program) during his stay in Nepal from September 1959 to February 1962. But unlike Nissen, his former colleague and predecessor, Divers himself did not pursue the ideas and initiatives for the development of an Institute of Public Administration!

During his tenure there was instead some marked deterioration in the status and facilities of the "institute" as an Administrative Training Centre. This Centre was first taken into the Administrative Board in February 1961. This Board was outside the jurisdiction of any ministry. But in September 1961 this Board was moved to the Ministry of Finance as the Public Administration Department. So the Centre was in effect reduced to the status of a section in a department of a ministry. By February 1962 the Centre had but one Under Secretary left working in it – and he was also the personal secretary to the Minister for Public Works, Transport and Communications!

And so S.T. Divers successor Dr. Merrill R. Goodall (U. S.) observed that:

By March 1962 the institute was defunct. It had no staff, no budget, and could not be said to exist. The rooms in the Singha Durbar (Civil Secretariat building) which were allocated to the institute were literally ankle-deep in rubble, and its office equipment, gift of a foreign aid mission, covered with dust. The institute's library of some three hundred volumes was unavailable to prospective users.[93]

Goodall had succeeded Divers as the Senior UNTA Advisor in Public Administration. He was in Nepal from March 1962 to August 1963. He brought an institutional perspective into the administrative development process. Goodall found that advisory efforts to date had been piecemeal, uncoordinated, and even competitive; and on the Nepali side the administrative development efforts seemed to be disjointed, fragmented, and lacking in any central design! He put emphasis on the institutionalization of an administrative development capability in Nepal, in particular on a Public Administration Department and on an Institute of Public Administration.

The 1962 Committee on Administration (in which Goodall and three HMG Secretaries were members) gave serious consideration to the establishment and program for an Institute of Public Administration. In its Report of 23 July 1962 it urged that the Public Administration Department should plan at once for the development of an Institute. It urged that the plans for the Institute should be developed jointly with the chief financing agency, AID/Nepal, and other of the substantially concerned foreign assistance groups; and the plans should not be rigid and should be subject to continuing experimentation.[94]

The responsibilities of the Institute were outlined broadly as: (1) internal technical assistance; (2) administrative training; (3) survey, research, and

---

[93] Merrill R. Goodall, "Administrative Change in Nepal" in Asian Bureaucratic Systems Emergent from the British Imperial Tradition, ed. Ralph Braibanti (Durham. N. C.: Duke University Press, 1966), p. 624.
[94] His Majesty's Government of Nepal, Committee on Administration, Report (Kathmandu, Nepal, July 1962), p.6.

documentation; and (4) to serve as a professional meeting-place and clearing-house of administrative materials for ministers, public servants, and professional colleagues (page 7). HMG gave no official response to this Report!

Goodall had suggested, in an earlier memo of 2 May 1962 to the Member Secretary of the National Planning Council, that the Institute should be attached to the Civil Secretariat rather than to the national university. The Institute was to be given the leadership of two men – an honorary director and a technical director. The honorary director was to be a senior Nepali possessed of a distinguished reputation in civic affairs and of unimpeachable community standing, who would represent the Institute publicly and at the highest levels of Government; this appointment would reflect the importance that His Majesty's Government attached to the improvement of public administration. The technical director would provide energetic, continuing, and professional leadership to the Institute. There was to be no Board of Directors. Instead the technical director would be advised by a Board of Consultants which would have senior Nepali officials and representatives of the concerned foreign aid agencies.

Goodall advised that HMG ask AID/Nepal to provide the services of a contract team from an American university to assume the training and management-consultancy responsibilities at the Institute. But this recommendation may have contributed to the ambivalence of some Nepali officials towards the proposed Institute, since they may have seen or portrayed it as constituting a potential and undesirable foreign (American) intrusion into the public administration system. The Indian advisors who had dominated the field in the 1950s would have agreed with this narrow perspective!

In an 18 December 1962 memo to the Secretary of the Public Administration Department, Goodall urged that HMG do the following to realize the Institute into being: announce formally that it embraces the goals and functions of a Nepal Institute of Public Administration; state what these goals and functions are; and appoint a Director who would assume responsibility for the overall forward planning for the Institute. The Director would be advised by an advisory committee in which representatives of the concerned foreign aid agencies would be included. The Director was to present plans and recommendations for the Institute to the Council of Ministers.

In this same memo of 18 December 1962 Goodall claimed that: there was no question of the willingness of Nepalis to fashion an Institute of Public Administration in local, realistic terms and he had no doubt of the strength of interest among HMG civil servants in the study, research, and training activities commonly associated with an Institute of Public Administration; that the technical and administrative staff that such an Institute would require was possessed in increasing degree by His Majesty's Government; that the Institute needed leadership and a physical facility, and these important resources were at hand; and that significant elements of the country's leadership were convinced of the need for rapid improvement in the administrative system.

Goodall thought that while motives might vary, the climate of opinion for the betterment of administration was receptive to changes that might lead to more effective public services and more competent public personnel. He was quite understandably mixing some exaggeration with advocacy on behalf of the Institute! In fact there was no widespread comprehension of the concept of an Institute in HMG. Most understood it to be at best a "training centre". There was not much support for the idea of an Institute of Public Administration at "higher levels", or appreciation of its significance for administrative development. It seems that he did not even have much support for the idea of an Institute from his principal counterpart, the Secretary of the Public Administration Department.

Perhaps the Institute idea had little place in this Secretary's administrative value system. Also he may have felt that the Institute might take away from his own Department. The Institute's functions seemed to parallel those of his Department, and the relationship between the two had not been clearly indicated. He may have felt that to cooperate with the Institute proposal would be tantamount to presiding over the dissolution of his own organization base. He was the seniormost Secretary in HMG, with access to the King. It would probably be fair to say that this lack of enthusiasm contributed to stalling Goodall's efforts and advocacy on behalf of the proposed Institute.

Goodall had persuaded AID/Nepal to make $106,000 available to HMG for the construction of a structure for the Institute of Public Administration. A firm of architects had also been hired, with Israeli aid, to draw site plans for the Institute and design its physical facilities. Then things got stalled. The $106,000, and possibly more, was frittered away in a not very successful attempt to convert an old Rana palace into an upgraded facility to house the administrative development functions of HMG. No structure was constructed for an Institute, and no Institute of Public Administration was established.

Goodall had hoped that an on-going, functioning Institute would have enhanced and energized the administrative development functions of HMG, and attract the interest and support of a number of donor agencies who might have been hesitant about getting involved till then. But it was not to be. Still, he must be credited with having resurrected the idea of an Institute of Public Administration that his predecessor Hartvig Nissen had initiated (but that Nissen's successor S.T. Divers had overlooked). But the idea of an Institute of Public Administration would keep coming up thereafter.

It is interesting to note that Goodall's views on the Institute were not shared by his contemporary A. Linsell (U.K.), who was the UNTA Training Advisor from March 1962 to June 1963. Linsell pointed out that there was no clear idea in Nepal of the concept of an Institute of Public Administration, and that most understood it to imply a training centre.[95] He thought that the Institute should be a longer-term objective, and that of much more urgency was the great deal of training that required to be done immediately.

Linsell thought that work on the training should start as soon as possible using the resources at hand, and this meant building up the role and capabilities of the Administrative Training Centre of the Public Administration Department. He felt that the Centre could perhaps be developed later into an Institute of Public Administration, as envisaged by Goodall (and Nissen). This was a more limited perspective, from a clerical-secretarial training specialist, but it was perhaps based on the limitations of the time.

Sir Eric Franklin (UK) succeeded Goodall as Senior UNTA Advisor in Public Administration. He also did not pursue the proposals for the Institute! This is a pity. His advocacy might have provided a strong and continuing boost for the Institute idea. But he gave only a brief mention of the Institute in his final report (December 1966). He basically took the same line as his compatriot Linsell. Also, by the time he came to Nepal (May 1964) the initiatives for the proposed Institute of Public Administration had passed over to AID/Nepal (the U.S. Agency for International Development).

The American aid effort in Nepal appears to have been tentatively committed to the Institute project since fiscal year 1959-60, when it had made available about $106,000 for construction of a building. But no such structure was built. As of 4 February 1963, less than twenty percent of this sum had been released, presumably to provide equipment for the rather notional "institute" that was the Administrative Training Centre.

By February 1963 this Centre had been located by turn in: (1) the Home Ministry; (2) an autonomous Administrative Board; (3) the Public Administration Department of the Finance Ministry; (4) then this Department was itself sent to the Home Ministry; (5) and then it became an autonomous Public Administration Department. This was an all too familiar odyssey in the context of government and administration in Nepal!

---

[95] Alfred Linsell, In-service Training in Nepal: March 1962 to February 1963 (Kathmandu, Nepal, February 1963), para 18.

The US AID/Nepal Interest

The Louis Kroeger Report of March 1962 can be considered to mark the formal and purposeful entry of AID/Nepal (the U.S.) into the field of technical assistance in public administration in Nepal.[96] But Kroeger also poured cold water on the idea of an Institute of Public Administration! He felt that such institutes were usually university-attached, and "demonstration is superior to academic instruction." [97]

It seems that Kroeger had a limiting perspective of: (1) the administrative training function; (2) the scope and need for it in Nepal; (3) the role of an Institute of Public Administration; and (4) its value and potential for administrative development. His opinion that there was no need for the construction of an Institute structure aroused concern in Nepali circles. It was thought that AID/Nepal was now trying to abandon the Institute project, for which it was considered the major aid donor.

But AID/Nepal did not use the Kroeger Report to withdraw from the Institute project (at least not immediately). It seems to have made the Institute project a central part of the public administration technical assistance effort that it contemplated. The scale of effort tentatively proposed for the Institute was indicated in an AID/Nepal document of 22 December 1962.[98] It stated that:

Assistance will also be offered in constructing and staffing an Institute of Public Administration and in training personnel to undertake broad administrative improvements in the operational agencies (of His Majesty's Government).[99]

With the assistance of the U.S. AID/Nepal Public Administration Training Advisor, (His Majesty's Government will) formulate and implement an in-service training program for administrative personnel. This Institute will eventually take over the public administration training functions both of in-service type training required by (HMG) personnel and for young Nepalese graduates planning government careers.[100]

---

[96] Louis J. Kroeger, A Public Administration Program for His Majesty's Government of Nepal (San Francisco: Griffenhagen-Kroeger Inc. March 1962).

[97] Ibid. p. 72.

[98] AID Form 10-120 (7-62), 22 December 1962. Government Management and Institutional Development (Goal AB), Nepal.

[99] Ibid. p. III AB-2

[100] Ibid

During F.Y. 1964 a three-man contract team will be recruited and this team will remain in Nepal for a period of three years in order to plan, in coordination with the U. S. AID/Nepal and the UN Public Administration Advisors, organize the curriculum of and teach in the Institute of Public Administration.[101]

It is planned that the new (Institute) building should take from one to one-and-a-half years to construct, and that the construction should be let as early as possible in F. Y. 1964, so that building completion will closely coincide with the arrival of the U. S. contract team.[102]

The Institute project was seen in a three-year perspective (fiscal years 1964-67). For this period AID/Nepal indicated a willingness to provide $643,000 for the construction, equipment, and operation costs of the Institute, and for the U.S. contract team. An additional $240,000 was offered for local and overseas training, and $60,000 was offered for establishing a Central Office Machine Repair Centre to be attached to the Institute.

It was in this background that Frank G. O'Neill (U. S.) came to Nepal as Chief of the Public Administration Division of AID/Nepal. He stayed from December 1963 to September 1964. The two other American advisors in his team were Harold L. Smock as O&M Advisor (June 1963 to June 1965), and George A. Melanson as Training Advisor (July 1963 to July 1965). O'Neill concentrated his efforts on the plans and proposals for an Institute of Public Administration. In this respect he might be considered a successor to his compatriot and former UNTA Advisor Merrill R. Goodall, who had left Nepal in August 1963. There is no mention of Goodall in O'Neill's draft report on the proposed Institute of Public Administration (March 1964).[103] But Hartvig Nissen (UNTA Advisor in Public Administration ---1957-60) is mentioned.

O'Neill's report did not differ too much from Goodall's earlier proposals for the Institute. The Institute's main functions were to be administrative training, research, and documentation. Like Nissen, but unlike Goodall, he put primary stress on the training aspect of the proposed Institute. He felt that in the following five-year period the highest priority should be given to the short-range training needs in administration, such as: executive development; supervision training; functional training; pre-service training for entrants into the Gazetted Service; and training for clerks, secretaries, and typists. He felt that the Institute might cooperate later with the university to provide graduate-level training in public and business administration.[104]

---

[101] Ibid
[102] Ibid., p. III 72-AA-4.
[103] Frank G, O'Neill, Draft Report on Proposed Public Administration Institute, Nepal (Kathmandu, Nepal, 3 March 1964).
[104] Ibid., pp 5-6.

O'Neill was not keen about locating the Institute within the university. He felt that this would overemphasize the academic aspect of public administration, and a better location for the Institute would be the Public Administration Department, which was then under the Chairman of the Council of Ministers. He thought that in that location the Institute would be protected from inter-ministerial rivalries, and that ideally the Institute should be a semi-autonomous organization within this Department.

O'Neal preferred that the Institute should eventually develop into a separate entity directly under the Chairman of the Council of Ministers, and that its affairs should be managed by a Board of Governors who would be working with a fulltime Director.[105]

Most Nepalis saw the proposed Institute of Public Administration as a training center. So by stressing the training function O'Neill was closer to the local concept of the Institute than Goodall had been. Also, O'Neill thought that the Institute should be located within the Public Administration Department, and that this would in effect have enhanced the resources and status of that Department. This contributed to support for O'Neill's proposal from within this Department. In Goodall's earlier proposal the Institute was to have been located outside this Department, and those attached to the Department would therefore have seen it as drawing resources and attention away from them.

It seems that O'Neill had closer rapport on this one with the Secretary of the Public Administration Department. Also, his proposals, which would also involve some major expenditure by HMG, were part of a projected funding effort by his own aid agency; whereas Goodall was working for UNTA but recommending an institution-building project whose major donor was to be another agency (AID/Nepal).

Local consciousness of the Institute idea was increasing with the ongoing discussions and passage of time. The earlier UNTA advisors like Hartvig Nissen and Merrill R. Goodall deserve much credit for this. The consciousness was also growing with the increasing number of Nepalis who were being exposed to the theory and practice of public administration, both within in the country and via foreign training opportunities.

The Government approved O'Neill's report on the Public Administration Institute. Plans for the institute building were completed. HMG allocated a site for the same within the spacious grounds of the Civil Secretariat building (Singha

---

[105] Ibid. p7.

Durbar).[106] Then AID/Nepal appears to have bowed out – and rather abruptly and unilaterally too! As a senior and knowledgeable local official put it:

> *After December 1965, U.S. AID/Nepal policy concerning the Institute building changed. The Project Agreement for construction of the building had been signed by both AID and HMG officials, but another Project Agreement deleting the construction portion was sent to His Majesty's Government again for signature without any explanation. Thus the beginning of the building construction was delayed, awaiting further study which never came through for reasons best known to AID. Consequently, recruitment of the full staff was postponed for fear that they would have to wait indefinitely before being used – leading to poor morale and working habits.*[107]

Perhaps American hesitation on the Institute project had started even earlier, around December 1964. Illness had forced O'Neill to leave Nepal prematurely in September 1964, after only ten months in the country. He seems to have been popular and effective with his Nepali counterparts, and his departure must have been a great loss to the Institute project. Harold L. Smock succeeded him as Chief of the Public Administration Division of AID/Nepal, and remained in that (acting) capacity till about June 1965. Smock seems to have felt that he had no role or responsibility for helping to establish an Institute of Public Administration. It seems that after O'Neill's departure the Institute project was "de-emphasized" by AID/Nepal. There seems to be no mention of the Institute in the bilateral General Public Administration Project Agreement of 5 April 1965. The earlier agreement of 7 April 1964 had been full of it!

The reasons for this rather abrupt change on the American side are not clear. On the Nepali side, it has been said that the then Director of AID/Nepal killed the Institute project. Some suggest that he did not have good rapport with either O'Neill or with the leadership of the Public Administration Department. On the donor side, it has been said that the blame might lie on the opposition and dilatory tactics of a senior Nepali official. It appears that there were disagreements on how the Institute should be run, and what say AID/Nepal should have as the principal donor. The abrupt U.S. withdrawal did cause some bitter feelings in the Public Administration Department, and it effectively killed the project on the Public Administration Institute.

---

[106] Nanda Lall Joshi, Evolution of Public Administration in Nepal (Kathmandu, Nepal: Centre for Economic Development and Administration, 1973), p. 64.
[107] Ibid.

Recommendation for an Institute of Public Administration

There is an immediate and urgent need for an Institute of Public Administration. Such an institute should make available to the system of public administration of HMG such services as: (1) internal technical assistance; (2) administrative training; (3) survey, research, and documentation; and (4) activities of a professional meeting place and clearing-house of administrative materials for ministers, public servants, professionals and academics, and students and the public.

In the current context such an Institute must enjoy the intimate and sustained support and attention of His Majesty the King. He should appoint a Secretary General to give the Institute energetic, professional, and continuing leadership. This person should be equivalent in rank to his principal counterpart in HMG – the Chief Secretary. There should be no Board of Directors. But a Board of Consultants might be appointed to: (1) advise the Secretary General; (2) discuss and approve the annual budget of the Institute; (3) audit the expenditures of the Institute; (4) assist the Institute in its relations with public and private sector bodies; and (5) report periodically to His Majesty on the performance of the Secretary General. This Board should include in its membership senior HMG officials, representatives of the academic community, and some distinguished and concerned members of the public. But the executive authority of the Institute should be vested in the Secretary General.

The Institute should enjoy intimate working relationships with the Administrative Management Department (AMD). This Department should be developed into a strong and effective central office of administration located under the Chairman of the Council of Ministers, and it should be given the fulltime leadership of the Chief Secretary of His Majesty's Government (HMG). But the AMD should not be amalgamated with the Cabinet Secretariat. As the central office of administration, it should be charged with the coordination, direction, and development of the administrative system of HMG. It should also be the principal agency of HMG charged with running the personnel administration system of the Nepal Civil Service in a coherent and coordinated manner. The AMD should be the principal client of a separate and autonomous Institute of Public Administration, and it should determine the scope and magnitude of services that the Institute would provide to HMG.

The Institute of Public Administration should be established by statute. It should be an autonomous institution outside the administrative and academic bureaucracies of the country. It should provide an institutional framework within which qualified staff could expect a full career in training, research, and consultancy. It should work to establish, develop and consolidate an indigenous capability for administrative development in Nepal.

CHAPTER 9

THE CENTRE FOR ECONOMIC DEVELOPMENT

Genesis, Rationale and Challenges

The Centre for Economic Development and Administration (CEDA) was established in accordance with the tripartite agreement signed on 15 May 1969 between His Majesty's Government of Nepal (HMG), Tribhuvan University (the national university), and the Ford Foundation.[108] The Centre's objectives were stated as:

1. To provide a high-level institution for both in- and pre-service training and career development for His Majesty's Government and other Nepal Government and private sector enterprise personnel. Special emphasis will be given to supplying specific skills required for effective planning and implementation of development activities in Nepal. That is, techniques referring to project formulation and evaluation; annual planning, programming and budgeting; short-term, medium-term, and long-term planning; regional planning; and the implementation of development plans are to be emphasized.

2. To provide facilities, and encourage and conduct on-going applied research, emphasizing the evaluation of development activities, and the accumulation of data to be used in planning, teaching, managing, and otherwise carrying on the work of the nation.

3. To develop a facility with competence for providing consulting services. This consultation will be focused upon the same areas being emphasized in the Centre's training program, i.e. effective planning, implementation and evaluation of developmental activities in Nepal.

4. To improve the capability of Tribhuvan University to fulfill its unique role of education in Nepal. (In CEDA's first progress report this latter objective was elaborated as consisting of cooperation with the University "in developing its curriculum, level of instruction, library, and research program, in the disciplines of economics, commerce, public administration and related social sciences"). [109]

---

[108] Agreement of Cooperation between His Majesty's Government of Nepal, Tribhuvan University, and the Ford Foundation for the Establishment of the Centre for Economic Development and Administration (Kathmandu, Nepal, 15 May 1969).

[109] Centre for Economic Development and Administration, Progress Report for the first Eighteen Months of Operation: July 1969- January 1971 (Kathmandu, Nepal: Centre for Economic Development and Administration, 1971), p. 1. There have also been two

The Centre for Economic Development and Administration appears to have been Douglas Ensminger's baby, with midwifery done by the then Finance Secretary in His Majesty's Government. Ensminger was the Ford Foundation Representative to Nepal and India (based in New Delhi) in the years 1953-70. He was the primary force behind the conception and establishment of CEDA. Since the early 1960s, the Ford Foundation's assistance to Nepal had been purposively directed to the areas of planning and economic analysis. Ensminger felt that Nepal was accepting massive foreign assistance without having well developed plans for its utilization. Without effective planning, foreign assistance was being utilized on unrelated projects and, often, the projects were priorities of the donors, and not Nepal's.

The Foundation's policy in Nepal was to support the country's planning efforts, as centered in the Planning Commission and Finance Ministry, with a phase-out as trained Nepalis took over themselves. CEDA was seen as the logical step in providing training and developing local competence in planning and economic analysis. The inspiration behind CEDA was primarily that of economics.

So why were the other areas of public administration and university development added to the core economic role envisaged for CEDA? The public administration area was added insofar as Ensminger and his colleagues saw it as economic development administration – as the implementation of plans and management of public sector projects and enterprises. Public administration appears to have been seen primarily as business economics and finance applied to public sector operations. The limitation of this particular outlook, and the inadequacy of its perspectives, would be apparent to most students of public administration. What it had done is to project a newer and partial, and financially and commercially determined emphasis of public administration, at the cost of prior and more substantive areas.

This limiting economist outlook, that mistook the part for the whole, was to have some negative consequences for CEDA's future. The Ford Foundation Advisor who concentrated on the proposal and plans for CEDA was not even aware of the previous reports of 1957 and 1962 that recommended the establishment of an Institute of Public Administration!

The inclusion in CEDA objectives of the development of higher education in the social sciences seems due mainly to tangential considerations. One was the

---

Progress Reports by the Centre -- in 1972 for the period February 1971 to July 1972, and in 1973 for the period July 1969 to July 1973. other Progress Reports by the Centre -- in 1972 for the period February 1971 to July 1972, and in 1973 for the period July 1969 to July 1973.

understandable desire to win the support of the academic community for the CEDA enterprise. The more important one was the desire to find a suitable institutional location for CEDA. Both Ensminger and the Finance Secretary in HMG felt that CEDA should be independent of Government but should be geared to serving its needs – as Ensminger and his colleagues perceived these needs.

These people felt that within HMG the Centre would not be a very exciting institution. It would more likely fall victim to vested political and bureaucratic interests and wither away. But they also felt that as a department of the University the Centre would not have had the freedom to be innovative and to formulate training and research programs designed to serve the needs of government. So it was decided to have CEDA established as an autonomous institution within Tribhuvan University, with substantial Ford funding to bolster its independence from HMG. It would appear that CEDA's university development responsibilities were the price to be paid for its institutional location-cum-autonomy. They were to be the cause of some headaches to CEDA later on.

In the tripartite agreement of 15 May 1969 (between HMG, the Ford Foundation, and Tribhuvan University) the Centre was given powers to:

1. Formulate its own regulations; 2. Appoint staff members (other than the Director) without reference to the University Services Commission; 3. Establish its own pay scales and conditions of employment; 4. Prepare and approve its own budget; 5. Establish and approve its own program for training, research, and consultancy services; 6. Award certificates to those completing its courses; 7. Publish and utilize results of research conducted by it; and 8. Enter into affiliation with other institutions without prejudice to the terms of the founding agreement.

These powers were vested in a Board of Governors. The Board was to run CEDA through an Executive Director nominated by HMG in consultation with Tribhuvan University and the Ford Foundation, and appointed with the approval of the Board of Governors. Since the Board of Governors tended to give a remarkably free hand to the Executive Director, it was he who in effect exercised CEDA authority, and who seems to have determined its policies, emphases, staffing, and direction.

But there were some stark truths behind the formal autonomy. In Nepal no institution can be created and sustained without HMG concurrence. CEDA autonomy was a grant of HMG that would have to be intermittently justified to it. This may have been forgotten at times by CEDA's leadership and proponents. Also CEDA was not established by statute. Its legal status remained unclear. This increased its institutional vulnerability to various designs within HMG and the academic community to control it. The lack of a statutory framework was an invitation to the various academic and bureaucratic factional interests to fish in CEDA's institutional waters.

The Centre's autonomy was vested in the Board of Governors. But this Board was very much under the control of His Majesty's Government. In theory there was a balance of interests in the Board. Its ex-officio Chairman was the Vice-Chancellor of Tribhuvan University. Two Members were nominees of HMG and two were nominees of the Tribhuvan University Syndicate. The Executive Director of CEDA was the Member Secretary.

But apart from the possible exception of one university nominee, the Head of the Economics Department, the rest owed their posts to HMG decision and could be transferred out of them as and when it desired. They were the Vice Chancellor, the Finance Secretary, the Governor of the Rastra Bank, a Member of the National Planning Commission, and the Executive Director of CEDA. Subsequent changes in Board membership highlighted the reality of government and the fact that CEDA autonomy was no more than a tentative grant of HMG. Tribhuvan University could hardly give CEDA a truly autonomous location; it was itself a dependent of HMG.

The substantial foreign funding did help CEDA autonomy. His Majesty's Government could be tolerant of an institution like CEDA that attracted substantial foreign resources and made limited claims on scarce local resources. Also CEDA could argue with considerable justice that only an institution like itself was likely to attract such outside funds for economic development research and consultancy. The Ford Foundation was the major funding agency. It contributed 50 percent of the building costs, as well as funds for consultancy and research, case studies, equipment and fellowships. It also provided full and part-time technical assistance services.[110] As of June 1973, the Ford Foundation had obligated some $800,000 to CEDA. In August 1974 it had indicated a willingness to obligate an additional $200,000 to CEDA.[111] In addition, U.S. AID/Nepal had, as of June 1972, obligated some $350,000 to CEDA, mainly for building, furnishing and equipment, and for the establishment of a Documentation Centre.[112]

---

[110] Ford Foundation provided the following long-term advisors to CEDA: Dr. John Dettmann (Business Administration) from January to March, 1969, and from August 1969 to August 1971; Dr. Arie Beenhakker (Economics), who was also made available to HMG/Nepal, from August 1967 to September 1971; Dr. Vijay Kelkar (Business Administration) from September 1971 to September 1973; and Dr. Jose Abueva (Development Administration) from May 1973 to June 1975. The foundation also provided a series of short-term consultants, such as Drs. Edwin Bock, Merrill R. Goodall, Amara Raksastaya, Ajit Bannerjee, Raul De Guzman, Norman Uphoff and Warren Ilchinan.

[111] Figure based on information from Ford Foundation/New Delhi.

[112] Nepalese-American Cooperation: A Summary of American AID to Nepal, 1951-72 (Kathmandu, Nepal: United States Agency for International Development/Nepal, 1972), p. 27.

Other donor agencies also provided support, mainly in the form of contracts for surveys and feasibility studies, and through the provision of advisors and fellowships. All this massive inflow of outside funding did unfortunately arouse some considerable local envy towards CEDA.

But even in the funding aspect the reality of HMG could not be escaped. The operational expenses of CEDA, as well as the costs of its training programs, were funded by HMG. It had also contributed to the building and furnishing expenses. CEDA's clients were primarily the economic, administrative, and academic institutions controlled by HMG, and outside funding to CEDA was channeled via HMG. So the reality of HMG was quite predominant.

The chances for CEDA autonomy were made problematical by the expansive attitude of Ensminger and his colleagues, and by the CEDA leadership. They wanted an institution that would be "exciting". They felt that it should have a major influence on government policies and play a key role in national development efforts. The Government was not likely to remain cool to such an ambitious institution. This expansive attitude may also have resulted in HMG being more concerned with CEDA funding and management than was necessary.

It was also the sort of attitude that got CEDA into the areas of public administration and university development – areas that were more than usually productive of political and bureaucratic concerns within Government. It might have been wiser for CEDA to have concentrated on providing services to HMG, and related institutions, in the more technical areas of economic analysis and consultancy. These areas were large enough to demand the full-time attention of CEDA. They tended to attract major local and outside funding. They might have helped CEDA to preserve and enhance its autonomy behind the veil of a highly technical image, authority, and set of functions. But CEDA was ambitious.

Proposal for an Administrative Staff College

In early 1970 the Chief Secretary had asked Dr. Merrill R. Goodall for a note on what had to be done if His Majesty's Government was to establish an effective Administrative Staff College. Goodall had been in Nepal twice before: as an Advisor in Public Administration (from April-May 1952 as a Fulbright Research Scholar; and then again from March 1962 to August 1963 as UNTA Advisor, when he had given strong advocacy for establishing an Institute of Public Administration). He then returned as the Fulbright Visiting Professor in Public Administration to Tribhuvan University (for the academic year 1969-70).

On 6 February 1970, Goodall submitted a memo to the Chief Secretary with the title "Planning for an Administrative Staff College in Nepal". He said that despite HMG's growing commitment to sound post-entry personnel training, the educational programs for civil servants in Nepal were still too narrowly conceived and tended to operate effectively only at the lower levels of the service.

Goodall felt that HMG was ready to develop a new series of educational programs for its senior and mid-career officers in the forthcoming plan period (1970-75). He proposed that an Administrative Staff College (ASC) should be set up for this, and he suggested a gradual development program for the ASC including: 1. A survey of training needs and resources by a small, high-level body of inter-ministerial officers; 2. An observation tour by HMG officers to various educational institutions for upper-middle and top-level administrators in Pakistan, India, the United Kingdom, France, the Philippines, and the United States; and 3. The determination and discussion of plans and proposals on the scope and magnitude of the College efforts. It seems Goodall saw the proposed ASC as an entity distinct from both CEDA and the Administrative Training Centre of the Administrative Management Department. He thought the role of the Centre was to conduct lower-level training for civil servants.

A little later another modified version was provided by the Administrative Management Department (from its Training and Research Division), which also managed the Administrative Training Centre. In this proposal the Administrative Staff College (ASC) was to provide the following kinds of training: 1. Preservice training for new recruits to the public services; 2. In-service (general) training for government officials at logical stages in their career, in such areas as supervision and management methods and principles; 3. In-service (specialist) training in specific skills such as accounting, tax and land revenue administration, and health services administration; and 4. Clerical-Secretarial training in typing, shorthand, correspondence, and so on. Instruction at the Staff College (ASC) was to be supplemented where necessary by core academic training in Tribhuvan University and in foreign universities.

The ASC was to be created by legislation. It was to be run by a Board. It was felt that this would provide it with the flexibility in the appointment of staff, and freedom in the management of expenditures, that would otherwise not be possible. It was felt that training should be made mandatory, with promotions made contingent upon the attendance of ASC courses, as only then would the proposed training efforts receive the support of the ministries and departments and stand a chance of success.

The ASC proposal looked like a commendable if tentative step by the Administrative Management Department towards fulfilling the broad training responsibilities given it by HMG. The proposal was designed to link training to promotions and to career development, and to the personnel administration system generally.

The ASC proposal owed much to the initiative of the Chief Secretary. He did not see it as a threat to CEDA. Indeed he saw CEDA as desirable, useful, and worthy of support. But he saw CEDA as being involved in economic development research and consultancy and in giving advanced training in economics and planning. He did not see it as a suitable institution to provide the kind of education and training that the ASC was to be responsible for. The ASC would obtain instructors from among senior and experienced officials and professors. By contrast CEDA had recruited young people with academic degrees but not much teaching and administrative experience.

The ASC proposal died for lack of foreign funding. The Government was not willing to meet the costs of its establishment and organization by itself. AID/Nepal was aware of the ASC proposal but did not support it. In its view the staff college proposal was limited to mundane, procedural matters, and there promised to be more flexibility, independence and larger scope at CEDA. It chose to offer financial support to CEDA. The Chief Secretary had hoped that the Ford Foundation would be a major funding agency for the ASC, and had hoped to secure its aid for building expenses, technical assistance for curriculum development, and for travel and study awards for the ASC faculty. He saw the Administrative Staff College as complementary to CEDA's role and status. But the influential others at the Ford Foundation and CEDA did not see it that way.

Ensminger (Ford Foundation) and the CEDA leadership and proponents saw the proposed Administrative Staff College as a threat to their own fledgling institution. With their limiting economist perspectives they failed to perceive the full scope and scale of the administrative training needs of HMG. To them public administration was primarily about the planning and management of public projects and enterprises, and they thought that CEDA could provide training in these areas, so to them there was no need for a competing Administrative Staff College with a claim to the limited resources. Ensminger himself was curiously reluctant to have the Ford Foundation enter into public administration technical assistance in Nepal. The planning and economic analysis drive became something of an obsession, based no doubt upon personal preferences and limiting perspectives on the significance of public administration. He seems to have persuaded himself that Nepal was not willing to accept help in the sensitive area of public administration. This was not so!

There was a noticeable preference in the Royal Palace and the Civil Service Secretariat to shift the Ford Foundation emphasis in the country from economic planning to the public administration field. This in effect is what HM King Mahendra told Foundation President McGeorge Bundy when he visited in February 1968. The reluctance was on the side of Ensminger and the Ford Foundation. Later, after repeated Nepali requests, the Foundation did provide some limited, fitful technical assistance in position classification. The priorities were Ensminger's, not that of HMG. Also, his perception of Nepali needs and realities was influenced by the then Finance Secretary in HMG, who was an economist trained in the US; his advice did little to inform Ensminger's perspectives on public administration.

Ensminger met with the then Crown Prince Birendra on 29 May 1970. He advised Him that Ford Foundation's future assistance to HMG would be focused on the development of CEDA as a strong institutional resource on planning, economic development, and administration. He recommended that HMG officials be deputed to CEDA to help with training in administration. One Secretary on deputation should be Visiting Professor and Director of Training in Administration. One more Joint Secretary should be deputed to provide needed strength to the working staff. In effect he was saying that the Foundation would not cooperate with the ASC proposal, and that the Foundation would support the administrative training function only if it was given to CEDA. The ASC proposal was aborted! It was thus, by the pre-empting of a prospective rival institution that CEDA moved into the field of public administration.

CEDA and Training and Research in Public Administration

A Cabinet Policy Statement of 28 October 1970 gave CEDA the function of administrative training for HMG personnel of Gazetted Class II (Under Secretary) level and above. CEDA was to cooperate with the Administrative Management Department (AMD) in the conduct of such training.[113] The Chief Secretary was inducted into the Board of Governors of CEDA as Vice-Chairman in early 1971. Prior to this the AMD did not have a representative on this Board. A senior Secretary was deputed to CEDA as Visiting Professor. But, compared to the scope and extent of the need in administrative training, what CEDA achieved in this regard was quite limited.

CEDA organized a seminar package including courses in Project Analysis and Management, Development Planning, and Development Administration to fulfill its training responsibility for Under Secretaries. These were part-time (non-residential) courses of a month's duration each, and repeated in a cycle of four sessions. The emphasis was economic, aimed at exposing the Under Secretaries to the techniques of planning, project analysis and management, and development administration. The program did not impart any substantial specialist expertise. It may also have been too technical for the average generalist, who was unlikely to be concerned substantially with economic planning, project analysis and management in his subsequent career.

The Under Secretaries were also not quite at the significant levels of decision-making in HMG. It is the Joint Secretaries and Secretaries who occupied such

---

[113] "Training Provision for Civil Servants". A Copy of HMG Cabinet Decision of 28 October 1970.

levels in the administrative system. The CEDA rationale seems to have been that the Under Secretaries would eventually occupy more responsible positions in the administrative system, and so constitute a force for change in the future. But many would not make it to these positions, and some of those who did would probably have let rust the skills in economic development that CEDA training may have imparted to them. Some might say that the function of in-service training is to meet present needs, not to second-guess the future. No regular programs were devised for Joint Secretaries and Secretaries. CEDA did organize two colloquia of two days duration each for the latter.

There was also a case study program started in spring 1971 with the Ford Foundation providing funding and the preliminary and short-term services of Dr. Edwin Bock. By mid-1973 some 24 case studies had been produced in mimeograph form in two volumes. The broad areas of development planning, project analysis and management, and development administration were covered. In general this helped to supplement, and even to dilute, the CEDA tendency to teach abstract planning perfections, with an actual Nepal-situation and problem-solving approach.

The Under Secretaries program had started in July 1971. By October 1974 some 150 participants had been given the Project Analysis and Management course; some 156 had gone through the Development Planning course; and some 122 participants had been given the Development Administration course.[114] The total number of Under Secretaries who took all three courses was probably nearer 100. In addition, some 80 HMG officials had been put through two two-week introductory courses in program budgeting, prior to the start of the Under Secretaries training program. Some 50 HMG Secretaries had also attended the two Secretaries colloquia referred to above. There were also two two-day seminars on problems of Nepali foreign policy, and a one-week seminar on law. This was the gist of four years of CEDA efforts in in-service training in public administration for civil servants of HMG.

CEDA did contribute to administrative training in another area. From 1970-73 it ran three diploma programs in public administration. This program had been started within Tribhuvan University in 1968. The program had been developed by Dr. Richard Podol of AID/Nepal and by Dr. McAlister Brown, the first of three Fulbright Visiting Professors involved in this project. The program was open to persons with a BA degree. It was designed to provide an overall background in public administration. When fully developed, it covered courses on: (1) principles of public administration; (2) problems of organization; (3) modern management practices and techniques; (4) personnel administration; (5)

---

[114] Centre for Economic Development and Administration, A New and Permanent Status for CEDA: To Enhance its Contribution for National Development (Kathmandu, Nepal: Centre for Economic Development and Administration, September 1974), Appendix I.

development administration; and (6) financial administration. Each course lasted a month and consisted of 64 hours of classroom instruction. Examinations were taken immediately after each course, and a post-graduate diploma granted upon completion of all six courses in the program.

Eighteen students were enrolled in the first program, some of them civil servants. Dr. Brown was succeeded by Dr. Merrill R. Goodall (1969-70) and Dr. Louis Hayes (1970-71), who were assisted by Dr. Prachanda Pradhan of Tribhuvan University. CEDA took over the program in 1970, as part of its move into the field of administrative training. It was a convenient move, since the groundwork had already been laid for this smoothly operating program, which was also being conducted with heavy foreign input. It was shrewd institution building – the acquisition of what seemed to be a smoothly working program and the credit for it, with little extra effort.

CEDA did very much better in its primary interest area of economic research and consultancy, where it did fill a much needed gap in Nepal. There were seminars in areas like business management, pricing policy, small-scale industrial development, resource mobilization, human resources management and industrial policy.[115] There was perhaps some scattering of effort, with variations in quality and impact for participants, and the heavy input of foreign expertise helped to shore up the qualitative aspect of things. No external evaluation was made of these activities. But these efforts did help to fill a vacuum and did not pre-empt anyone in the process.

CEDA did very good work in the areas of survey analysis and consultancy. Among the surveys it conducted was one on the impact of development programs on the Pokhara Valley, and another on an analysis of barter and barter-like trade in Nepal. Among management surveys was one on the Royal Nepal Airlines, another on the National Commercial Bank, and another on the Transport Corporation. Feasibility studies were conducted on topics such as real estate investment, the proposed malt industry, and various transportation projects. Policy related studies were conducted in such areas as land revenue taxation by local governments; choice of technology in road construction; pricing policy in public enterprises; and regional planning.

Between fiscal years 1969-75 CEDA had conducted, or was slated to complete, some 36 such efforts in survey, analysis and consultancy.[116] These efforts attracted substantial local appreciation, and a good deal of outside attention and funding. Demands for CEDA expertise in these areas grew very rapidly indeed, and funding patterns were both flexible and considerable. These areas were demanding and expanding enough to call for the full-time attention

---

[115] Ibid., Appendix 2
[116] Ibid. Appendix 3.

of CEDA. They were areas in which CEDA was unchallenged, and their technicality tended to deter political and bureaucratic attention from within HMG. It is where CEDA should have concentrated!

There was not much logic in CEDA's acquiring the administrative training function. The Centre was an economics-oriented, multi-purpose institution, and it was unlikely to be able to devise and conduct training programs in administration to the extent envisaged in the Administrative Staff College proposal, or as per HMG needs.

The CEDA leadership and proponents did not comprehend the extent and nature of these needs. Even at Gazetted Officer level these needs cover more than the areas of planning and project analysis and management. They also include specialist training in "tool" areas such as accounting, auditing, budgeting, organization and methods, and job classification. There are "field" areas like personnel administration, land administration, revenue administration, public health administration, education administration, district administration, and customs administration. There are "policy" areas like administration and the constitutional system, land reform, family planning and birth control, trade and transit and land-locked situation, and decentralization and local government.

There is also general in-service training of the type indicated in the public administration diploma program, and also pre-service training of the civil service academy type. There is also the need for research and development in administrative training; and the need to train, develop and sustain Nepali trainers (training of trainers) within a favorable institutional and career framework.

If CEDA had seriously intended to serve these manifold needs, it would in all probability have ceased to function as an institutional resource in economic planning, research, and consultancy. Also, the focus and staff resources of CEDA did not indicate such a possibility. Its staff was young and academic, with a strong bent towards economic planning, research, and consultancy.

CEDA had developed no noticeable staff capability in administrative training and research.[117] It depended heavily on senior HMG officials and foreign expertise for such training. Also, CEDA was reluctant to engage in higher-level training of Joint Secretaries and Secretaries, in part because it anticipated resistance to send such officers to be trained by relatively younger, less experienced persons; and CEDA had not itself hired the senior staff to conduct such training.

---

[117] As of September 1974 only 2 out of 29 permanent officers of CEDA appear to have had their major degrees in public administration. Three others had them in political science. By contrast 19 officers had major degrees in commerce, business administration, and economics. (See Table 9.1).

Table 9.1. Academic Background of CEDA Permanent Officers.*

Discipline	Jan 1971	July 1972	July 1973	Sept. 1974
Economics	5	8	12	12
Commerce	2	4	3	4
Business Administration	1	1	2	3
Public Administration	1	1	1	2
Political Science	-	1	3	3
Sociology	-	1	3	1
Anthropology	-	-	1	1
Statistics	1	1	2	2
Accounting	-	1	1	-
Library Science	1	1	1	-
Engineering	1	3	-	-
Other	-	-	-	1
TOTAL	12	22	29	29
Ph. D.	3	2	4	2
M.A.	5	14	22	19
B.A.	All	All	All	28
Below	-	-	-	1

*Temporary Officers, Consultants, Visiting Professors and Advisors, and Supporting Staff excluded. (Source: CEDA Progress Reports and various other CEDA documents)

Administrative training in Nepal is a substantive and substantial enough function to justify separate institutional treatment. There is little logic in splitting it, and then subordinating a substantial chunk of it within an institution oriented primarily towards economic analysis and consultancy. Administrative training in HMG can only be effective within the context of a unified and comprehensive system of personnel administration, with oversight by a central personnel agency that is located close to the source of executive authority in government. Such an apex agency would be more likely to cooperate closely with an institution designed primarily to service its needs. This would be more likely than with an institution like CEDA, with its unique location in Tribhuvan University, and oriented primarily to economic development and consultancy.

The CEDA experience appears to make the case for an Institute of Public Administration as strong as ever. Such an Institute should be dedicated to meeting the training, research, and consultancy needs of the administrative system of HMG, and it should provide an institutional framework for staff careers in training and research in administration.

Problems of Perspective and Autonomy

The administrative training function proved to be a problem for CEDA. The Chief Secretary and the Administrative Management Department (AMD) had been constrained to drop the proposal on the Administrative Staff College (ASC) because CEDA acquired a major administrative training function, and they cooperated on the assumption that it would evolve in the direction of a Staff College. They became disillusioned when this did not happen. A senior official of the AMD, who was in charge of its training function, exerted constant pressure on CEDA to evolve in the ASC direction. In mid-1971 he went on temporary assignment to the Royal Palace Secretariat, and his pressure, with the support of a key official there, became intense.

Pressure was put on CEDA to either develop into an Administrative Staff College of HMG, or merge with Tribhuvan University as one of its constituent institutes. Neither choice involved the sort of autonomy that CEDA wished for. CEDA had acquired a very demanding client in the AMD. That Department had no intention of surrendering its training responsibilities. CEDA had acquired operational responsibility for some of the training in administration, so the AMD tried to exercise as much influence on CEDA as possible.

Perhaps in response to this the CEDA leadership began to concentrate more and more on relationships with the Administrative Management Department and the Civil Secretariat, at the cost of attention to links with institutions like the Tribhuvan University and the Planning Commission. This at a time when the Civil Secretariat was declining in weight, while the University and the Planning Commission were the objects of increasing official attention, and were forging closer links with people of influence within the Royal Palace Secretariat. The Civil Secretariat was resentful of any CEDA moves to forge closer links with the Palace Secretariat, and there was also a general feeling among civil servants that CEDA was not responding to their needs. It was a difficult situation that CEDA had brought upon itself by trying to be too many things to too many people.

Tribhuvan University had cooperated in the establishment of CEDA, and its uniquely autonomous location within it, on the assumption that the Centre would play a significant role in the development of its social science programs, and also act as a funnel for foreign assistance into the university system. These expectations were not fulfilled. CEDA acquired a high profile separate from the university, and itself absorbed the substantial funding available to it. Its unique autonomy within the university; the great deal of leeway given to its Executive Director by the Board of Governors; its flexible administrative structure;

comparatively high staff salaries; and relative affluence of funds and facilities, all contributed to resentment within the University faculty. This made things difficult for the Vice-Chancellor of Tribhuvan University, since he was also the Chairman of the Board of Governors of CEDA.

Changes in the Board of Governors also weakened the ability of CEDA to withstand pressures upon its autonomy. The first Board had been a very good one for CEDA. Five of six members were economists, and four were Ph.Ds. All seemed well disposed to the CEDA Director. The Finance Secretary who had worked with Ensminger (the Ford Foundation) in establishing CEDA was a member. He had access to the King and was influential within HMG. He facilitated the highly delegated style of operations which the Board adopted, but he left in July 1971. The induction of the Chief Secretary as Vice-Chairman of the Board in early 1971 was also helpful for the building of bridges between CEDA and the Civil Secretariat and its Administrative Management Department. He was supportive of CEDA and its Executive Director, and had access to the King. But he left in January 1972. A year later the Board looked to be a rather weak one. None of its members was especially supportive of institution building or the research function. Only one was an economist, and only one was a Ph.D. Five of the six members were career bureaucrats in the civil service and university administration. It looked like a relatively weak Board that was passive and unable to withstand unfavorable pressure from outside.

Some rather strong and negative pressure appears to have come from the influential Vice-Chairman of the National Planning Commission. He did not like CEDA's high profile and plenitude of resources, and appears to have looked on it rather negatively as "that trans-Atlantic organisation"! From this perspective, perhaps the "foreign" profile in CEDA, especially of the Ford Foundation, was higher than was wise. To the more youthful and cosmopolitan staff and leadership of CEDA this was perhaps not a problem. But it exposed CEDA to some negative undercutting. CEDA's first Executive Director was young, energetic, intelligent, educated and cosmopolitan. He led it during its four years of autonomy (1969-73). But he had a capacity to attract strong personal feelings, and seems to have had a fair share of detractors in HMG and academia. For them it was difficult to distinguish CEDA from its Director. This blurring of identities may also not have been to CEDA's benefit.

Also, it cannot have been wise for CEDA to assume for itself the role of critic to HMG. To say that such criticism was meant to be constructive was not helpful, since in Nepal there is not a very great appreciation of the function of "loyal opposition". To the extent that such an opposition was tolerated it would more likely be from within something like a legislature or political party. CEDA was not these things and was not set up to do so. Its task was to present findings emanating from its research in a clear, objective, and judicious manner and provide constructive analyses, based upon documented facts and figures.

In an address to the Conference on Institution Building and Development (26-30 June, 1971), the Executive Director of CEDA characterized the Government as a "monopolistic institution" and called this situation unhealthy and productive of a "stale atmosphere" detrimental to the flow of ideas and initiatives and likely to lead to involutionist thinking! He saw it as CEDA's duty "to bring in new options and ideas and to provide alternatives of policy and decision to the government."[118] At the same seminar another senior CEDA official suggested that there was an "establishment" running the Government! He felt that it was CEDA's function to provide alternative ideas to those of this "establishment", and to test these ideas "in the cauldron of public opinion". He said that CEDA's role was winning it popularity with the general public, and was "bringing the spotlight to bear on CEDA."[119]

This may not sound unusual to some. But in the Nepali context it was not very wise to openly claim the role of critic to Government, especially for a relatively new institution with no local roots. HMG was not interested in funding its critics, and according them prestige and autonomy, and then again not those who courted the spotlight and public popularity in the bargain.

This self-appointed role of HMG critic also highlights the image of CEDA as an institution of young, bright, and ambitious personalities with all of the privileges of criticism but none of its restraints. There were those in administration and elsewhere who dared not criticize HMG and resented CEDA's claim to such a function. Such an attitude also put CEDA in an unnecessarily political light. In 1971, barely two years after its establishment, CEDA's first Deputy Director was elected to the National Assembly on a rather radical ("anti-Government") platform. His consistent and unusually critical attitude to Government eventually landed him in jail. He was a bright young person who had only recently returned from the USA with a Ph. D. in Business Administration. It did little to improve CEDA's image within HMG.

On 16 July 1973, the Centre for Economic Development and Administration lost its autonomous status within Tribhuvan University. It was absorbed into the newly established Institute of Business Administration, Commerce, and Public Administration (henceforth "Institute of Business") of the university. The Centre lost its Board of Governors, and also its first and energetic Executive Director. This "Institute of Business" was not an Institute of Public Administration as envisaged by advisors like Nissen, Goodall, and O'Neill. Nor was it even a close approximation to the proposed Administrative Staff College. This new Institute of Business that replaced CEDA was an academic entity within Tribhuvan

---

[118] Conference on Institution Building and Development: June 26 to 30, 1971 (Kathmandu, Nepal: Centre for Economic Development and Administration, 1971), p.11
[119] Ibid. pp. 84-85.

University; a sort of untidy combination-department of Business Administration, Commerce, and Public Administration within a university.

The decision to downgrade CEDA was made by the National Education Board (NEB) in two meetings on 24 April and 15 May 1973.[120] The composition of this Board is interesting. It had the outgoing Executive Director of CEDA. It also had the Vice-Chairman of the National Planning Commission, who it seems did not much like the CEDA Director, and who spoke disparagingly of the Centre as "that trans-Atlantic organization"! With the grace and favor of the King, and strategic connections in the Royal Palace Secretariat, this Vice-Chairman had become quite influential in HMG. The other five Board members were from the academic community; two were ministers and three were university administrators. The Board membership might be viewed as a six-to-one composition against CEDA! The NEB had no members from the Civil Secretariat or from its Administrative Management Department. The NEB decided to move CEDA into the new Institute of Business, within which it would be set up as a separate unit for research and counseling; and it added that "Whether this arrangement is to be retained or ended, is to be decided on the basis of its usefulness and effectiveness."[121]

That CEDA was not immediately wiped-out as a distinct entity was due mainly to its foreign connections and funding. Some contracts were still in effect between HMG and donors, and perhaps it was felt that these projects should be completed before CEDA's separate identity was more completely demolished.

Without royal support for a strong and independent CEDA it could not survive academic and HMG efforts to control it, or failing this, to downgrade or disintegrate it. The Royal Palace Secretariat was becoming the real policymaking unit in the country – not the Civil Secretariat, and not the Council of Ministers. The Royal Palace Secretariat worked in close coordination with "technocrats" like the Vice-Chairman of the National Planning Commission. Quite a few of these "technocrats" seem to have cooled to CEDA. At that stage perhaps the Royal Palace Secretariat was also cool to CEDA, though maybe not to the extent of wanting it to be fully demolished.

Meanwhile CEDA lost its Documentation Centre to the Tribhuvan University Library. This center had been established with the assistance of AID/Nepal, and it had developed a useful collection of some 5,000 books, articles, and documents, in Nepali and English, with a particular concentration on economic development matters.

---

[120] Copy of the Decision taken by the National Education Board (A mimeo dated 15 May 1973).
[121] Ibid. p. 3.

In a meeting on 4 May 1973 the National Education Board also sabotaged the resurrection of the Administrative Staff College proposal. In this matter CEDA and the academic community were in agreement, as neither wanted to allow the growth of a potential rival outside their own particular institutional set up. They also had no adequate comprehension of the scope and scale of the administrative training needs of HMG. The Board (NEB) felt that the New Education Plan (whose principal author was one of its own members) had intended that post-school education and training needed for HMG programs and projects should be met through the Tribhuvan University only, via its relevant constituent institutes, and with no other separate arrangements!

So responsibility for administrative training was given to this composite Institute of Business.[122] In other words the need must conform to the plan, rather than vice-versa! The members of the NEB had not bothered to study the nature and extent of the need. The new arrangement repeated most of the disadvantages of the old one, with the added problems that the composite Institute of Business did not enjoy CEDA's flexibility of operations; nor did it look like the sort of institution that was likely to attract donor funding and technical assistance in public administration. Its resources looked to be inadequate, and its location and programs too mundane, for an institution charged with the responsibility for administrative training and development.

CEDA was not easy to digest! It had hardly been taken into the composite Institute of Business than it began to struggle to get out. In this it got strong support from Dr. Jose Abueva, who in May 1973 had come to CEDA as the Ford Foundation Advisor and as Visiting Professor in Development Administration. The Dean of the Institute of Business had looked upon Abueva as a key resource in easing CEDA's transition problems and in building bridges between himself and the CEDA that was now under him. But CEDA had a tendency to attract strong commitment from the donor community, and Abueva himself soon identified quite completely with CEDA. He worked closely with its leadership in undercutting the Dean's position. The struggle was soon characterized as "the battle for CEDA autonomy from (the Dean)." It became unsavory at times, getting personal and communal, as some things tend to be. In identifying with CEDA, Abueva found himself on one side of an intense institutional struggle. It was not an ideal situation for a foreign technical consultant.

The institutional struggle quite inevitably involved the Royal Palace Secretariat. The new (and third) CEDA Director even managed to get a 40 minute audience with the King. The latter appears to have been favorably disposed to his idea of converting CEDA into a National Development Academy. He asked the Investigation and Inquiry Centre (*Janch Buch Kendra*) that was attached to the Royal Palace Secretariat to look into the matter. A task force was formed

---

[122] Ibid. pp. 4-5.

with the CEDA Director and an official of the *Panchayat* (Local Government) Training Institute as members and with the Joint Secretary of the Administrative Management Department (in charge of its training responsibilities) as chairman. He had been involved in the earlier (aborted) Administrative Staff College proposal. What the task force did is not clear.

In December 1974 another committee was set up to draft a comprehensive plan to make CEDA capable of formulating necessary development projects for the country, and also preparing the manpower needed for their implementation. This committee was headed by the same Member of the National Planning Commission who had previously been the second Director of CEDA from July 1973 to April 1974. It was thought that by mid-1975 CEDA would be restored to a separate status within Tribhuvan University.[123] But it seems that this had not transpired as of November 1975.

Two documents, authored by Dr. Jose Abueva among others, are worth mentioning with regard to the existential question of CEDA's future. The first document of 8 March 1974 dealt with a proposed reorganization for the new developmental role of Tribhuvan University.[124] It called for the conversion of CEDA into a Tribhuvan University Development Centre (TUDC), which naturally meant getting it out of the Institute of Business. Another stated purpose of the TUDC proposal was to "render unnecessary any move to establish another Administrative Staff College in Nepal."[125] The proposed TUDC was to have a Director who would be responsible for running its affairs. There would be a Council above him to give him broad policy directions, as in the case of the CEDA Board of Governors.[126]

The proposed TUDC was to be given a mind-boggling mix of roles and functional units.[127] These were: 1. A Development Policy Council for development policy research; 2. A National Development Research Council for advisory and consulting services; 3. An Administrative Staff College to develop the administrative and managerial competence of executives in His Majesty's Government, the public corporations, and private enterprises; and 4. Four separate units for "university development" – (a) The University Development Service; (b) The Administration Service; (c) The Information and Publication Service; and (d) The Centre Facilities Service. In addition to this the TUDC was to have the roles of "enlightenment of public opinion" and "constructive criticism

---

[123] Nepal Press Digest, Vol. 18, No. 51, 23 December 1974.
[124] Centre for Economic Development and Administration, Reorganising for the New Development Role of Tribhuvan University (Kathmandu, Nepal, 8 March 1974).
[125] Ibid. p. 9.
[126] Ibid. p. 6.
[127] Ibid. 6-7 and passim.

and inducement of change." [128] This was quite a mixture of roles and responsibilities and very broad-based too!

Where was the institutional leadership and capability for all this? What logic was there in combining this plethora of roles and functional units? The combination looked to be devoid of logic, whether considered from the perspective of organization by "clientele" or by "purpose". The only logic seems to lie in organization by "special purpose" – to resurrect CEDA to its former autonomous status, and indeed to enhance it considerably. It seems that Abueva (and others) had a limiting comprehension of the nature and extent of administrative training needs in Nepal. Perhaps it was a perspective clouded by too close identification with an embattled and egotistical CEDA.

About six months later another document of September 1974 proposed a new and permanent status for CEDA – to enhance its contribution to national development needs. [129] It was something of a rehash of the earlier TUDC proposal. It was based ostensibly on an opinion survey of CEDA staff (by CEDA staff), which not surprisingly indicated their desire to see CEDA restored to its former autonomous status. There was some confusion, since they wanted CEDA to retain its name, but also to become an Administrative Staff College of Nepal (ASCON). It seems that the purpose of the ASCON twist was to thwart pressures to convert CEDA into an Administrative Staff College. It appears from the document that the CEDA staff did not wish to give up their previous bent towards economic analysis and consultancy.

Some of the functions proposed were quite unusual for an ASCON![130] Among them were: 1. To provide policy-makers with some of the conceptual, empirical, and value premises for shaping developmental policies, plans and programs; 2. To assist policy-makers to evaluate the formulation and implementation of such policies, plans and programs; 3. To recommend alternative policy ideas and decisions to policy-makers; 4. To help Tribhuvan University in its various programs, to enhance its role in national development; and 5. To foster intelligent and informed discussion of issues and problems in Nepali public affairs, so as to promote the formation of an enlightened, concerned and influential public opinion. Such an institution was not very likely to meet the comprehensive administrative training needs of HMG!

These two documents of March and September 1974 were not very convincing. They emanated from an embattled CEDA that was desperate for

---

[128] Ibid. p. 1.
[129] Centre for Economic Development and Administration, A New and Permanent Status for CEDA: To Enhance its Contribution to National Development (Kathmandu, Nepal: Centre for Economic Development and Administration, September 1974).
[130] Ibid. pp. 10-11.

resurrection to its former role and status. They reflected institutional angst rather than institutional logic!

CEDA as a National Institute for Economic Research and Development

CEDA had its existential problems because it was too ambitious. These ambitions may have clouded perspectives, and may have caused its proponents and leadership to have gotten ahead of institutional realities – or the lack of them.

There is place for a national institute of economic research and development (and consultancy) in Nepal. CEDA did rather well in this capacity, and this is what it should have been developed into. Such an institute should operate with the sort of autonomy that was given to the original CEDA. It might also have an institutional location that is close to, but independent from, the National Planning Commission and Tribhuvan University, among others.

The administrative training function, that CEDA had so unwisely acquired, should go into an Institute of Public Administration that is separate and autonomous from, but works in close relationship with, the Administrative Management Department (or a Ministry of General Administration).

There is also space for Tribhuvan University to develop separately, but in tandem with them, in the academic disciplines of economics and government and administration. This would separate roles and emphases that are substantive and substantial enough to merit separate attention. It would facilitate the institutionalization of two broad and vital functions in Nepal, of administrative development and economic research and development, and locate these institutions closer to their respective major clients and support bases.

CHAPTER 10

TRAINING IN ADMINISTRATION

In Rana times there was an administrative school of sorts called the *Shrestha Pathsala* (Accounts School). It was started circa 1905 and was operated by a *Gurju* (High Priest), apparently at his own residence. The studies at this school led to an examination called the *Char Pass* (four passes), successful completion of which facilitated (but the absence of which did not necessarily restrict) entrance to the lowest clerical level of the civil service system. The passes referred to were in the four subjects of accounting, arithmetic, handwriting, and administrative rules and regulations. It seems that in the immediate post-Rana years no concrete efforts were made to improve training in Nepal. The Indian advisors appear to have done little if anything for the development and institutionalization of the administrative training function in the country.

Training Programs and Efforts at Institutionalization

The government of Prime Minister Tanka Prasad Acharya (January 1956 to July 1957) did make some purposeful moves towards the development and institutionalization of the administrative training function. The UNTA Public Administration Advisor Hartvig Nissen (Norway) was intimately involved in these efforts. He was principal advisor to two sub-committees of the Administrative Reorganization Planning Commission (1956-57) that recommended that an Institute of Public Administration be established in Nepal, and drew up plans for the Institute.[131] The proposed Institute was directed initially at the in-service training of civil servants. But the Commission itself did not survive beyond the typically short tenure (for Nepal) of the Tanka Prasad Acharya government that had created it (18 months).

It appears that an "institute" was established notionally in early 1958 when a number of in-service training courses were commenced in the Civil Secretariat building. These courses included: 1. Functional seminars for officials at Deputy Secretary level; 2. A course for departmental Directors; 3. A four-month training program for a small group of development officers to be sent to the districts; 4. Basic short-term training for a large number of lower-grade officers in job

---

[131] Ad Hoc Advisory Committee Regarding an Institute of Public Administration in Nepal, Report (Kathmandu, Nepal, 1957), and Committee on the Institute of Public Administration in Nepal, Report (Kathmandu, Nepal, 1957),

instructions, methods and relations; 5. Special training for about 500 civil servants in the use of the new Secretarial Manual; and 6. Three courses in elementary bookkeeping. Senior Nepali officials and aid mission staff served as instructors.

The notional "institute" was formalized in February 1959 when His Majesty the King declared open the *Prashasan Prashiksan Kendra* (Administrative Training Centre). So the existing in-service training courses that took place in a few rooms of the Civil Secretariat building were given the institutional but largely declaratory framework of a Centre. No full-time director or full-time instructors were appointed. It was a useful beginning, but the Centre or "institute" was at this stage a rudimentary affair with a very tentative existence.

Herbert Arnold McKinnnon Billings (U.K.) was the first In-Service Training Advisor provided to the country from UNTA. His initial one-year term (March 1960 to February 1961) was not renewed. His terms of reference were rather broad:

1. To assist the Nepal Government in the planning and conduct of a broad program of in-service training for personnel of its central ministries and its field and regional offices.
2. To examine existing clerical methods and office practices and organize appropriate training courses in such work with special application to staff at the clerical and middle-supervisory levels.
3. To develop Nepali staff trainers through appropriate use of special courses in training methods, on-the-job teaching of assigned junior aides, and recommendations for UN or other fellowships.

All this called for the services of an expert in administrative training – and an unusually good one in the difficult Nepali context. Billings was not this. He had risen from the clerical levels of the U.K. civil service to its middle-supervisory levels. On the way, he had acquired much administrative experience in the Ministries of Health, and Pensions and National Insurance. Some of this was in the supervision of training in office procedures and O&M for clerical level officials. His technical assistance experience prior to, and after, his assignment in Nepal, had been as a social security expert in Brunei, Indonesia, and Pakistan.

This was perhaps a not sufficient background to indicate a capability to identify, to shape, and to establish a broad-based, in-service, administrative training program in Nepal. That UNTA proposed Billings as a training expert, and that the Government accepted him, may indicate an insufficient comprehension of the scope and scale of the training needs in administration and of the magnitude of the challenge in doing something concrete about them.

It seems that Billings did not achieve much beyond the state of the administrative training function as it was at the time that his predecessor Nissen had left it in, in early 1960. He was not even asked to submit a formal report at the end of his term. He wrote the writer that he did leave behind "copious notes for lectures etc.," but it appears that this material became sort of "fugitive" when he left. His successors do not indicate having used them.

There was a rapid deterioration in the state of the administrative training function in the year following Billings' departure. The times were difficult for any efforts aimed at administrative development in the country. The Royal Coup of December 1960 had been followed by a massive purge of civil servants in February 1961. Among the fallen was the Planning Secretary, who had been ex officio Director of the Administrative Training Centre since its inception. In February 1961 the Centre was combined with the O&M Office into an Administrative Board. This Board was an autonomous entity outside any ministry. It had a full Secretary at its head and was located directly under the seniormost Cabinet Minister. But in September 1961 the Board was absorbed into the Finance Ministry, where it became the Public Administration Department under a Joint Secretary. The Administrative Training Centre had thus fallen to the status of a section, within a department, of a ministry.

By March 1962 the Institute was defunct. It had no staff, no budget, and could not be said to exist. The rooms (in the Civil Secretariat building) which were allocated to the Institute were literally ankle-deep in rubble, and its office equipment, gift of a foreign aid mission, covered with dust. The Institute's library of some three hundred volumes was unavailable to prospective users. [132]

It seems that things had regressed to square one. His Majesty's Government (HMG) then requested that the successor to Billings (U.K.) be "from a small country like ours so that he may be able to understand and help in solving the problems of administration in Nepal very easily."

Alfred Linsell (U.K.) succeeded his compatriot Billings as the In-Service Training Advisor from UNTA. He was in Nepal from March 1962 to June 1963. He had some good qualifications. He had some fifteen years of experience of technical assistance in clerical-secretarial training in Sudan, Egypt, Iran, and Burma. He was given the same terms of reference as Billings; and it might be said that these were very broad for an expert in clerical-secretarial training.

Linsell's efforts were facilitated by the enhancement in the status of the Public Administration Department (PAD). His contemporary Merrill R. Goodall,

---

[132] Merrill R. Goodall, "Administrative Change in Nepal" in Asian Bureaucratic Systems Emergent from the British Imperial Tradition. ed. Ralph Braibhanti (Durham, N.C.: Duke University Press, 1966), p.264.

who was at the time the UNTA Public Administration Advisor, deserves some credit for this. In July 1962 the PAD was taken out of the Home Ministry. (It had recently been transferred there from the Finance Ministry in May 1962, to where it had been transferred previously in September 1961. Prior to that it had been the Administrative Board that was created in February 1961 and that reported to a senior Cabinet Minister). This new or rejuvenated PAD was given an autonomous status outside of any ministry. It reported directly to the Vice Chairman of the Council of Ministers (His Majesty the King was Chairman), and it had the full-time leadership of the seniormost Secretary in HMG. The training function was put under the Training Division of the Department. There it was to enjoy a four-year locational stability.

Some good progress was made during Linsell's tenure in Nepal – especially when one considers that work in administrative training had to recommence almost from scratch. An induction course was conducted for 25 newly appointed Gazetted Class officers, and another for 29 new Non-Gazetted Class staff. He conducted three courses on: administration for civil aviation personnel; office management for accountants; and management for the Nepal Industrial Development Corporation. Some 64 personnel received these courses.

Another 154 civil servants were given training in typing, shorthand, and records management. The classes on typing appear to have been an innovation as well as a cooperative effort: three instructors were loaned by the Indian Aid Mission; HMG provided counterpart personnel who later became instructors themselves; the Colombo Plan donated 12 Nepali-language typewriters; and AID/Nepal sent two Nepali trainees to India for courses in typewriter maintenance and repair. Linsell wrote the Report on Secretarial Management which became the basis for courses on this subject.[133] These courses led to the revision in 1963 of the 1958 Secretariat Manual. But the new Manual was not formally adopted or put into practice.

Linsell helped to reestablish the administrative training function in HMG. But the progress was mainly in the area of clerical-secretarial training. There were still huge gaps to be filled in the overall field of administrative training, and there was still a long way to go for its institutionalization. Linsell observed that despite the increase in Gazetted staff of the Public Administrative Department to 25 in the year from March 1962 to February 1963, only two were concerned with training!

In his final report Linsell recommended that the training function of the Public Administration Department should be given the full-time leadership of a Director of Training with the upgraded rank of Joint Secretary. He urged the need

---

[133] Alfred Linsell, Report on Secretarial Management (Kathmandu, Nepal, 1962).

to properly staff and equip this function, and to put it in a building that would be suitable to its activities.

But Linsell did not support Goodall's push for an Institute of Public Administration! He felt that the immediate need was to concentrate training efforts at the "grassroots" level. He felt that it was at this lower (clerical-secretarial) level that the bulk of government officials were located, and where methods and processes were most in need of improvement.[134] As a specialist on training at the clerical-secretarial level, he was perhaps less likely to have sympathy for Goodall's larger vision of a broad-based Institute of Public Administration.

Linsell's one-year term was extended by a few months to June 1963, but not renewed. This was because AID/Nepal wanted to provide its own in-service training advisor, as part of a planned effort that included the establishment of an Institute of Public Administration. HMG felt that it could not coordinate the efforts of two in-service training experts from two different donors (UNTA and AID/Nepal); and the donors themselves were also concerned about possible duplication of efforts, and inclined to have a given area of technical assistance to themselves, or to leave it to the others. George A. Melanson (U.S. AID/Nepal) replaced Linsell as In-service Training Advisor (from July 1963 to July 1965). His terms of reference were as follows:

Advise and assist HMG of Nepal to upgrade their administrative personnel and to help implement improvement through in-service training; help to make training needs surveys; conduct training for higher echelons; prepare training course materials; train local trainers; and assist in organizing and establishing an Institute of Public Administration. [135]

Melanson's two-year tenure coincided with increased activity in the training function of the Public Administration Department. During the period from July 1963 to January 1965 the numbers of civil servants trained were: 1. Some 562 Gazetted and Non-Gazetted Class officials trained in Scientific Organization and Improved Supervision; 2. Some 501 Non-Gazetted officials trained in government rules and procedures; and 3. Some 297 Non-Gazetted Class officials were trained in typing and filing.[136]

---

[134] Alfred Linsell, In-Service Training in Nepal: March 1962 to February 1963 (Kathmandu, Nepal 1963).

[135] His Majesty's Government of Nepal and U.S. AID/Nepal, General Public Administration Project Agreement, 7 February 1964.

[136] Nanda Lall Joshi, Evolution of Public Administration in Nepal (Kathmandu, Nepal; Centre for Economic Development and Administration, 1973), p. 63. He quotes from an AID/Nepal document entitled "Technical Assistance Project History and Analysis Report, General Administration Project, July 1963-January 1965."

Training efforts were also taken to the field. Three mobile training units were formed. Seven instructors in administration, and three in typing, were recruited to staff them, and they were given three months of intensive training in in-service training methods and on course content. [137] These teams covered several districts annually, and by mid-1974 they had covered 62 of the 75 districts in Nepal. The remaining 13 districts were to be covered in the next two years. But it seems there was no provision for refresher training in the districts covered.

Melanson also cooperated with his counterparts in surveying training needs, defining training policies, preparing basic training material and training trainers, and laying a sound foundation for a broad in-service training program in HMG.[138] But the training capability that he helped to develop was primarily in the clerical-secretarial area.

In summer 1964 plans were prepared to provide pre-service training to the newly recruited graduate entrants (Section Officers) to the Administrative Service. A program of instruction was devised in seven major areas: general administration, financial administration, the *panchayat* system of government, economic planning, law, history, and geography. It was a three-month residential program, for which an old Rana palace was rented. Instructors were drawn from among senior HMG officials and from the foreign aid community in Nepal.

Two residential programs were run successfully, then the residential requirement was withdrawn. The lack of dormitory facilities was one reason given for this move. [139] Another likely one is that the residential requirement was not too popular with the trainees, quite a few of whom had homes and families in the Kathmandu valley area. The three-month pre-service training program became a common feature of the administrative training efforts of HMG. But some observers have thought that perhaps three months may be too short a time for the broad sweep of subjects in the program. Also, if resources permit, then there may be some wisdom in a residential program. This might facilitate concentrated efforts by staff and students, with more freedom from outside distractions. "Residential" is not only about dormitory facilities, but also about recreational, social and study activities. Group-life during training can help students to learn from teachers and from each other. It can help to stimulate the trainees, and facilitate exchange of ideas and experiences. But residential programs should not become too monastic, or too elitist.

---

[137] Ibid.
[138] Ibid.
[139] Ibid,., pp. 64-70

A major disappointment during Melanson's tenure was the failure to establish the Institute of Public Administration. AID/Nepal had intended that ultimately all HMG administrative training activities would be encompassed by, and become a part of, an Institute of Public Administration; and when fully functional this Institute would be responsible for fostering, developing and conducting administrative training on a government-wide basis. [140]

Frank G. O'Neill, the AID/Nepal General Public Administration Advisor, had drafted a report on the proposed Institute of Public Administration (March 1964).[141] Heavy emphasis was put on the in-service training functions of the proposed Institute. HMG had approved the report. But illness had forced O'Neill to leave the country rather prematurely in September 1964, and AID/Nepal inexplicably withdrew from the Institute project circa December 1964.

AID/ Nepal was supposed to be the major funding agency, so its abrupt withdrawal killed the Institute project. Some possible reasons for the withdrawal were: (1) disagreements with the Nepalis as to how the proposed Institute should be run, and what say AID/Nepal would have as the major donor; and (2) the leading officials in AID/Nepal and HMG were unwilling or unable to reconcile their differences. AID/Nepal may have felt chagrin and lost patience as a result. The abrupt end to the Institute project dealt a serious blow to the hopes of enhancing the administrative training capabilities of HMG above the clerical-secretarial level.

Then the Public Administrative Department was itself dissolved in April 1966. Its personnel and administrative reform functions went into the newly created Cabinet Secretariat. Its administrative training function went into the Economic Planning Ministry. There it was organized within a Central Training Department with its own special Secretary.

Sir Eric Franklin, the then UNTA Senior Public Administration Advisor, did not like this move. He thought it was an institutionally retrogressive step. He felt that the administrative training function was related functionally to the central personnel function and should be organized in tandem with it. In his final report he urged that the Central Training Department be brought back into the central office charged with administrative improvement in HMG.[142]

---

[140] HMG and AID/Nepal, General Public Administration Project Agreement, 7 February 1964.
[141] Frank G. O'Neill, Draft Report on Proposed Public Administration Institute (Kathmandu, Nepal, 3 March 1964).
[142] Sir Eric Franklin, Development of Public Administration in Nepal (Kathmandu, December 1966), pp. 62-63.

Sir Eric was perhaps correct from the perspective of consolidating and enhancing the capability for administrative development within HMG. The blow of the move was perhaps softened by the fact that: (1) the then Economic Planning Secretary was a young, energetic, influential and development oriented individual; (2) the Central Training Department had an enhanced status with its own Secretary to lead it; and (3) the Cabinet Secretariat was itself not a very suitable location for the administrative development and training functions of HMG.

The Central Training Department (that had been moved to the Economic Planning Ministry) was given the following broad functions: 1. To formulate the training policy of His Majesty's Government; 2. To survey and determine HMG training needs; 3. To coordinate various departmental training programs, bring about uniformity in them, and give clearance for the conduct of these programs; 4. To approve training programs abroad; 5. To conduct general administrative and other training required by government agencies; 6. To evaluate different training programs and to provide guidance to make them more effective; 7. To prepare and produce training materials; and 8. To conduct research and provide consultancy services.[143]

This was a very broad training responsibility. All this heralded a substantial increase in the scope of efforts expected of the Central Training Department, which was to be the central training agency of HMG. It was located in an old Rana palace, and it received AID/Nepal assistance for training materials, equipment, building renovation and furniture.

Various kinds of training programs were organized and conducted almost entirely by local people. Indigenous training materials were developed, a library was organized, visual aids were assembled, and training films were collected. All these were used extensively in the training programs. [144]

Howard L. Grigsby (U.S.) succeeded Melanson as Training Advisor to HMG. He was in Nepal for two years from September 1966 to September 1968. AID/Nepal got his services from the Public Administration Service (PAS) of Chicago, where he had been since 1966. Prior to that he had been a training officer in the Federal Communications Commission (1964-66); a management development officer of the Internal Revenue Service (1958-64); a training liaison officer to the Chief of Finance, U.S. Army (1956-58); and instructor-trainer at the U.S. Army Adjutant General's School (1953-56). But the Nepali situation was difficult and unusual. It seems Grigsby could not adapt to it. The PAS advisor found it very difficult to adjust to the administrative environment of

---

[143] Joshi, Evolution of Public Administration in Nepal, p. 69. Quoting from Public Service Training in Nepal (Kathmandu, Nepal: Central Training Department, His Majesty's Government of Nepal), pp. 2-3
[144] Joshi, Evolution of Public Administration in Nepal, p. 70.

Nepal. The type of management training required in Nepal was less than that required in a more sophisticated management or administrative environment. The result was little effective work or improvement in this area.[145]

It seems that Grigsby could not achieve very much during his two-year term. There was some progress on course content and training techniques. But it seems that the Central Training Department could not benefit much from his expertise. He appears to have run into a myriad of problems during his term as the Training Advisor to HMG. "Language was a barrier."[146] The instructors at the Central Training Department taught in Nepali, and the course content was also in this alien (to him) language. Thus he found it difficult to evaluate the content of the training courses and the capability for training of the instructors. The efforts to translate course content into English may have caused some dislocation of training efforts and demands of time, and the English of the instructors may not have been that good either!

The General Public Administration Project Agreement of 7 February 1964 between HMG and AID/Nepal had provided for the establishment of a translation pool in the Public Administration Department, to translate administrative training materials into Nepali. It seems that this pool did not exist several years later when Grigsby came (1966-68). There is need for such a pool. A lot of research, development and writing in public administration takes place abroad. This material must be translated and given wider dissemination in Nepal.

Grigsby found that the morale of the training instructors was rather low, because being "development" personnel they were in the temporary employ of HMG, and therefore were not entitled to the tenure and pension benefits given to "regular" civil service personnel. At this time "development" personnel were quite agitated about their insecure status in HMG.

During Grigsby's tenure the training effort was supposed to also include middle and top management officials of HMG. This was not achieved during the project period.[147] It seems that these officials refused to be trained by the instructors of the Central Training Department, who were of a lower grade than they were! The alternative would have been to have a training program conducted by senior HMG officials and by members of the aid community. It seems this was not done. This "status" issue points to the need for an Institute of Public Administration that is outside the hierarchical and bureaucratic set-up of HMG.

---

[145] Public Administration Service, Project for Improving Government Organisation and Methods and Management Training, Government of Nepal: Final Report (Chicago: Public Administration Service, 29 May 1969), p.6
[146] Ibid.
[147] Ibid.

In April 1968 the Public Administration Department was resurrected in the form of the new Administrative Management Department (AMD). This Department was given the equivalence (not formally) of a separate ministry of His Majesty's Government, with the full-time leadership of its own Secretary. Into it went the administrative reform and personnel functions that were with the Cabinet Secretariat; and the Central Training Department was taken out of the Economic Planning Ministry and became a division within the AMD. But this was a loss in status for the Central Training Department from being a semiautonomous department to becoming a subordinate division, and from having the full-time leadership of a full Secretary to being led by a more junior Joint Secretary.

Grigsby had difficulty in establishing rapport with the Secretary of the new Administrative Management Department. Already burdened with a sense of a failure, the change in status and location of the training function proved to be the last straw for him. After April 1968, "the limited progress that was being made by the advisor came almost to a standstill," and "his enthusiasm for the project waned," especially with management training for middle and top management officials. [148] He left in September 1968 without having had much impact on developing and institutionalizing the administrative training function.

Starting from April 1968 the responsibility for oversight of the central training function in administration was placed with the Training and Research (T&R) Division of the Administrative Management Department (AMD). The Division was led by a Joint Secretary. It administered the Administrative Training Centre, where the AMD conducted its training courses. In the years since 1968 there seems to have been quite a gap between the AMD's broad-based training responsibilities and the actual work done. The T&R Division seems to have confined its activities to basically running the Administrative Training Centre. Its range of some ten programs (as of September 1974) emphasized: (1) limited general administration training (pre- and in-service) for the junior level of the Gazetted service (Section Officers); and (2) clerical-secretarial training in typing, shorthand, and office procedures.

A survey of the AMD in September 1968 reported that the T&R Division's training programs had become routine and ritualized, rather than dynamic and changing. [149] Little attention was being given by the Division to such other responsibilities as: (1) formulating training policies; (2) determining administrative training needs; (3) conducting research related to its training activities; and (4) evaluating training programs. The survey recommended that

---

[148] Ibid., p.7.
[149] Administrative Management Department, HMG/Nepal, Management Survey of the Administrative Management Department of His Majesty's Government of Nepal (Draft Report, Kathmandu, Nepal, September 1971, p. 54.

there should be a clear separation of the T&R Division and the Training Centre, with both reporting directly to the Secretary of the AMD. [150] The survey thought that this would facilitate fuller attention to the broad-based training responsibilities of the AMD.

Some Observations and Recommendations

There appears to be room for considerable improvement within HMG as regards appreciation of, and support for, the administrative training function.

The fact that between mid-1971 and early 1974 no permanent Joint Secretary was named to lead the Training and Research Division speaks volumes. The resulting lack of leadership dissuaded AID/Nepal from offering a training advisor to help the AMD assume its broader training role. There were many staffing problems. The Gazetted Class Officer training section had no permanent instructors. They were usually drawn on an ad hoc basis from various ministries and departments. It seems that what was taught was closer to the inclination of visiting instructors than to the training needs of the participants. There were also problems of career development for the eleven instructors in the section for training Non-Gazetted Class staff. Six of the instructors were Section Officers, but since there was no dedicated post of Under Secretary immediately above them, they would have to be transferred out if promoted; and the five typing instructors, all Non-Gazetted Class I officials, had no opportunity for advancement within their functional position at the Training Centre.

The absence of an effective central personnel agency in HMG is a serious problem. This has led to the existence of a rather fragmented civil service system in Nepal. This has also been a major reason for the lack of an effective and comprehensive career development scheme in administration. It has also contributed to neglect of policy formulation, and research and development, regarding the administrative training function of HMG. Without such a central personnel agency it will be difficult to persuade the ministries and departments to utilize to the fullest the training programs made available to their staff by the Administrative Management Department. Without such an agency the administrative training function of HMG will continue to seem rather disoriented and with a limited perspective.

The administrative training capability of HMG, as it exists in the Administrative Management Department, appears to be limited largely to clerical-secretarial training, with some little capability in induction and refresher training for the lowest level of the Gazetted Class (the Section Officers). This is a very limited capability when compared to the scope of the administrative training function, and the magnitude of HMG needs in this area.

---

[150] Ibid. p.66.

The administrative training function is a very broad one. It may be divided into pre- and in-service training. It may consist of orientation and induction training before, or early in an official's career, and of refresher and retraining at later career stages. It may be classified into general administration training, clerical-secretarial training, management training, and specialized training. Specialized training may be classified into "tool" areas like personnel administration, O&M, and revenue administration; and into "policy" areas like land reform, family planning, law and order, decentralization and local government. So far the AMD with its Training Division and Training Centre seems to have touched only the tip of the training iceberg. [151]

Table 10.1 Administrative Training Centre: HMG Staff Trained (1956-74).

Five-Year Plan Period	No. of Persons Trained			
	Gazetted	Non-Gazetted		Total
		Centre	District	
First (1956-61)	334	1,291	-	1,625
Second (1962-65)	257	691	548	1,496
Third (1965-70)	1,124	1,208	1,346	3,678
Fourth (1970 up to July 1974)	1,591	2,223	1,122	4,936
TOTAL	3,306	5,413	3,016	11,735

Source: Administrative Management Department, HMG/Nepal, Management Survey of the Administration Management Department of His Majesty's Government of Nepal (Draft Report, Kathmandu, Nepal, September 1974)

---

[151] Despite all the problems the point should not be overlooked that the Administrative Training Centre in various manifestations has been involved in the training of a large number of HMG employees over the years – about eleven thousand in the period 1956-74 (See Table 10.1).

The problem is basically one of institutionalization of the administrative training function within HMG. This will remain largely unresolved until there is an improved perception of the role of the training function in administration and for administrative development; and until due value is given to the potential contributions of the training function, so that HMG is willing to divert some of its own scarce resources to sustain and enhance this function with the priority that it deserves. The institutionalization problem might be summarized as: (1) lack of adequate comprehension and appreciation of the administrative training function in HMG; (2) lack of top-level executive support for this function; (3) lack of assurances of sustained and sufficient resources for this function; and (4) lack of adequate institutional bases and relationships for this function. The basic institutional problems relate more to attitude and perception, than to training.

What is needed is a massive effort of will, imagination and leadership for the promotion of administrative training and administrative development in Nepal. The problem of institutionalization is broad-based and must be tackled in a coherent, coordinated, sustained and purposeful way. This also requires an effective central office of administration, with authority to run the personnel administration system, and to direct, coordinate, and develop the public administration system. In the training field such an office would formulate training policies, determine administrative training needs, and evaluate training programs.

There is need for an Institute of Public Administration that is separate and autonomous from such an office, but that has an intimate working relationship with it. This Institute would conduct training courses; do related research; and train, develop, and sustain Nepali instructors and research staff within a favorable institutional and career set-up. This Institute should also provide inputs into other aspects of public administration like: (1) survey and research; (2) internal technical assistance; and (3) information, exchange, and communication.

The Institute of Public Administration should be autonomous from both the civil administration and university bureaucracies. In the current situation it ought to be given the close and constant support and patronage of His Majesty the King. It should enjoy the greatest possible flexibility in budgeting, staffing, programming and operations. It should be established with Nepali money, materials, staff and leadership. The donor input should be supplementary.

Utilization of Overseas Training Opportunities

The foreign advisory efforts in public administration were supplemented by the provision of participant training opportunities outside Nepal. UNTA Training Advisor Alfred Linsell noted in his final report that in the period from 1951-61 some 2,163 scholarships were granted to Nepalis for overseas training. Some 53 Nepalis were sent abroad for training in administration from 1951-61, but that at the end of this period only some 13 were known to be employed in government! The disposition of some 37 of them was quite unknown.[152]

In the period 1951-73 the U.S. AID program in Nepal sent out some 2,060 Nepalis for training in various fields.[153] Of this some 159 Nepalis were sent out for training in public administration, and 126 for community development training.[154] The AID/Nepal document from which these figures are taken also indicates the position held by each trainee at the time these statistics were compiled in 1973. The figures below give a best assessment of the number of trainees sent abroad for training in selected areas of public administration who in 1973 were in posts in HMG in which their acquired expertise was likely to be substantively used. The figures indicate the number of trainees and (in parentheses) those in posts related to their field of training: 1. Organization and Methods – 15 (2); 2. Personnel Administration – 11 (5); 3. Administrative Training – 10 (4); and 4. Local Administration – 57 (39)

These figures are indicative of the general need for improvement in the utilization of trained expertise within the civil service system. There is also considerable room for improvement in its personnel and training policies. One problem is the vague and limiting generalist perspective that appears to pervade much of administration. The result is that many officials are not put in the job for which they were trained, and where their expertise could be utilized for the maximum possible benefit. A related factor is the lack of an effective and comprehensive career development program in administration. Such a program is unlikely to be successfully instituted in the absence of a strong and effective central personnel agency.

---

[152] Alfred Linsell. In-Service Training in Nepal. He derives these figures from Table 20, Section 5, of a May 1962 UNESCO report entitled Education Planning in Nepal and its Economic Implications.
[153] Cancelling out for multiple training, there was a total of some 1,918 Nepalis who were sent out by AID/Nepal for participant-training in various fields in the period from 195173.
[154] Participants Directory, HMG-U.S.AID (Kathmandu, Nepal: United States Agency for International Development/Nepal, 8 March 1974).

There have been attitudinal problems regarding the optimal utilization of overseas and participant training opportunities. It seems that they have not been adequately appreciated as a means of acquiring and developing valuable expertise in administration, and indeed of enhancing knowledge and skill levels more generally in the country. A senior and experienced Nepali observer and administrator points to the tendency in the past to treat such participant training opportunities as "subsidized tourism"![155]

There seems also to be a "distributive approach" to the selection of people for these training opportunities. Such a "distributive approach" often conforms to considerations that are primarily: departmental (to divide up the opportunities to travel abroad between departments, irrespective of relevance); patronage (to provide opportunities to those linked to senior politicians and bureaucrats); political (distribution according to party affiliation, communal, regional or other criteria seen as vital to system maintenance); and protectionist (to exclude those seen as "outsiders" to the system and those with a "western" education). Such limiting and wasteful attitudes hamper the optimal utilization of training opportunities, and of the expertise that may be acquired for the development of public administration, and the development of the country itself.

Not surprisingly, there appears to have been a somewhat poor acceptance cum utilization rate of participant training opportunities that have been made available. It is the old paradox of Nepal not only lacking the resources for its development, but of also being unable to more fully utilize the resources that are offered! It seems that in 1962 Nepal utilized only one-third of the fellowships made available by the UN! In 1972 Nepal could utilize only half of the participant training slots offered by various donor agencies! In earlier years a major problem appears to have been the lack of an adequate system to process and utilize the training offers; but later it may have been a case of too much system, with very inappropriate perspectives of distribution, reward and punishment, nepotism, protectionism and envy. So many offers lapse yearly because people cannot cut through the pettiness and red tape, or are not allowed to!

It seems that under the new scholarship rules (instituted in 1972) the foreign training opportunities are processed through some eight separate bureaucratic processes involving some six separate HMG entities! The results can be unfortunate. In fall 1973 two training slots in management analysis, at an American university, could not be utilized because of insufficient time to process the nominations under the new scholarship rules. It seems that in 1973 AID/Nepal offered HMG eight training opportunities as part of its Administrative Management Training Project, but the National Planning Commission (NPC) decided to curtail the number of AID/Nepal training

---

[155] Joshi, Evolution, p. 59.

opportunities! The Administrative Management Department protested strongly, and succeeded in having three of the eight seats restored.

It was said of the then Vice Chairman of the Planning Commission that he was a British-trained technocrat with a rather parochial and ethnically "Gurkha" thought process and preferences. He had strong links to the Palace Secretariat and a disdain for most things American. He had referred to the Centre for Economic Development and Administration (CEDA), whose principal sponsor was the Ford Foundation, as "that trans-Atlantic organization"!

There is a need to ensure that manpower "planning" does not degenerate to the level of manpower "policing"! The chronic under-utilization of overseas and participant training opportunities is beyond reasonable in the context of the country situation, and of the need for development of public administration in Nepal, and the development of the country generally. The penchant to restrict foreign study opportunities to those in government, or to those close to the political dispensation, is very wasteful in the context of national development.

The proprietary and exclusionary approach to the foreign training opportunities that have been made available to the country, and the chronic underutilization and mis-utilization of these opportunities, perhaps also reflect embedded perspectives amongst political leaders and bureaucrats who see politics and public administration as means of entitlement rather than of public service. It might also be observed that this is much more unfortunate for the country when it is considered in the context of the broader, chronic reality that the civil service in general, and more so at its senior levels, is not in its composition a very close reflection of the general composition of Nepali society in its varied connotations of caste, ethnicity and so on. This is the same at the leadership levels of the political parties and the various and ever-changing "governments" that they have been "leading".

Thus overseas training may not have had an optimal impact upon administrative development in Nepal. Its effects upon the administrative environment are limited by a number of constraints. One of these is the relatively small number of trainees compared to the range and numbers of qualified staff required. This might be made more problematic by the parochial, distributive, or political approach to the opening of training opportunities, and selection of candidates. There is then the further problem of the underutilization, or perhaps even non-utilization, of returnees in their areas of acquired expertise.

Another possible challenge that may have to be faced is the reassertion of cultural norms and political realities against innovation, and the inability of trainees to adapt what they have studied, and their acquired expertise, to local needs and realities. Edward Weidner refers to these problems in his book on technical assistance in public administration. [156]

Despite this, overseas training has made some useful contribution to administrative development in Nepal. It has helped to impart specialist expertise. To the extent that the expertise has not been properly utilized, or nurtured and developed, it must be regretted, and redeemed. Overseas training has helped to introduce the administrator to foreign concepts, processes and systems, and it has brought awareness of the possibilities for administrative change and reform.

Overseas training has helped to make the trainees more development oriented, and some trainees have held useful positions at senior levels of administration, and in agencies like the *Janch Bujh Kendra* (Investigation and Inquiry Centre) and the Administrative Management Department. It has contributed to positive moves for administrative improvement.

Foreign Advisory Assistance and Training Opportunities

Foreign advisory assistance is about the transmission of information between the donor and recipient. For this to succeed there must be some degree of complementarity between the originators and recipients of the communications. The recipient system must develop a capacity to absorb, analyze and utilize the information that is transmitted through the technical assistance process. [157] Participant training can play a vital role in imparting such expertise and inculcating a perspective that is conducive to reform and development.

But administrative development can only be a sufficient and sustained reality where the capability for this has been adequately indigenized and institutionalized. In this respect participant training overseas can be a more useful method of technical assistance than some of the more general and fragmentary foreign advisory efforts of the past. Such training may be more cost effective than in maintaining an intermittent and relatively expensive series of foreign advisors. Also the advisor's expertise is lost to the host country when he departs, in many cases after too short a stay. By contrast, the participant trainees bring their hopefully newly acquired expertise back to the home country – to stay.

---

[156] Edward W. Weidner, Technical Assistance in Public Administration Overseas: The Case for Development Administration (Chicago; Public Administration Service, 1964).

[157] John T. Dorsey, Jr., "An Information-Energy Model" in Papers in Comparative Public Administration, eds., Ferrell Heady and Sybil L. Stokes (Ann Arbor, Michigan; Institute of Public Administration, The University of Michigan, 1962), pp. 52-53

Participant training overseas exposes Nepalis directly to foreign concepts and processes and systems in a different and often more developed learning environment, and then challenges them to relate and adapt them to their own. It introduces Nepalis to the possibilities of change and reform, while hopefully enhancing their capability for research and analysis, and adaptation. It remains for Nepalis and their country institutions to decide how best this new experience and expertise might be utilized for administrative development.

This complementary approach would seem to be closer than foreign advisory assistance per se to the best tradition of helping people to help themselves. It might be less likely to produce those human and social costs and tensions, such as inferiority complex and dependency syndrome, that more direct and exclusive foreign advisory assistance can generate on its own. The two approaches must be complementary, at the very least.

Technical assistance efforts in public administration ought to put emphasis on helping the Nepalis to develop a capability to decide for themselves what they need by way of administrative development, and to generate the local expertise to do the necessary about it. The stress must be on indigenization and institutionalization. This calls for greater emphasis on institution-building in Nepal and on complementary participant training overseas.

CHAPTER 11

PERSONNEL SYSTEM AND ADMINISTRATION

The Civil Service System

The Nepal Civil Service system covers all civilian employees of the ministries and departments of His Majesty's Government (HMG). The university (Tribhuvan University) is outside this system and has its own set of personnel rules and regulations. The employees of the "public corporations" (government-owned enterprises) are outside the civil service, except for persons on deputation to the corporations from the various ministries and departments.[158]

In the personnel structure of the Civil Service there is a vertical distinction between "Gazetted" and "Non-Gazetted" posts. Gazetted posts are used for administrative, professional, and technical types of work. Non-Gazetted posts are used for clerical and sub-professional types of work. In general, a person must have at least a Bachelor's degree to be eligible for initial entry to the Gazetted level. There are four levels (ranks) of Gazetted posts: Special Class (Secretary), First Class (Joint Secretary), Second Class (Under Secretary), and Third Class (Section Officer), in descending order of seniority. Similarly there are four levels (ranks) of Non-Gazetted posts: Class I (*Nayab Subba*), Class II (*Kharidar*), Class III (*Mukhiya*), and Class IV (*Bahidar*) in descending order of seniority. At the lowest level of the system is the labor-messenger group, designated as peons and equivalent.

The Gazetted posts are divided horizontally into eleven cadres or Services and two broad groups (administrative and technical). The administrative group includes the Administrative, Foreign, Judicial, Auditing and *Panchayat* Services. The technical group covers the Education, Health, Agriculture, Engineering, Forest, and Miscellaneous Services. There are no Special Class posts of Secretary

---

[158] The legal basis of HMG Civil Service is provided by the following: Part 13 of the Constitution of Nepal, 12 December 1962 (Amended 27 January 1967), relating to the Public Service Commission; the Public Service Commission (Working Procedure) Act, February 1964, and the Public Service Commission (Working Procedure) Rules, 24 August 1970; the Nepal Civil Service Act, 11 September 1956, and the Nepal Civil Service Rules, 22 March 1965, which on being promulgated replaced the earlier Nepal Civil Service Rules of 8 December 1956. The Acts and Rules mentioned have been subject to amendment since their dates of promulgation.

(normally the administrative head of a ministry) in the technical Services. The Services vary in size, as can be seen from Table 11.1.[159]

Yet another distinction between posts is that between "permanent" and "temporary" (previously called "regular" and "development") posts. The distinction was initially made to identify those temporary "development" posts created to carry out development projects, which were usually financed primarily from foreign aid. The idea was that when these "development" projects were terminated, those of their staff who were no longer needed could be separated so much more easily from HMG service. These "development" personnel were in the temporary employ of HMG and therefore ineligible for the service tenure and pension benefits granted to permanent or "regular" HMG personnel.

The "development" personnel appear to have resented their insecure status and suffered in morale. The problem was compounded by the large increase in development posts, many of which began to acquire de facto permanence. Foreign advisors often cited this distinction between "regular" and "development" posts as being harmful to the national development efforts, as well as constituting bad personnel administration. Starting around 1968 a large number of posts were converted from "development" to "regular" status.[160]

A Ministry of General Administration was created by the first post-Rana government formed in February 1951. Besides responsibility for general and district administration it was charged with central responsibilities in personnel administration, such as: 1. Appointments, postings, promotions and transfers of all *Bada Hakims* (district governors) and Heads of Department; 2. General references from the Public Service Commission; 3. General terms and conditions of service; and 4. Conduct and discipline of Government servants.[161]

The Ministry of General Administration was merged with the Cabinet Secretariat in 1952. The resulting entity was called the Prime Minister's General Administration Department. In May 1957 this department was dissolved, and its central personnel responsibilities went into the Ministry of Home Affairs.

---

[159] The Administrative Service has itself been divided into the following sub-groups, primarily for purposes of selection for overseas training: General Administration (personnel administration, public administration, field administration, community development, defence, education, and rules and regulations interpretation); Statistics; and Finance (economics, commerce, industry, taxation, and customs and excise).

[160] The above broad description is derived in part from Lee. D. Bomberger, "The Need for Civil Service Reform in Nepal", in Prashasan (The Nepali Journal of Public Administration), Yr. 4, No.2, July 1973, pp. 33-43.

[161] Nepal Administrative Reorganization Committee, Report (New Delhi: Ministry of External Affairs, Government of India, 1952), p. 147.

Table 11.1 Gazetted Class Officials in HMG Civil Service (July 1973).

	Classes - Ranks				
Service	**Special (Secretary)**	**First (Joint Secretary)**	**Second (Under Secretary)**	**Third (Section Officer)**	**Total**
Administrative	63	98	532	1,301	1,994
Administrative	39	52	362	994	1,447
Foreign	11	9	17	47	84
Judicial	9	31	91	113	244
Panchayat	1	1	7	17	26
Auditing	2	4	19	74	99
Other[1]	1	1	36	56	94
Technical	-	185	597	1,789	2,571
Education	-	33	174	288	462
Health	-	50	193	492	735
Agriculture	-	36	94	241	371
Engineering	-	37	74	294	405
Forest	-	19	39	64	122
Miscellaneous		10	56	410	476
Total	63	283	1,129	3,090	4,565

[1] The "Other" or "Miscellaneous" Service is a general category including political appointees and those not in any other Service.
Source: Records of the *Nizamati Kitab Khana* (Civil Personnel Records Centre).

Rule 9 of the HMG Transaction of Business Rules (1962) stated that: "The Ministry of Home Affairs shall, unless the case is fully covered by instructions or advice given by that Ministry, be consulted in all matters involving: (a) the determination of the methods of recruitment and conditions of service and general application thereof to Government servants in civil employ; and (b) the interpretation of the existing laws and orders of general application relating to such recruitment or conditions of service; provided that the Ministry of Home Affairs shall consult the Ministry of Law in respect of matters mentioned in clause (b)."

The Home Ministry was a government entity with a plethora of functions and a primary orientation to law and order, control and regulation. It was not very likely to give the personnel administration function the specialist attention that it deserved. Sir Eric Franklin, the Senior UNTA Public Administration Advisor to HMG from May 1964 to December 1966, urged that this function of the Home Ministry should be transferred to the Public Administration Department (PAD), which at the time was an entity outside of any ministry, reporting directly to the Chairman of the Council of Ministers, and under the senior most Secretary of HMG.[162] (See Chapter 5 above for the mutations and migrations of the PAD).

This Department (PAD) already had the function of examining proposals for the creation of positions or their alteration in status, and of forwarding its recommendations to the Finance Ministry. It also had the function of receiving and assessing periodic efficiency reports on all Gazetted Class officials. This Department was also supposed to function as the principal instrument for administrative improvement in His Majesty's Government. In April 1966 the personnel functions of this Department, as well as of the Home Ministry, were combined within the Management Improvement Division of the newly established Cabinet Secretariat. In April 1968 the Public Administration Department was resurrected as the Administrative Management Department (AMD). The AMD took over the administrative reform and personnel administration functions of the Cabinet Secretariat, as well as the administrative training function that was at the time with the Ministry of Economic Planning.

The AMD, through its Personnel Administration Section, was responsible for administering the Administrative Service. This included: 1. Posting new Section Officers (fresh entrants to the Gazetted Class) to various ministries and departments; 2. Initiating transfers, or approving them if so requested by ministries or employees; 3. Approving requests for "acting" status; 4. Maintaining individual files for each officer; 5. Reviewing ministry recommendations for incentive awards; 6. Acting as a communications channel between the ministries and the Public Service Commission; 7. Administering the

---

[162] Sir Eric Franklin, Report on the Development of the Public Administration Department (Kathmandu, Nepal, September 1964), pp. 25-26.

Reserve Pool (*Rekh Dekh Daudaha*); 8. Collecting information on and investigating cases of disciplinary action recommended by the ministries and departments; 9. Processing requests for deferred retirement; 10. Converting personnel from temporary to permanent status; and 11. Approving requests for deputation.

The Administrative Management Department also seems to have responsibilities (not clearly delineated) for the Miscellaneous and Foreign Services. Other Services are administered by their own ministry – e.g. the Health Service by the Health Ministry, and the Education Service by the Education Ministry. The "Service" concept does not apply to Non-Gazetted posts (with the exception of the Judicial Service). Each Ministry appoints its own Non-Gazetted employees from lists of eligible persons certified by the Public Service Commission (PSC), determines their assignments, and decides on promotion or otherwise.

The Administrative Management Department also has certain responsibilities for all Services. It collects personnel description forms, reviews them for compliance with the Civil Service Rules, and forwards them to the Public Service Commission; it maintains a file for each officer who has submitted a personnel description form; and it approves requests for employees posted in the districts to come to Kathmandu on official duty, in cases where their intended stay is for more than seven days.

The AMD has a Position Management Section that is charged with the function of reviewing requests to create additional posts, and modifying the status of existing posts. The AMD has a Rules and Regulations Section which provides opinion and interpretation on specific cases related to the Civil Service, when this is requested by various ministries and departments, and where necessary it seeks the opinion of the Law Ministry, the Finance Ministry, and the Public Service Commission on such matters. It also drafts amendments to the Civil Service Act and Rules, the Public Service Commission Act and Rules, and various rules and regulations prescribed by the Department itself, and submits them for higher approval. It also reviews requests for contracts and makes recommendations on the same. In addition there is a Position Classification Section that is charged with helping to establish and operate a position classification system within the Nepal Civil Service. Such a system has not yet been established. The AMD is also responsible for administering the Civil Personnel Records Centre (*Nizamati Kitab Khana*). The AMD's Training and Research Division is responsible for the general survey, planning, and coordination of the training needs and activities of the Nepal Civil Service. It operates the Administrative Training Centre where the training is conducted.

The Public Service Commission (PSC) is responsible for the conduct of examinations concerning recruitment, and has a strong influence on promotions and policy changes affecting the civil service (see also the separate section on the PSC below). The Ministry of Law submits its opinion to the AMD on various aspects of the law, and on rules and regulations on the civil service.

With regard to foreign training the Finance Ministry receives requests from the ministries for training assignments abroad. It looks at the availability of foreign aid funds for this purpose, and submits proposed overseas training assignments to the Council of Ministers for final approval after the assignments have been subject to the prior review and approval of the Scholarship Review Committee. The Finance Ministry advises the AMD on the financial liabilities of proposed rule changes. It receives requests to evaluate the need for general salary adjustment, refers such proposals to the Pay Commission for comment, and submits recommendations to the Council of Ministers. The Finance Ministry also receives recommendations from the AMD on the proposals from ministries and departments for the creation of new posts, or for changes in the status of existing ones. It (Finance) looks at the availability or otherwise of funds and forwards its recommendations to the Council of Ministers for its final decision; but in the case of Non-Gazetted posts its own decisions appear to be the final stage.

The National Planning Commission is charged with determining and planning for the manpower needs of HMG and suggesting ways to meet them. There are also inter-ministerial bodies that deal with matters of pay, promotion, and overseas training opportunities: such as Promotion Committees, the Pay Commission, and the Scholarship Review Committee.

The Council of Ministers must give its approval on a host of matters. In the case of Gazetted Class officers and posts it must approve such matters as: the creation of posts and the modification of existing ones; initial appointments into the Civil Service; overseas training; transfers within a Service or between Services; promotion; disciplinary action; and extension of the retirement age. It must also approve such matters as changes in Acts and Rules related to the Civil Service, and proposed general and individual salary adjustments.

It seems that some of these matters also go to the Royal Palace Secretariat for review, comment and approval. Working closely with the Royal Palace Secretariat is the *Janch Bujh Kendra* (Investigation and Inquiry Centre) that is also tasked with looking into the functioning and problems of the Civil Service, and recommending improvements. It is this very strategically located Centre that produced the New Promotion Rules which came into effect in September 1971, and the "Plan for Strengthening the Public Service Commission" (1971), which is expected to come into effect with some modifications.

All this indicates a quite complicated system of personnel administration involving individual ministries, the Administrative Management Department, Public Service Commission, Finance Ministry, Planning Commission, Law Ministry, the Council of Ministers, the Royal Palace Secretariat, and several committees and commissions. There seems to be no central agency with overall responsibility for directing and coordinating the plethora of agencies and functions that are responsible for personnel administration in the civil service. A Nepali observer who has studied the system, and spent many years of service within it, pointed out that since the personnel function was everybody's business, nobody took it upon himself to improve the system as a whole! [163]

Dr. O. Glenn Stahl, who was the Personnel Administration Advisor to HMG from March to June of 1969, pointed out that the personnel organization was unnecessarily divided and complex, providing neither adequate central direction and control, nor adequate managerial discretion in the Departments.[164] This is not as anomalous as it may seem. Where authority is weak, disorganized, or divided, there will be a reluctance to delegate. To delegate authority adequately one must first possess it in sufficient degree and with sufficient clarity and confidence. Stahl noted that despite the many bodies with personnel functions, certain functions were not being performed by anyone, e.g.: 1. Continued and detailed review of jobs; 2. Regular and periodic review of salary and allowance levels; 3. General personnel audit – a continuing inspection of what is going on by way of personnel administration throughout His Majesty's Government; and 4. Grievances – there was no point towards which complaints about the system could be directed.[165] Stahl added that there was too much emphasis on daily "traffic control" and too little on executive responsibility and on simple procedures, and this deprived HMG of full managerial control and knowledge through inspection of what was actually going on.[166]

This fragmented system of personnel administration results in many deficiencies. There is the lack of an adequate system of planning to meet the manpower needs of HMG. There is no comprehensive scheme for the Nepal Civil Service. Related to this is the lack of adequate and effective machinery to assess training needs, and to develop and conduct training programs to meet them. There is no coherent direction of the system of personnel administration, and overall emphasis seems to be on regulation rather than on development.

---

[163] Nanda Lall Joshi, Evolution of Public Administration in Nepal (Kathmandu, Nepal: Centre for Economic Development and Administration, 1973), p.93
[164] O. Glenn Stahl, A Strong Civil Service for Nepal (Kathmandu, Nepal, June 1969). Reprinted in *Prashasan* (The Nepali Journal of Publication Administration), Yr. 2, No. 1 April 1970, p. 62.
[165] Ibid. p. 58.
[166] Ibid., p. 44

Another problem is the delay in filling up vacant posts in administration. An internal survey of the Administrative Management Department, whose results came out in September 1974, revealed that there were 93 files pending in its Position Management Section. These files included requests for a total of 430 Gazetted Class posts and 3,164 Non-Gazetted posts. The oldest file had been with this seemingly overworked and understaffed Section for fifteen months! If to this sort of delay is added the time needed to fill posts after going through the process of recruitment, examination, appointment, and induction training, then the problem looks to be very irksome. The time lapse between requests for posts, and when somebody actually shows up to begin work in them, seems to be much too long in too many instances.

A major characteristic of a fragmented personnel administration structure is the lack of an effective and comprehensive career development program in the civil service. There are other problems related to this. An internal survey of the AMD (1974) revealed that apart from its O&M Section the Department itself did not have job descriptions for its employees! If this is the case with the department charged with the leadership role in improving the civil service system of HMG, then one can imagine the situation in the rest of the administrative system!

A good job description scheme becomes the reference point for most activities in an efficient and effective personnel administration system. Without an adequate job description system it becomes difficult to fit the right man to the right job, to let the individual know what is expected of him, and to evaluate his work for purposes of promotion and career development.

Job descriptions were not alien to Rana administration. Letters of authorization were given to some individuals, charging them with a certain task, authorizing the use of some specified authority and resources, and even giving some general guidance as to the conduct of their work. It seems that this useful practice, and some others in Rana administration, got lost in the process of "modernizing" Nepali administration starting with the Indian advisors who were sent over in 1951. The Nepal Administrative Reform Commission (1968-70) called for a comprehensive job description scheme for all civil service employees.[167] The need for a proper job description scheme had been urged by practically all the personnel administration advisors to His Majesty's Government. But such a scheme has not yet been instituted.

The deficient concern with career development is shown also in the highly inadequate grade structure in the Nepal Civil Service. There are but four levels

---

[167] The Administrative Reform Commission (1968-70) was established by HMG in April 1968. It was given the task of surveying the administrative machinery of HMG with a view to making it more effective, efficient, and development oriented. The Commission submitted one Report each in 1968, 1969, and 1970.

each in the Gazetted and Non-Gazetted ranks. This means that the typical employee in the Gazetted ranks can expect no more than two grade promotions in the course of his service career. The problem is worst at the two lower levels of the Gazetted ranks (Section Officer and Under Secretary) where the stagnant grade structure results in frustration and debilitation of morale. The main casualty is work, and any interest or enthusiasm for it. The four-grade structure seems to be unsuited to Nepali needs, and even less suitable now in the context of an enlarged Nepal Civil Service.

The Indian advisors (1950s) helped to create this inadequate grade structure. The subsequent foreign advisors have repeatedly criticized this grade structure and suggested that in the Gazetted ranks alone it could be expanded to between six and eight grades. Such suggestions were made by Sir Eric Franklin (196466), Wilson Hart (1965), Edward McCrensky (1968), and O. Glenn Stahl (1969), among others.

It is interesting to note that there were some fourteen grades in Rana administration, with the grades about equally divided between what is today the Gazetted and Non-Gazetted Classes. So is this a case where "modernization" has actually brought about some regression?

Related to this deficient grade structure is a tendency for the bureaucracy to be top-heavy in the decisional sense and bottom-heavy in personnel. Elitism may also be a factor in keeping the top levels rarefied in personnel and cluttered with decisional authority, while having the exact opposite at the lower levels. There is room for rationalization. It must begin with appreciating that bureaucracy exists to serve the public rather than to cater to the egos and employment needs of bureaucrats and "leaders"! But overall political constraints must be noted.

There is also a general and chronic tendency to have frequent transfers of employees in HMG. This means that individuals do not get the time to do justice to their jobs, and will probably lack the motivation to acquire any expertise in them. This may be due to a negative sort of generalist elitism which prefers that administrators not be tainted with anything hinting of "specialist" expertise. But it may be better to have administrators whose generalist perspective is derived from expertise built upon a succession of competently held posts. There is need for a more positive approach and a better career development scheme.

The rather high turnover rate in administration has negative consequences for administrative development. The continuous shifting of senior administrators can inhibit sustained progress, and result in a loss of continuity and a need for restarts. The frequent rotation of competent administrative officials out of their posts can have such negative effects as: (1) seriously limiting the input they can give to the administrative development process; (2) making it more difficult to organize the administrative development process in a coherent, coordinated, and continuous manner; and (3) hindering the building-up of an indigenous capability for administrative change and reform. The high turnover rate also makes it more difficult to more fully and effectively utilize foreign-trained Nepali officials upon their return to the home country. The high turnover rate in administration has been repeatedly criticized by many personnel administration advisors to HMG. But the problem is still very much there!

The Public Service Commission

The Public Service Commission (PSC) was established in June 1951 pursuant to the relevant enabling Articles in the Interim Government of Nepal Act of April 1951, also known as the Interim Constitution. Article 64 states that there shall be a Public Service Commission for Nepal consisting of a Chairman and as many other members as the King may prescribe. Article 65 laid down that they were to be appointed by His Majesty's Government, and their salaries and terms of service were to be the same as that for judges of the High Court (*Pradhan Nyalaya*). Article 67 laid down the duties of the PSC. These duties might be classified in the following order: 1. To conduct examinations for appointment to all services of His Majesty's Government of Nepal; and 2. To be consulted on the following matters: (a) All matters relating to methods of recruitment to Civil Services and for civil posts; (b) All principles to be followed in making appointments to Civil Services and posts and in making promotions and transfers from one service to another; (c) On the suitability of candidates for appointment to Civil Services and posts and in making promotions and transfers from one service to another; and (d) On disciplinary matters affecting persons serving under His Majesty's Government of Nepal, including memorials and petitions relating to such matters.

The sections on the PSC in the Interim Constitution were, with some modification, lifted from the relevant sections of the Constitution of India. This is not surprising, since both the Interim Constitution and the Public Service Commission have their origin in the technical assistance given to the Government by the Indian Advisors in the immediate post-Rana years of the early 1950s. It seems that the PSC was created and assigned its duties more in imitation of Indian models than with any independent analysis of what might best serve Nepali needs. The PSC seems to have been designed as a protective screening device rather than as an instrument for locating and recruiting talent according to need and availability.

The intention seems to have been that the PSC should be more than a "watchdog" agency and an advisory body for the civil service system on the general principles and methods relating to the civil service system; it was also to decide on the suitability of individual candidates for appointment, promotion and transfer. This mix of watchdog, advisory and operational roles may not have been very wise. The PSC was given a sort of privileged and "constitutional" position outside the administrative structure of HMG. Insofar as the PSC was too proactive in carrying out its operational role this might weaken the executive branch in its control over personnel matters. It might reduce the willingness or ability of other agencies of the civil service system to address problems and needs of personnel administration and weaken their interest in studying, analyzing, and reforming the personnel administration system. Such a PSC might also be in the way of the creation of an effective central personnel agency that is responsible for running a coherent and coordinated system of personnel administration.

Curiously, some had felt that there was nothing in the Interim Constitution of 1951 that said that the advice given by the PSC (set up in 1951) was mandatory!

Unfortunately the circumstances were such that the Public Service Commission could not do justice to its statutory functions. The number of civil servants recruited on the recommendation of the Public Service Commission, between the dates of its creation to the promulgation of the Civil Service Act and Rules (late 1956) was not encouraging. Few cases of promotion or discipline were referred to the Public Service Commission.

Most of the top civil servants, who happened to be at the top by the same procedure prevalent during the (Rana) family rule, did not think it wise to advise the ministries (ministers?) that the Commission must be consulted at least on cases of appointment. Nor did the ministers, who felt that they would be despised as lacking in human feelings and party-loyalty if they did not acknowledge it as their duty to see their needy friends and relations and party workers were placed on the public payroll at the earliest possible opportunity, realize their constitutional responsibilities.

Things became worse. The discipline which was maintained very strongly during the family rule (the Rana autocracy from 1846-1951) was a dream of the past. The efficient, honest and sincere clerks, who could expect promotion during the family rule on the recommendation of the head of the office or the head of the department, as the case may be, found that it was not equally possible now.[168]

Thus the personnel administration situation seems to have been unsatisfactory and confused, with the PSC being a largely formalistic and ineffectual body. Walter Fischer, who was Personnel Administration Advisor from December 1957 to September 1958, felt that: the PSC was not being fully utilized in its statutory functions; that the existing Acts and rules and regulations were not being fully implemented; that knowledge of these was not sufficiently

---

[168] B.P.Khanal, "Personnel Management in the Nepal Public Service--Some Suggestions," in *Prashasan* (The Nepali Journal of Public Administration), Year 5, No.1, February 1974, p. 17. (This was originally a paper presented by the author at Manchester University in May 1963).

widespread, even at senor administrative levels; and that personnel matters tended to be handled on the basis of rules in practice during the Rana regime, which had been abolished in early 1951.[169]

Since then, the PSC has perhaps been ignored with less impunity than the case above. But it appears to retain most of its past inadequacies. Insofar as HMG has acted on the PSC it has been to broaden its area of operation and enhance its status, rather than to rationalize its duties by turning it into an advisory and watchdog agency stripped of its operational role.

The 1959 Constitution of the Kingdom of Nepal sought to fit the PSC into the new parliamentary context by giving it the duty of presenting HMG with an annual report on the work done by it. The Government was then to cause a copy thereof to be laid before Parliament, together with a memorandum explaining the cases, if any, when the advice of the PSC was not accepted, and the reasons for this. Such a constitutional provision could be of significance where the legislature was strong and effective, and where legislators were interested in the professionalism and probity of the civil service and matters of personnel administration, and appreciated the importance of this. Many would question whether this has been the case in Nepal!

The Constitution of Nepal (12 December 1962 and amended 27 January 1967), gave teeth to the consultative function of the Public Service Commission. Article 78 (2) states that:

A person who is henceforth appointed by recruitment to a civil post without consulting the Public Service Commission shall not be entitled to pension.

The Public Service Commission (Working Procedure) Rules, August 1970, would seem to indicate that PSC recommendations regarding appointments are virtually compulsory. Rule 24 indicates that the appointing authority shall make appointments in vacant services or posts according to a list of candidates drawn up in order of merit by the PSC. The Rules suggest strongly that PSC recommendations should ordinarily be followed on all matters where it is to be consulted. The rules also require the consulting authority to notify the PSC within a month (15 days in case of appointments) on what action has been taken on matters requiring consultation with the Commission, together with an explanation for non-compliance.

The PSC net was extended to the public corporations (government enterprises). Article 78(3a) states that the PSC shall be consulted by the appointing authority on matters relating to any service or a post specified by law,

---

[169] Walter Fischer, Personnel Administration in Nepal: Final Report (Kathmandu, Nepal, October 1958), p. 6.

of a government owned corporate body. Section 4(8) of the Public Service Commission (Working Procedure) Act, February 1964 (amended August 1970), says that appointments to public corporations and quasi-government institutions must be filled by prior consultation with the PSC.

This extension of the operational role of the PSC seems to be diametrically at odds with the recommendation of advisors like Sir Eric Franklin (1964-66) and O. Glenn Stahl (1969) that its role should be limited to that of a statutory watchdog of the system of personnel administration. But it seems to be in line with the seemingly opposite recommendation of some earlier advisors like Walter Fischer (1957-58) and Louis Kroeger (1962) that the PSC should be developed into a central personnel agency of His Majesty's Government!

Thinking in Nepal on personnel administration matters continues mainly along protective lines. The stress has been on enhancing or protecting the "integrity" of the civil service system. Perhaps there is also a general distrust of the individual and a preference for the rigidities of rules and regulations. Perhaps this is a sort of manifestation of administration by distrust. In this atmosphere "protectionist" organizations like the PSC continue to thrive, despite a general inability to do anything really developmental for the civil service system.

So it is not surprising that the Nepal Administrative Reform Commission (1968-70) made recommendations designed to further enhance the operational and protectionist role of the PSC. Thus the recommendation that where consultation with the PSC was mandatory, its recommendations must also be mandatory. It also recommended that the PSC net be extended to include public corporations. Also that the PSC be consulted in crossing "efficiency bars". It seems that HMG accepted the protectionist spirit behind these recommendations.

The Plan for Strengthening the Public Service Commission, prepared by the *Janch Bujh Kendra* (Investigation and Inquiry Centre) circa early 1974 seems to be an attempt at enhancing the efficiency and effectiveness of the PSC in its current mix of roles. The plan indicates that the executive branch was not satisfied with the work of the PSC and points out such weaknesses as: 1. Lack of coordination and cooperation between the PSC and the executive branch; 2. Lack of administrative experience of the PSC members (whom some also accuse of having an excessively legalistic orientation); 3. Deficiencies in organization, work distribution and methods, and in staff-quality; 4. Absence of short- and long-term manpower perspective; and 5. Preoccupation with routine work.

But the Plan prepared by the *Janch Bujh Kendra* (JBK) does not seek to divest the PSC of its mix of roles – protective, advisory, regulatory, and operational. It makes no recommendation to rationalize the fragmented system of personnel administration, or to create an effective central personnel agency. It does not seek to focus the PSC on its watchdog function, while also leaving operational matters to a new and empowered central personnel agency. It seems that this Plan of the JBK seeks to strengthen the PSC within its old mix of roles by increasing its staff and enhancing its organization; while leaving its protectionist orientation as is.

Protectionism and Developmental Imperatives

The personnel system of HMG administration struggles between the desire to maintain the integrity of the merit objective and the need to meet vital manpower and managerial needs, without finding the best way to harmonize these objectives.[170] The struggle may not be intense! Given that jobs are scarce and mostly governmental, and that competition for them is intense, the protectionist side of the struggle tends to win! Concern for civil service "integrity" is often a convenient belief (more convenience than belief) that serves to limit access to government jobs, while protecting the interests of those who are already in, and who will be selecting the similar sorts who will join them!

In this context, and given the emerging developmental needs of the country, it cannot be wise to stifle the personnel administration system with such a protectionist orientation. This could stiffen recruitment procedures and hamper recruitment of suitable personnel with requisite expertise to meet the various administrative and technical needs of HMG. There is need for more positive personnel administration geared to the recruitment of the best people for the jobs, within an effective and comprehensive career development scheme.

The protectionist orientation can be seen in several negative aspects of the personnel administration system. The Services within the Nepal Civil Service are a reflection of a "closed-career system". This system tends to recruit personnel only at the base, filling higher posts by means of promotion of those already in the service; there is also restriction of advancement opportunities to insiders. There is almost absolute closure to lateral entry above the lowest level (Section Officer) in the Gazette ranks. This can work to prevent the infusion of new blood (personalities, ideas, skills) at levels where it is likely to be most effective. There is a need for relaxation here. Several personnel administration advisors have urged the need for a more open civil service system with more lateral entry. It is interesting to note that these advisors tended to be mostly American, such as Wilson Hart (1965), Edward McCrensky (1968), and O. Glenn Stahl (1969). Their advice for openness was not taken!

A closely related problem is the age-bar for entry into the Nepal Civil Service. Section 2 (2c) of the Civil Service Rules, 22 March 1965, states that persons who have completed the age of 35 years shall not be appointed in the Civil Service or in civil service posts. Exceptions were made in the case of those

---

[170] Stahl, A Strong Civil Service for Nepal, p. 43.

in the permanent employ of HMG whose posts had been made redundant, or those who had served in temporary "development" posts for at least 5 years and were being considered for conversion to the "permanent" side.

Many foreign advisors have been critical of this age limitation.[171] They have pointed out that this limitation has a stultifying effect, leaving little room for lateral entry of new blood from time to time. It provided no opportunity for lateral entry by persons who had demonstrated their ability outside the government service. They have assumed quite rightly that there were people over 35 in Nepal who possessed skills and capabilities needed in government. A nation with limited resources of manpower cannot afford the luxury of too low maximum age limits. The need for talent should supersede any desire to ensure internal promotion of staff. Some lateral entry need not significantly reduce promotion opportunities; there was in any case a continuous expansion of government programs and of the personnel required for them.

But the protective orientation and interest in its preservation has been too strong and too deeply ingrained. The Administrative Reform Commission (1968-70) went against the spirit of the foreign advisory efforts by recommending that the maximum age limit for entry to Gazetted ranks be reduced from 35 to 30, and in Non-Gazetted ranks from 35 to 25! It recommended that the retirement age be lowered from 63 to 55! This when advances in health and medical science is keeping people healthier and active over a longer life span!

HMG did seem to have opened up a bit in the 10th Amendment (12 April 1974) to the 1965 Civil Service Rules, where an exception has been made in the case of ex-servicemen and police personnel who are to be appointed to the Civil Service or to civil posts. In their case the upper age-limit was raised from 35 to 45. It is interesting to note that the new exception was designed to accommodate persons with a security background; and it too was probably made despite the objections of the civil servants. Their own preference cum protective orientation is reflected in the action of a Foreign Secretary who had the maximum age-limit for entry to the Foreign Service reduced from 35 to 26 years of age! So potential diplomats of qualification, background and ability do not exist above 26? There is room for a more sensible approach to age limits in the Nepal Civil Service!

The excessive concern for "integrity" seems also to have led to a fixation upon seniority as a presumably objective general principle for promotion. The 1956 Civil Service Act held that promotion was to be granted on the basis of seniority. Exceptions were made in the case of promotion to the top ranks of Secretary and Joint Secretary, where merit (not clearly defined), was to be the

---

[171] Once again they are mainly American, for instance Louis Kroeger (1962), Wilson Hart (1965), O. Glenn Stahl (1969), and Lee D. Bomberger (1970-74); and they were not listened to!

criterion, and also in the case of a clearly incompetent senior or an exceptionally qualified junior. Did this mix of rigidity and vagueness facilitate the promotion of quite a few whose virtue lay in seniority of service or the favor of a patron?

The Civil Service Act (1956) was amended on 27 September 1967 to read that promotion to all higher posts was henceforth to be made on the basis of efficiency, with seniority being the deciding factor only in those cases where two civil servants possessed equal qualifications. The 24 March 1969 Amendment to the Nepal Civil Service Rules made the first attempt at defining "efficiency" and operationalizing the promotion system accordingly. It laid down that three aspects were to be considered for purposes of evaluation of efficiency, with 100 marks to be given for each (i.e., equal weight was given to them): 1. Seniority (years in service) and Experience (work of different kinds; work in different geographical areas; and increase in technical skills); 2. Educational Qualifications (degrees, diplomas, certificates); and 3. Departmental Report, which on a scale of one to six purported to measure such personal qualities (fourteen in all) as interest in work, efficiency, speed, capacity to control subordinates, initiative, general conduct, and capacity to get along with superiors and subordinates.

This was perhaps a commendable attempt to introduce an element of objectivity and rationality in the promotion system, provided that it can be properly done. But there can also be problems. It may not be entirely wise to give the promotion process an unduly mathematical and mechanical air, especially if it serves as a mask for subjectivity. It may de-emphasize the informed and objective judgment of supervisors, and may reduce their interest in the career development of subordinates. Badly done, it might become a manifestation of administration by distrust, with stress put on mathematical processes over human judgment. There can be no one model of an ideal civil servant. Different qualities are required in different jobs, at different times, in different professions, in differing situations of interaction.

Sometimes the qualities that are sought are more importantly the intangibles, such as the capacity for innovation, initiative, decision-making ability, good judgment, ability to work under stress, resourcefulness, creativity, human relationship capability, and so on. A B.A. with ten years of service and a good mix of such qualities might be more preferable than say an M.A. with twenty years of experience but a not very favorable mix of intangibles. It is often in the intangibles where the best human and administrative capabilities lie. But evaluation of these tend to depend more on personal observation and judgment, and to be often short-circuited in a mechanical-mathematical evaluation system. Should degrees as such be given equal weight to seniority, experience, or a wide mix of intangibles? There is the risk of injustice to intangibles and to the human factor in administration and development.

The New Promotion Rules produced by the Investigation and Inquiry Centre (*Janch Bujh Kendra*) of the Palace Secretariat, and promulgated 24 September 1971, have not necessarily solved these problems, or materially improved the 1969 evaluation and promotion system that they replaced. The three general categories of subjects were increased to five: education, seniority, experience, special capacity and assessment of work. The provision to give equal weight to each category was also dropped. It seems that there was a general increase of marks for everything, educational qualifications included; and marks were also given for such additional things as medals, letters of commendation from His Majesty the King, health, and published research work. Perhaps the main purpose of this change was to please as many as possible, and to placate the civil servants; their opposition had stalled the implementation of the previous promotion and evaluation scheme of 1969.

The Confidential Report which purports to measure the individual's work performance, and his personality, character, and merits, seems to have become a bone of contention. It seems that since September 1971 this report was no longer confidential, at least not from the employee being evaluated, and the result has been a general tendency to evaluate everyone favorably but not too exceptionally. The foreign advisors have themselves been divided on this question of confidentiality. Walter Fischer (1957-58) from Austria supported it on the grounds that otherwise the superior would be reluctant to evaluate his subordinates to the best of his objective capacity, and without fear of subsequent embarrassment. But American advisors like Louis Kroeger (1962) and Wilson Hart (1965) felt that the employee had the right to know about his deficiencies and how to correct them. Fischer probably assessed the Nepali situation better, though Kroeger and Hart were closer to the ideal of openness, consultation and counseling. There is no easy answer to this one! It may be a question of moving from the one to the other in a phased manner, with balance and maturity.

The promotion and evaluation system in Nepal shows the effects of an excessive concern with protection of the "merit" objective (which might be seen within a background of emphasis on degrees, ability to pass entrance exams, seniority, personal and cultural loyalty, and so on). It is mechanical and mathematical. It does too little justice to human intangibles. Merit is not only a question of comparison between individuals, but also between individuals and the job to be filled. This seems not to be adequately appreciated. The promotion scheme also tends to encourage a tendency to take training courses, to acquire paper qualifications, and to write scholarly articles, primarily for the sake of the marks obtained. Such an attitude cannot do justice to individual improvement, or the quality of education and research.

There is a certain generalist bias in the Nepali Civil Service, though one is not certain that this need necessarily constitute a major defect in the system. In general, professional personnel from the technical Services are excluded from promotion to the highest level of the Civil Service, that of Secretary to His Majesty's Government (usually the administrative head of a ministry). American advisors like Wilson Hart (1965), Edward McCrensky (1968), and Glenn Stahl (1969) had felt that there was an inadequate recognition by rank and level of the real importance of many posts of professional personnel. They felt that such personnel ought not to be kept out of the executive posts with a primarily administrative content, provided they have the capability for this. But the Administrative Reform Commission (1968-70) very clearly disagreed with this. In its Preliminary Report of September 1968 the Commission recommended that HMG should discourage the use of technicians for administrative jobs:

The ARC (Commission) was convinced that involving technical officers in departmental administrative work would not only weaken the administrative machinery but would prevent their technical knowledge from being used properly. In order not to prevent these technicians from upgrading their professional qualities, the ARC thought it best to discourage the tendency of engaging them in departmental administration except as advisors.[172]

There is some merit in this. Technical and professional skills are relatively in short supply in Nepal, and ought to be utilized and developed to the maximum in their specialist capabilities. This is where the national interest lies. Perhaps professional logic also points in this direction. It is not easy to appreciate specialists with a burning aspiration for generalist authority. Some might suspect the dedication of such people to anything but ambition and ego. In the Nepali context it can lead to a waste of qualified human resources that are scarce.

This is not to say that all is well with the generalists. They could do with a broader perspective, and have greater respect for specialists and appreciation of their vital role in the service of the nation. There may be ways of encouraging the specialists other than by elevation to the higher level "status" of generalist posts. They might be given more attractive pay and service conditions and better and more frequent foreign training opportunities, and be encouraged to develop greater professionalism. A range of prestigious advisory roles might be created for them. The generalists must respect them and honor their expertise, while coordinating their work in the broad mosaic of government and administration.

Between fiscal year 1951-73 the number of civil service personnel of HMG had increased from some 7,000 to about 50,000. (See Table 11.2.). In the same period the total annual budget of HMG went up from some 30 million Nepali Rupees to about 1,000 million Nepali Rupees. In the same period the annual development expenditure went up from probably less than 10 million Rupees to about 600 million Rupees. Despite these immense strains, it would be too dramatic to suggest that the public administration system of the country is in

---

[172] Joshi, Evolution of Public Administration in Nepal, p. 102.

imminent danger of collapse and disintegration. It continues to survive and function. But the need for change, and for reform and development, is obvious.

Table 11.2 HMG Civil Service Personnel *

Year (Mid-July)	Gazetted Class	Non-Gazetted Class	Peon and equivalent	Others [1]	Total
1951 (Jan)	-	-	-	-	7,521
1958	706	8,910	14,158	-	23,774
1961	1,050	10,691	15,531	-	27,272
1962	1,139	12,419	15,005	-	28,593
1963	1,291	11,219	15,100	1,300	28,910
1964	1,553	12,996	14,534	978	29,761
1965	1,660	13,004	14,787	552	30,003
1966	1,933	13,694	14,768	443	32,208
1967	2,303	14,913	14,752	240	33,467
1968	2,571	15,851	14,549	496	35,076
1969	2,796	17,272	14,712	296	35,076
1970	3,251	21,548	17,188	184	42,171
1971	3,847	23,606	17,137	266	44,856
1972	4,023	25,705	18,415	190	47,833
1973	4,570	28,405	17,725	140	50,850

*As registered at the *Nizamati Kitab Khana* (Civil Personnel Records Centre).   [1] Their Scales do not fit with the others.
Source: Records of the *Nizamati Kitab Khana*.

Since the "democratic revolution" of 1951, the hopes and expectations and urgency of development over the entire spectrum of national life – social, political, and economic – have placed immense strains upon the administrative system of government, which previously had been oriented primarily to the traditional functions of control and revenue extraction. This has naturally posed challenges to, and put strains upon, the system of public administration and the system of personnel management of the Nepal Civil Service.

There will be merit in moving away from the "closed system" approach, where the concern with "integrity" and "merit" may have more to do with the protection of turf and the privileges of the insiders. Some feel that there is also an ingrained system bias against western-oriented education, and against experiences and perspectives that are gained from outside.

There will also be merit in a bureaucracy that is not marked by any casteist cum exam-oriented elitism; the two do seem to go together! There will be merit in a bureaucracy that is much more optimally inclusive of all the Nepali people, in their wide variety; and it must be at all the various levels of its composition.

The inward-looking and narcissistic concern with the "integrity" of the civil service is not the same as concern for the integrity of public administration that is embedded in professionalism; and that is not subordinated to the ideological imperatives of the political parties, or to their political conveniences.

At its best it must be integrity that is tied to such values as selflessness, dedication to public service, probity, performance and professionalism. Concern with the "integrity" of the civil service in the narrower sense of the protection of processes, personnel, privileges, access and image of exam-oriented cum casteist elitism and exclusiveness is not the same as the integrity of public administration in the sense of administration that is in the best interests of the public.

It may be said of administration and the related personnel processes in Nepal that there is a very obvious and indeed quite chronic need for more openness and development of the system. Also, all of this must be pursued in the context of country realities, past experience and emerging needs, and with attention to both "system" and "attitudes".

CHAPTER 12

THE PERSONNEL ADMINISTRATION ADVISORS

It could be said that at least some of the defects of the system of personnel administration of His Majesty's Government arose from the disinclination and inability to consciously inherit and adapt from the best in Rana administration.

The reason for this lack of conscious and positive continuity is twofold. The Nepali leadership that succeeded the Rana autocracy in 1951 was largely inexperienced in government and administration. These new leaders had been mostly schooled in the ideological ferment and conspiratorial politics of India during and after the final stages of its struggle for independence from the British. They were effective in toppling the Rana autocracy with significant and indeed crucial Indian assistance, and with the backing of King Tribhuvan, who had fled to the grounds of the Indian Embassy in Kathmandu and then went on to exile in India. But they seem to have been unprepared for the challenge of having to run the government and administration of a separate and sovereign country.

Also, these elements had spent a great deal of their energies and intellect in the conspiracy against the Rana autocrats. They were therefore generally disinclined to do any finessing between Rana politics and Rana administration. They damned both. The Indians, by contrast, had borrowed freely from the administrative and other systems of their former British rulers. It is not unusual to meet educated and intelligent Nepalis whose dislike for the Rana autocracy (1846-1951) led them to believe rather uncritically that there could not have been such a thing as "administration" during the century of Rana rule! Therefore what was inherited and continued was despite the new leadership and elites rather than because of conscious and reasoned choice on their part. Thus what is inherited can quite possibly be the worst rather than the best.

As far as personnel administration is concerned, the Rana autocrats appear to have operated a civil service system that was quite flexible, open, and unified. The minimum age for entry to government service was sixteen. There appears to have been no maximum age ceiling on entry to government service, and no formal retirement age. There were no particular levels at which entrants to government service had to be inducted. There was no rigid distinction and career barrier between administrative and clerical levels. Promotion was based upon the discretion of the Prime Minister, seniority of service, and upon merit which was not specifically defined. There were at least fourteen grade levels in the civil service, about equally distributed between what would later be distinguished as the administrative (Gazetted Class) and clerical (Non-Gazetted Class) levels.

The top levels of Rana administration were reserved for family members only. But below them there was in effect a unified civil service system with scope for vertical and horizontal movement.

The attributes of unity, flexibility, and relative openness were principally due to the authority and discretion of a strong and sufficiently empowered Prime Minister. In his *Mukhtiyar* (Senior Minister) he had a powerful and strategically located deputy charged with administration-wide responsibilities of supervision and coordination. The *Mukhtiyar* was assisted in this task by the powerful central office of administration that was the *Muluki Adda* (Home Office). Unity and coordination were facilitated by the clear chain of command up through the *Mukhtiyar* to the Prime Minister – where the buck stopped. It seems that there was a relatively clear set of expectations as to roles and responsibilities. This was facilitated by the political authority of the strong Prime Minister. It was also facilitated by the practice of granting documents of appointment and authorization to individual officials, which might detail their functions and authority, the manner of their operation, and the resources that would be made available to them for the job to be done.

Problems of Inducement

India had dominated the field of technical assistance in public administration in the immediate post-Rana years (1951-56). The Indian Advisors did not really understand the Nepali administrative system. It is not clear that they seriously attempted to! Rather they tried to convert the local system into the Indian frame of reference that they did understand, and that they had inherited and continued in large measure from their former British rulers of British India (*British Raj*). The Indians may not have felt that they were doing anything negative. They considered Nepal to be like a smaller and less developed princely state of India. They did not appreciate that Nepal had inherited its own rather elaborate administrative system from the Ranas (and from before the Ranas).

Nepal had not experienced some two centuries of government and tutelage from a metropolitan Anglo-Saxon power, as was the case with India under its British rulers. Nepal's needs and realities were likely to be somewhat different from that of India. It is possible that the Indian Advisors were convinced of the superiority, and widespread applicability, of their own British-induced system of administration, with the elitist Indian Civil Service (ICS) at its apex. In general they seem to have disregarded the local system while transplanting their own British-derived Indian models. The result was a confusing amalgam of the imitated (by inducement) and the inherited (by default), to which so many of the defects of the Nepal Civil Service might be traced; and the Service became closed, fragmented, and primarily concerned with "integrity".

It was the Indian Advisors who were instrumental in establishing the Public Service Commission (PSC) in 1951. The model was Indian. The PSC seems to have been designed as a protective screening device rather than as an instrument for locating and recruiting talent according to need and availability.

The net result of this inward orientation and obsession with bureaucratic "integrity" was the less than desirable levels of flexibility of operation vis-à-vis the needs. Some may argue that the spirit of protectionism, and what they see (and label) as the inward-looking cultural and intellectual involution ("sanskritization") and the casteist elitism ("brahmanism"), that they see as a problem of the Nepal Civil Service system (and a challenge to the development of public administration), can be traced in part to the Indian advisors and inducement of Indian models upon the Nepali system.

The Civil Service Act and Rules of 1956 constitutes an attempt to give form and substance to the personnel system of the Civil Service of post-Rana Nepal. Much credit for the Act and Rules, as for most legal drafting at the time, must go to B. G. Murdeswar (India). He was the Legal and Constitutional Advisor to His Majesty's Government from 1954-61. His services were provided via the Colombo Plan.

The Civil Service Act and Rules of 1956 are not without some defects. They are vague in places, and the Act in particular constitutes skeleton legislation giving Government broad powers to fill-in at will, and when they are specific the Act and Rules indicate a general drift towards protectionism. Seniority was enhanced as a general principle of promotion. Restrictive age ceilings were instituted to govern entry to, and retirement from, the civil service. The inadequate grade structure developed by the earlier Indian Advisors was enshrined, and the basis for a closed-career system was well and truly established.

The personnel system that was thus established was obliquely criticized by some foreign advisors as being imitative of the worst features in other civil service systems! Louis Kroeger (1962) found the system to be negative, protective, too much oriented to the procedural, and not likely to facilitate the sort of personnel administration that was required for a dynamic program in the public interest.[173] Wilson Hart, another Advisor to HMG (1965), thought that this system of personnel administration was an unsuitable imitation of the Indian Civil Service. He noted a tendency towards abstract administrative perfection

---

[173] Louis J. Kroeger, A Public Administration Program for His Majesty's Government of Nepal (San Francisco: Griffenhagen-Kroeger Inc., March 1962), pp. 41-42.

and an inclination to see public administration as an end in itself rather than as an instrument of public service!

Searching for Direction

Walter Fischer (Austria) was the first UNTA Advisor in Personnel Administration to HMG. His tenure was from December 1957 to September 1958. He is remembered by his Nepali contemporaries as a generalist without the specialist expertise in personnel administration that they had hoped for. In the course of commenting on Fischer's final report [174] one of his Nepali contemporaries observed that:

Although Fischer's report pointed out some weaknesses in the system and the bureaucracy, his report was a sort of review and did not provide the kind of personnel program which the UN had sent him to Nepal to develop.[175]

The same observer has characterized Fischer's recommendations as being of a general nature and not requiring expert advice.[176] The recommendations made by Fischer did have a potential to be useful. It is just that the Nepali side expected more from him than a rather general effort. He did not, for instance, help to shape any program for the development of the personnel administration system of HMG. He did conduct a seminar for some ten Nepali officials from May-October of 1958. Some of these officials helped compile a Manual of Personnel Administration (1958). They also developed detailed suggestions for the introduction of a personnel evaluation scheme in the form of a confidential efficiency report. But the officials did not feel that the seminar had given them any specialist expertise in personnel administration.

Fischer's main recommendation was for the strengthening of the Public Service Commission (PSC). He wanted it enhanced as a central personnel agency that would be more than a constitutional watchdog – it would have been at the center of coordination and direction of the entire personnel administration system of the HMG.

Was this a good idea? Such a PSC, with its privileged constitutional position outside government, might have been inclined to emphasize the protective aspects of the civil service, and to deprive the executive branch of control over personnel matters. With its relative isolation from the executive branch, such a

---

[174] Walter Fischer, Personnel Administration in Nepal (Kathmandu, Nepal, October 1958).
[175] Nanda Lall Joshi, Evolution of Public Administration in Nepal (Kathmandu, Nepal: Centre for Economic Development and Administration, 1973), P. 90.
[176] Ibid.

PSC might have caused the personnel system to be less responsive to the developing and expanding needs of the operating agencies.

Fischer does appear to have seen the need for a strong and effective central personnel agency to give the personnel administrative system the unified, coordinated, and coherent leadership it deserved. But to convert the PSC into such an agency would have been to err on the side of protectionism, as with the Indian advisors. HMG ignored this recommendation, as indeed it ignored Fischer's report in general. What was not ignored was the manner in which he criticized HMG's system of personnel administration in his report. He was forthright but too blunt, and his bluntness was not saved by the grace of expertise. Fischer suggested that the HMG personnel system was corrupt and undemocratic, and that the average civil servant was deficient in education, training, discipline, and team spirit, among other things! [177]

Fischer did not correctly gauge the sensitivity of his Nepali colleagues to such blanket criticism of themselves and their system. He left behind the impression of a rather irksome backseat driver who was more critical than competent in his area of expertise. He gave the impression of an advisor who comes to Nepal with all his prejudices, but which he does not manage to put in perspective while doing his job as a technical assistance expert. In his final report he said that the personnel administration system of HMG was not "democratic", but does not explain what he means by this; or what "democratic" administration is; or how well the "democratic" administration that he had in mind could have fitted into the socio-political ecology of Nepal. To fling around words like "democratic" or related derivatives in this fashion is all too common a habit, but it is not a very intelligent one; or indeed very useful.

Fischer also called for some sort of trade union for civil servants. This appears to have been part of his "democratic" system of administration. The recommendation may not have been suitable in the Nepali context, where the civil servants may have been unduly politicized in any case. They were, especially at the Gazetted Class levels, already part of the privileged elite groups in the country – being better off academically, socially and economically than the vast majority of the Nepali people. Perhaps many of them were even better off than the majority of the rather weak and ineffective politicians who flitted across the unstable political landscape. Unionizing them might have politicized them further, and made them even more elitist, stronger and more privileged.

---

[177] Some might say that Nepali society was basically consensual and the conflict of ideas had yet to be internalized as a general social value; and criticism was not seen in the same useful light as in some other societies. Fischer may not have seen this. He gave the impression of criticizing the system rather than of suggesting positive changes to it. A good advisor will try to do the latter without appearing too very overtly to be doing the former.

It may have made for some "democracy" for civil servants – but it is doubtful that it would have made them more people-oriented, or facilitated the establishment of an inclusive and "democratic" system of public administration that was dedicated to the service of the vast majority of the people. Fischer's excursions on "democracy" and unionization did not enhance respect for his technical assistance.

Some years later, in June 1963, UNTA again offered his services as personnel administration advisor to His Majesty's Government. The offer was declined with due courtesy and some delicacy and diplomacy! HMG said that though Fischer's work in his previous assignment was greatly appreciated, there was nevertheless a need at that time for an Advisor who was rather more senior, and with a much better command of English!

In January 1962 Louis J. Kroeger, of the San Francisco based consulting firm of Griffenhagen-Kroeger Inc., came to Nepal to conduct a survey of the public administration needs of His Majesty's Government, and to make recommendations in this respect to HMG and AID/Nepal. The survey was funded by AID/Nepal. Kroeger did his job in some five weeks and submitted his report.[178] A Nepali observer thought the report was dull and pedantic, and the sort of thing that could be taken off the shelves of a consultancy firm. He observed that:

The report suffers from its lack of a clear-cut course of action and a program leading to a step-by-step improvement of administration in terms of institutional development. The findings and efforts were not based on sustained intellectual effort and inquiry.[179]

Like Fischer had done before him, Kroeger also made a general listing of some broad problem areas of personnel administration that needed attention. But AID/Nepal did not take up his recommendation to begin technical assistance in personnel administration. It may have felt that this was too sensitive an area for bilateral technical assistance, and that any meaningful reforms in this field would be seen as too threatening by too many people to be acceptable to bureaucrats, politicians, and the Royal Palace. It stayed out.

Wilson Hart (U.S.) was the next UNTA Advisor in Personnel Administration after Walter Fischer (who left in 1958). Hart's tenure was from February to December of 1965. He was given some very broad terms of reference. His job description stated that: 1. He was to advise and assist HMG on the special requirements in Nepal for a modern, effective, and adequate system of personnel

---

[178] Louis J. Kroeger, A Public Administration Program for His Majesty's Government of Nepal (San Francisco: Griffenhagen-Kroeger Inc., March 1962). .
[179] Joshi, Evolution of Public Administration in Nepal, p. 92.

administration; 2. He was to prepare and develop materials relating to the selection, recruitment and promotion of personnel, and general conditions of service; and 3. He was to collaborate with various public administration experts in Nepal to help develop training programs for public service personnel and for an Institute of Personnel Administration.

Hart was not very effective during his short tenure in Nepal. This was not necessarily due to any lack of expertise on his part. His last post before coming to Nepal had been that of Chief, Labor Relations Branch, Defense Supply Agency, Washington, DC. Prior to this he had held the positions of Director or Deputy Director of Personnel in various U.S. defense establishments. These were commendable qualifications, but they did not necessarily suit him for the difficult and unusual environment in Nepal, where an approach was required that was at once less sophisticated but also very much more creative and pioneering.

Hart was disadvantaged by the fragmentation of the civil service system, and by the rather limited degree of institutionalization of the administrative development functions in general, and of the personnel administration function in particular. He was attached to the Home Affairs Ministry, where the major portion of the central personnel function of HMG was then located. This was a ministry with a primary orientation to law and order, and control and regulation. It was unlikely to give the personnel function the specialist and developmental attention that it deserved. It seems that the Home Affairs Ministry simply did not know how to use Hart. It was at the time struggling to retain its central personnel role against the claims of the Public Administration Department (PAD). Sir Eric Franklin, the then UNTA Senior Public Administration Advisor, lent his influential advocacy to the claims of the Department (PAD). This may have made matters more difficult for Hart, who was himself an UNTA Advisor. The struggle seems also to have disoriented the Ministry and made it disinclined to undertake major initiatives in personnel administration.

During Hart's tenure there was no noticeable sense of urgency regarding the development of the personnel administration function of HMG. His principal Nepali counterpart in the Home Affairs Ministry appears to have been primarily involved with matters other than personnel administration. Initially, Hart's main area of work was to be a study of the civil service pay and classification system. But the Council of Ministers had him sidelined on this one because in early 1965 it was itself involved with sensitive political issues concerning pay raises for HMG employees. The raises were announced in June 1965. Hart was not asked to get back into the pay and classification area. He was instead asked to look into the new Nepal Civil Service Rules of 22 March 1965. Perhaps this job was to keep him preoccupied, rather than as a reflection of any felt needs. It is interesting to note that it took the Home Affairs Ministry some ten weeks to provide Hart with an English copy of the new Civil Service Rules!

Two aspects of Hart's final report are worth mentioning.[180] He recommended a manpower development program for HMG that was much too complicated for the time. His own experiences in Nepal ought to have taught him that. The manpower program he outlined had all the trappings of the sort of thing one might find in the United States: manpower planning; human resources management; job engineering; position classification; a unified civil service with career fields and career ladders; a comprehensive career development scheme; and a very American-sounding reduction-in-force (RIF) scheme. The best that can be said is that Hart could not have seriously believed that HMG would adopt and implement this program. It did not.

Hart noted the fragmented nature of the system of personnel administration. Fischer had recommended that the Public Service Commission (PSC) be made the central personnel agency of His Majesty's Government. Kroeger supported this idea. But Sir Eric Franklin recommended that the PSC role be limited to that of a statutory watchdog. He wanted the Public Administration Department to be developed into a strong and effective central personnel agency of HMG, where this function was to be joined with some other functions of HMG like O&M and administrative training.

But Hart came up with yet another novel recommendation. He suggested that a separate Central Manpower Agency be established. It was to function in addition to the existing agencies handling the personnel function in HMG. It was to be constituted as an executive board or committee with the Chairman of the Council of Ministers as its Chairman, a Secretary to HMG as its full-time Vice Chairman and Executive Director, and with the Secretaries of the various government agencies charged with significant portions of the overall manpower program as members. The functions of this Central Manpower Agency would be to coordinate and give general directions to, and to inspect and assess, those aspects of the operations of the HMG agencies that were related to the personnel administration function. This recommendation for a Central Manpower Agency was also not accepted by HMG.

Hart's main reasons for avoiding both the Fischer and Franklin lines were: (1) that the personnel functions were being competently performed by the existing agencies of HMG; and (2) that uniting the functions under one agency might cause confusion and chaos, however temporary. Both contentions were debatable. His own Central Manpower Agency would more likely have further fragmented the personnel administration structure of HMG. The executive board that Hart had proposed for it would most likely have added a further layer of indecision to the already somewhat confused personnel administration system. The executive board idea ought to be viewed with the greatest possible caution. Quite often it simply does not work.

---

[180] Wilson R. Hart, Draft Final Report (Kathmandu, Nepal, 13 January 1966).

Hart left Nepal with no noticeable impact on the personnel administrative system of the civil service. He is remembered kindly by his Nepali counterparts as a nice person who felt that only the Nepalis could best understand and develop their public administration system. He felt that UNTA ought to hold off on advisors on personnel administration until HMG was clearer about its administrative development priorities, and about the specific areas in which it wanted outside technical assistance.

Sir Eric Franklin (U. K.) was Wilson Hart's contemporary and the Senior UNTA Public Administration Advisor to His Majesty's Government (May 1964 to December 1966). In his 1964 Report on the Development of the Public Administration Department, Sir Eric urged the transfer of the HMG central personnel function from the Home Affairs Ministry to the Public Administration Department (PAD). He felt that the Home Affairs Ministry was a general and regulatory agency with a primarily law and order function. It was not likely to give the central personnel function the specialized attention it deserved. The PAD was already charged with the O&M, training, and administrative coordination functions. He thought the central personnel function would be better located there.[181]

Sir Eric did not agree with Walter Fischer and Louis Kroeger before him that the Public Service Commission should be developed into the central personnel agency of HMG. He seems to have been critical of the PSC's operational role in the personnel processes of the civil service system. He felt it should focus on the more indirect role of constitutional watchdog of the system of personnel administration.[182]

Sir Eric felt that the Public Administration Department should become the central personnel agency of HMG. He recommended that this Department be developed into the central executive office of HMG, and be given the formal status of a ministry; and that it should be led by the Chief Secretary, and report directly to the Chairman of the Council of Ministers.[183] He saw such a transformed Public Administration Department developing eventually into a nerve-center of the entire public administration system of government.[184] In making these recommendations Sir Eric appears to have been expressing the felt

---

[181] Sir Eric Franklin, Report on the Development of the Public Administration Department (Kathmandu, Nepal, September 1964), pp. 25-26.

[182] Sir Eric Franklin, Report on the Development of the Public Administration in Nepal (Kathmandu, Nepal, December 1966), pp. 54-55.

[183] Franklin, Development of the Public Administration Department, pp. 32-34.

[184] Edward McCrensky, Proposal for a Unified Civil Service for His Majesty's Government of Nepal (New York: United Nations, 10 June 1969). An earlier version had been printed in Kathmandu, Nepal, on 15 November 1968.

desires of his counterparts in the Public Administration Department, and quite possibly of some other senior HMG officials.

Then in April 1966 the Public Administration Department was replaced by the newly established Cabinet Secretariat. This Secretariat was led by the Chief Secretary of HMG, and was placed directly under the Chairman of the Council of Ministers. The functions of central personnel administration, O&M, and administrative coordination were located within this new Secretariat. The training function of the former Public Administration Department was, however, sent to the Economic Planning Ministry. Sir Eric thought that this was a retrogressive step, and he urged that this function be relocated to the central office charged with administrative improvement in HMG.

The Cabinet Secretariat also functioned as the Secretariat of the Prime Minister and of the Council of Ministers. The new arrangement appears not to have been very successful. The general staff functions of the Cabinet Secretariat appear not to have mixed too well with its administrative improvement functions. Primacy of attention tended to go to the former, and the latter areas tended to suffer as a result. Then in April 1968 the administrative improvement functions were located separately in the newly established Administrative Management Department. Here they were joined by the administrative training function of the Economic Planning Ministry. But the Administrative Management Department has not developed into a strong and effective central personnel agency of HMG.

The central personnel function continued to suffer from excessive fragmentation and lack of unified and effective leadership. This function seems to have been taking the lion's share of the time and attention of the Administrative Management Department, possibly over 80 percent of the time of the Secretary. But attention tends to go mainly to routine matters of personnel administration, and areas such as administrative training and reform appear to suffer from inadequate attention.

So the need remains for a strong and effective central personnel agency with administration-wide authority and responsibilities. Such an agency might be more effective if it is also charged with the direction, coordination and development of the public administration system. It would be a central office of administration, with the dedicated leadership of the Chief Secretary, and be located directly under the Prime Minister. It should be kept separate from, but in close relationship to, an Institute of Public Administration, to which would go the research and development and consultancy aspects of administrative development, and the conduct of training.

Proposal for a Unified Civil Service

Edward McCrensky (U. S.) was UNTA Advisor in Personnel Administration after Wilson Hart (who left in December 1965). McCrensky was at the time the Inter-Regional Advisor in Public Administration (Personnel and Training) with the UN, and he was in Nepal from 4 to 18 November, 1968. He was asked to review various policy and procedural issues of the system of personnel administration under consideration, including the possible introduction of a system of position classification.

The invitation to McCrensky was a calculated attempt by some elements in the Administrative Management Department, and its Secretary, to urge HMG to move towards the establishment of a unified civil service system with a watered down version of position classification. They felt that their own advocacy alone would be insufficient to win serious consideration for this and they wanted him to lend the prestige of his advocacy to their proposals. In short he was to be a catalyst for change. It is not surprising that he wrote his proposal for a unified civil service in fourteen days![185] His local counterparts had been ready with their ideas, preferences, and information. He put these in his proposal that was more advocacy than plan of action.

McCrensky recommended to HMG that it establish a unified civil service system that would do away with the exclusiveness of the eleven separate Gazetted services, and the invidious distinction between the Gazetted and Non-Gazetted classes, as he saw it. And there was something very American in his recommendation that the designations based on rank should be abolished. This may not have been agitating the Nepali mind! There is a natural instinct for hierarchy in societies in general and bureaucracies in particular. The point is how best to utilize this. The unified civil service system that he proposed consisted of four Services: (the HCS: Higher Civil Service; the AFS: Administrative and Foreign Service; the PTS: Professional and Technical Service; and the CTSS: Clerical and Technical Support Service). Also, there were to be five Zones; and twelve Grades. (See Table 12.1).

The Higher Civil Service, at the apex of the proposed system, was to be government-wide in concept, and to operate without special reference to specialization acquired. Promotion into the top two Zones (IV and V) was to be made via government-wide competition. Promotion between Zones was to be made after required consultation with the Public Service Commission. Promotion within Zones was to be made by departmental management, and it would not necessarily involve any change in the position held. It appears that a competent

---

[185] Edward McCrensky, Proposal for a Unified Civil Service for His Majesty's Government of Nepal (New York: United Nations, 10 June 1969). An earlier version had been printed in Kathmandu, Nepal, on 15 November 1968.

civil servant could normally expect such in-zone promotions after completing the required years of service. Up to 10 percent of annual vacancies in Zones III and IV (the mid-career levels) were to be filled by lateral entry from outside the civil service. So it seems that the existing closed-career system was to be opened a bit.

McCrensky also recommended the adoption of a position classification scheme, and of salary policy evaluation, as part of the unified civil service system that was proposed.

Table 12.1 Proposed Unified Civil Service

Existing		Proposed		
Classes	Service	Zone	Grade	Minimum Service Requirements for Promotion Within and Between Zones.
Special and Gazetted Class I	HCS	V	12	17 years total
	AFS/ PTS	IV	11	2 years in 11 for 12
			10	3 years in 10 for 11
Gazetted Class II	AFS/ PTS	III	9	2 years in 9 for 10
			8	3 years in 8 for 9
	AFS/ PTS	II	7	2 years in 7 for 8
			6	3 years in 6 for 7
Class III Gazetted	AFS/ PTS	I	5	Entrants to AFS/PTS must serve 5 years here for eligibility to G-6
Non-Gazetted Classes I-IV	CTSS		4	Service Requirements to be determined.
			3	
			2	
			1	

Note: HCS: Higher Civil Service; AFS: Administrative and Foreign Service; PTS: Professional and Technical Service; CTSS: Clerical and Technical Support Service.

McCrensky was a transitory consultant. His proposals had a certain prepackaged flair about them. They did look rather simple, but in fact they implied a major conversion of the civil service system. It is perhaps unusual to be making such sweeping recommendations after a fortnight's stay in the country! But his proposals did help to persuade HMG to pursue further analysis and reform of its system of personnel administration. HMG acted on his recommendation that it seek further technical assistance in the area of position classification and salary policy evaluation. In this sense Edward McCrensky did do quite well as a catalyst for change.

Dr. O. Glenn Stahl (U. S.) was the next Personnel Administration Advisor to HMG. He stayed in Nepal from March to June 1969. His services were provided by the Ford Foundation, with whom he was then working as its Public Administration Consultant for Asia and the Pacific. Prior to this he had worked with the U.S. Civil Service Commission as Director, Bureau of Policies and Standards, from 1965 to 1969. He appears to have been a person of considerable experience in personnel administration and position classification. HMG asked him to evaluate and suggest improvements in its personnel system, with particular reference to its job structure and promotion system, its assignment practices, and its compartmentalization.

Stahl's final report was a comprehensive and impressive critique of the many shortcomings in the system of personnel administration of the Civil Service.[186] It received attention at the higher levels of government and administration. He urged the adoption of a modern and comprehensive position classification system as the foundation of a strong civil service for Nepal. In this, his efforts were a continuation of those of McCrensky, and of the small, progressive element within the Administrative Management Department. He got things moving a step further when HMG acted on his recommendation that it seek further technical assistance (from the Ford Foundation) to help institute a position classification scheme for its civil service.

Stahl's other major recommendation was for the creation of a strong and effective central personnel agency for the civil service. In this he took a similar line to that of Sir Eric Franklin. Like Sir Eric he also felt that the Public Service Commission (PSC) should confine itself to the role of a constitutional watchdog and a quasi-judicial agency concerned with protecting the merit system. He felt that the PSC should avoid an operational role since it was neither fully informed about, nor involved in, the daily operations of the ministries and departments.[187]

---

[186] O. Glenn Stahl, A Strong Civil Service for Nepal (Kathmandu, Nepal, June 1969). Reprinted in Prashasan (The Nepali Journal of Public Administration), Yr. 2, No. 1, April 1970.
[187] Ibid. pp. 62-63, and 77.

He called for the Administrative Management Department to be reconstituted as a Ministry of Administrative Policy and Standards. This Ministry was to direct and operate the overall personnel program, including recruitment and related matters, through its own organization; and, as necessary, by delegation to other ministries. It was to be placed under the Prime Minister, who was to be accountable for its work.[188] Stahl saw the establishment of such a ministry as a vital first step towards purposeful and sustained efforts for the development of a strong civil service for Nepal.

But HMG did not act on Stahl's recommendation that the Administrative Management Department should be reconstituted into a new and empowered Ministry of Administrative Policy and Standards. Stahl had seen this as a crucial recommendation for a strong and effective central personnel agency for the civil service. Lack of progress on this might be attributed to a general disinclination in government and administration to have the central personnel function dominated by one agency, and possibly by one individual. This may be a reflection of a general distrust against endowing any official or agency with meaningful authority, and of pessimism that such authority could be controlled by legal and institutional means. Such pessimism can itself lead to the usual expedient of securing control and responsibility by denying meaningful authority.

Lee D. Bomberger (U.S.) was the Public Administration Advisor (O&M) to HMG from August 1970 to September 1974. His services were funded by AID/Nepal. He wrote copiously on personnel administration matters.[189] In this respect his efforts might be considered the consolidation and repetition of what he felt were the still germane observations and recommendations of the previous personnel administration advisors. He supported and gave continuation to the advocacy and recommendations that in the period since 1969 had sought to institute a position classification scheme for the civil service. Bomberger was no specialist in personnel administration, and while he gave a faithful advocacy of position classification, he did not add any new perspectives on the matter in the Nepal context. Perhaps HMG did not expect this of him anyway.

---

[188] Ibid., p. 78.

[189] Lee D. Bomberger, "Proposed Work Plan" (A memo to the Chief Secretary of His Majesty's Government of Nepal, 11 September 1970); "The Need for Civil Service Reform in Nepal," *Prashasan* (The Nepali Journal of Public Administration), Yr. 4, No. 2, July 1973, pp. 33-43; "A Positive Approach to Personnel Management," Paper presented at the Top Management Seminar, Centre for Economic Development and Administration, Kathmandu, Nepal, 4 December 1973; "Manpower Development Training Project," *Prashasan*, No. 10, June 1974, pp. 7-11; Organizing for Improved Personnel Management in His Majesty's Government of Nepal (Kathmandu, Nepal, December 1970).

CHAPTER 13

POSITION CLASSIFICATION

Idea, Advocacy and Endeavours

Position Classification is a tool of personnel administration. It is based upon the ideal value that there should be equal pay for equal work under like conditions. It seeks to measure the contents of a job-position – chiefly its duties and responsibilities and consequent qualification requirements. Positions involving duties and responsibilities calling for substantially the same qualification requirements are then arranged into distinct classes, within which the positions are given similar treatment in the personnel process. A class might be defined as "a group of positions sufficiently alike in respect of their duties and responsibilities to justify common treatment in the various employment processes."[190]

A class (e.g. Civil Engineer-II) consists of an occupation (Civil Engineer) and a level or zone of difficulty usually expressed in terms of a grade (G-II). For purpose of convenience and consolidation several classes might be brought under a distinct occupation group (e.g. Engineers). Such occupation groups might in turn be grouped under separate services--e.g., Administrative and Foreign, Scientific and Technical, Clerical and Secretarial, and Labour and Messenger.

Pay is determined by the class to which a position is allocated (classification level), and by the contents of the job rather than by what the advocates of position classification consider to be the more "personal" criteria of other systems.

Position classification is based on the concept "that the contents of a given position or class of positions be the hub around which the personnel actions and indeed management should revolve." [191] Such contents and the resulting classification of positions into classes become the reference point for most activities in the field of personnel administration – such as recruitment, placement, compensation, promotion, transfer, training and efficiency rating.

---

[190] O. Glenn Stahl, Public Personnel Administration (Calcutta: Oxford and International Book House Publishing Company 1962), p. 156

[191] Frederick C. Mosher, "The Public Service in the Temporary Society." Public Administration Review, 31 (January-February 1971): 58.

Position classification seeks to bring about the greatest possible element of objectivity in personnel administration. It attempts this by replacing a significant element of human discretion by objective measurement and mechanical processes of personnel administration.

Advocates of position classification claim that by contrast to this the "rank classification" approach concentrates on the individual and his personal characteristics rather than the job and its contents. Thus pay is determined by the rank of a person rather than by the contents of his job. The same might be said of other aspects of the personnel process, since other personal attributes might also be considered – such as seniority of service, education and other qualifications, and medals and honors.

The advocates of position classification claim that in the "rank classification" system personnel administration revolves around the person and his personal attributes, rather than on the position and job attributes. They claim that rank classification also leaves a greater deal of leeway for human discretion, and there is less stress on the "objectivity" that comes via the precision of measurement and mechanical processes of personnel administration.

But it might be argued that the rank classification system does not entirely ignore the job and its contents, or the concept of equal pay for comparably equal work under like conditions. It does not necessarily pursue or promote a human discretion that is unfettered by a desire for objectivity, or that is not at all informed by the regularity and uniformity and requirements of relevant laws and rules and regulations.

It may not be necessary to look at the two systems of "rank classification" and "position classification" in dichotomous terms. For instance, the rank classification system could acquire some of the more positive emphases of the position classification system by incorporating a well-developed and more comprehensive job description scheme.

A job description might be defined as a detailed description of duties, typical tasks, and standard education and other requirements expected of any person holding a particular job. The job description then becomes a valuable tool and point of reference for the personnel process. While the stress remains on the individual, that person can then be referred to against the specificities of the job that is held or is to be assigned. Some of the weaknesses of the personnel process of the civil service in Nepal can be said to be due to the absence of such a comprehensive and effective job description scheme, and the absence of a strong and effective central personnel agency to establish and oversee the operation of such a scheme.

Walter Fischer (Austria), the first Personnel Administration Advisor to the Nepal Government from UNTA (United Nations Technical Assistance Program), had recommended the institution of a job description scheme for the civil service in his final report (1958). But he had not recommended the replacement of the existing rank classification system by that of position classification.

Even Louis Kroeger (U.S.) had not recommended such a change in his 1962 survey report – and he came from a consulting firm that had experience with helping to institute the position classification systems in the United States. Kroeger said that:

His Majesty's Government should indeed have a position classification plan – sometime in the future. It is a refinement, however, which can well await the greater maturity of the administrative staff and the future development of the administrative philosophies found best suited to Nepal's purposes. [192]

Some of the American advisors who followed were not so cautious. Wilson Hart (U.S.), the UNTA Personnel Administration Advisor to HMG from February to December 1965, had not been able to be very effective during his short advisory tenure. He must have been aware of the problems of getting HMG to institute and sustain any real change and development in its system of personnel administration. But he recommended the institution of a sophisticated manpower development program that, for the actual Nepal situation, was lacking in an underlying sense of reality and of priorities and perspective.[193]

But Hart's heady concoction indicated to his Nepali hosts the sort of gadgetry that was available for the personnel processes, and position classification was one such "new" gadget.

It was at about this time (1965-66) that the personnel process of the civil service began to receive some fresh interest from amongst some Nepalis themselves. A contributing factor was the transfer of the central personnel function from the regulatory framework of the Home Ministry to the relatively more developmental ambit of the Public Administration Department – or to the Cabinet Secretariat that succeeded it in April 1966. The transferred central personnel function was given the initial leadership of an energetic and reformist Joint Secretary who, in April 1968, became the Secretary of the new Administrative Management Department. He put emphasis on three particular areas of personnel administration – merit and its evaluation; a unified civil service system for Nepal; and position classification.

---

[192] Louis J. Kroeger, A Public Administration Program for His Majesty's Government of Nepal (San Francisco: Griffenhagen-Kroeger Inc., March 1962), p. 37.
[193] Wilson R. Hart, Draft Final Report (Kathmandu, Nepal 13 January 1966).

There were some other progressive elements in the civil service. They were often young and had had some training and education in public administration in western countries – often in the United States. They had brought back an awareness of how things were done abroad, and how they might be done in Nepal to greater advantage. Some of them tended to be impatient with the inadequacies of their own administrative system, and often despaired of achieving anything concrete through evolutionary schemes. Such schemes also demanded the sort of time, patience, imagination, adaptability, and political and institutional support that may not always have been available to an adequate degree. Some of these progressive elements may therefore have had a preference for more radical change and reform, and with this they may also have had an insufficiently critical preference for some of the more sophisticated practices and gadgets of Western, and particularly American, systems of administration.

It is not always clear that these progressive elements understood the implications of that which they sought to adopt – some might even say to imitate. One can imagine the quite limited level of comprehension of such gadgets in the rest of government and administration! The series of transient foreign advisors cannot have helped matters very much with their penchant for advocating their own systems and gadgets of administration as the one best way of doing things.

It might be said that these progressive elements tended to have only a peripheral place in the scheme of government and administration in Nepal. Often their relative youthfulness became the basis for suspicion and diffidence in local eyes – and this might often have resulted in some rather negative undercutting of their efforts at change and reform.

Perhaps there was also an unfortunate but not entirely inaccurate belief amongst some of them that their very Nepaliness was the cause of their being taken less seriously than was desirable by their compatriots in the administration and by the powers-that-be in the government. Hence they would often seek the services of a foreign advisor to lend the prestige of his advocacy to their own proposals and preferences. It might be said that the absence of solid institutional bases for administrative development in Nepal often resulted in such efforts at change and reform sometimes taking on a flavor that was perhaps the worst of combinations – too foreign, too esoteric, and too power-oriented.

It was at the urging of the then progressive leadership of the Administrative Management Department that HMG invited UNTA Advisor Edward McCrensky (U.S.) to come to Nepal and review various policy and procedural issues of personnel administration that were then under consideration, including the introduction of a system of position classification. McCrensky stayed a mere fortnight (4-18 November 1968). It is interesting that in that short time he found it possible to present HMG with a wide-ranging proposal for a position classification system and a unified civil service.[194] Perhaps the groundwork had already been laid for the preparation and presentation of his proposal. It was no surprise that HMG did act on his advice to seek further technical assistance in the area of position classification and salary policy evaluation.

A few months later HMG acquired the services of Dr. O. Glenn Stahl (U.S.) from the Ford Foundation. Stahl stayed in Nepal from March to June 1969. He was asked to evaluate and suggest improvements in the personnel system, with particular reference to the job structure and promotion system, the assignment practices, and compartmentalization. Stahl was the first foreign advisor who specifically and in some detail recommended the adoption of a position classification system to HMG. Stahl noted in his final report that: Modern job analysis and classification is the only means of avoiding the limitations of a cadre system and assuring the best matching of men to jobs on a continuing basis, as well as pay commensurate with duties and responsibilities.[195] He proceeded to recommend that:

A thorough job survey should be started as soon as possible to arrange all positions into occupations and levels, with common qualification requirements and pay ranges for each, leading to elimination of artificial categories and their replacement by defined occupational distinctions only maintained on an up-to-date basis by continuous job audit. This approach may be represented by an Administrative-Professional group of occupations, a Clerical-Mechanical group, and a Labour-Messenger group.[196]

This approach included the institution of a unified civil service system. There was to be no artificial bar to movement based upon group or service. Personnel would be free to move from one job or grade or occupation to another, provided that they met the qualifications required by the job to be done.[197]

Stahl combined teaching with advocacy. He held a class on position classification for some twenty civil servants. The hope was that some of them might be developed into a nucleus of position classification analysts. It appears that Stahl also talked on the subject at the national university (Tribhuvan University) and at the Administrative Management Department. The then Chief Secretary of HMG was a vigorous advocate of the position classification concept

---

[194] Edward McCrensky, Proposal for a Unified Civil Service for His Majesty's Government of Nepal (New York; United Nations, 10 June 1969). An earlier version had been printed in Kathmandu, Nepal, on 15 November 1968.

[195] O. Glenn Stahl, A Strong Civil Service for Nepal (Kathmandu, Nepal, June 1969). Reprinted in *Prashasan* (The Nepali Journal of Public Administration), Yr. 2, No. 1, April 1970, p. 44.

[196] Ibid. p. 45.

[197] Ibid., p. 82

during his own term of office (January 1969 to January 1972). At an 11 June 1969 meeting of the Secretaries of HMG it was decided to begin work on a job description survey, preliminary to eventual decision on the introduction of a comprehensive position classification system for the Nepal Civil Service.

The Government also accepted Stahl's recommendation that it seek the services of an American or Canadian job evaluation expert for at least six months, and possibly longer, to assist in conducting a job survey and in setting up a classification plan. [198] It turned to the Ford Foundation for technical assistance.

It may be that, in his strong advocacy for position classification in the Civil Service, Stahl was acting more from a dogmatic belief in its being the one best way of doing things than from any deep appreciation of Nepali needs and realities. Such certainty can be persuasive (it was), but it might get the client into an area whose pros and cons are not fully comprehended, and whose future implications are not well understood. This may have been the case in Nepal, where the more youthful and progressive elements might have had a natural, but maybe not critical, preference for "modern gadgets" like position classification.

After Stahl, the Ford Foundation provided the services of William F. Danielson (U.S.) as Public Administration Advisor for the Position Classification Project. He stayed in Nepal from October 1969 to March 1970. Danielson's job was to: (1) introduce the concept of position classification; (2) train a Nepali Classification Team to carry out work on Gazetted posts, and on Non-Gazetted posts at a later date; and (3) to assist His Majesty's Government to develop and install a classification plan of posts within the Nepal Civil Service.

Danielson was quite well qualified for the job. He had been Director of Personnel at Berkeley (California) from 1955-69, where he had acquired extensive classification experience. He had worked on the installation of some 24 classification plans prior to Nepal. The Nepal effort was unique in that it was the first time he had had to leave a survey site before the whole work was completed.[199]

The time perspectives behind the donor and advisory efforts for the introduction and installation of the system of position classification in Nepal proved to be quite unrealistic! Six months was too short a time for the introduction of an alien concept like position classification, to train a local classification team, and to install a classification plan. Some Nepali proponents of position classification may have underestimated the complexities of the installation process, the lack of comprehension of the concept of position

---

[198] Ibid., p. 81
[199] William F. Danielson, Interim Report on Survey Classification of Posts for His Majesty's Government of Nepal (Kathmandu, Nepal, 19 March 1970), p. 7.

classification, and the local unease about it. Also, their influence in government and administration, and their capacity for effective advocacy, was perhaps much more marginal than they thought.

Perhaps the donor did not adequately comprehend the possibility and the pace of change in Nepal. Some responsibility for the inadequate perspectives on the timescale and the possibility of change must lie with the donor agency, in this case the Ford Foundation, which conducted its technical and development assistance efforts in Nepal from New Delhi in India. Its leadership there seems to have had a decidedly economist bias, which led it to concentrate its Nepal efforts largely on economic planning and development and business administration. Its support for the broader area of reform and development of the system of public administration seems to have been more ambivalent as to involvement, and fitful and parsimonious as to assistance.

None of the three Ford Foundation advisors that were provided to support the position classification installation effort seem to have considered their tenure in Nepal to be adequate for the job to be done! Danielson, who came after Stahl, felt that 18 to 24 months would have been more realistic for the job. He got hardly six months! The failure of the position classification effort in Nepal is thought to have been due, in some measure, to the inability of the Ford Foundation to sustain its advisors for a sufficient duration to see the Position Classification Project through to completion. The Project could be broken-up into the following basic stages:

1. Job Description and Analysis.
2. Arranging Positions into Classes.
3. Preparation of Class Standards and Classification Plan.
4. Installation of Classification Plan [200]

The timetable below indicates the approximate dates of completion of each of these stages as: (I) proposed by Danielson in his initial timetable; (II) timetable revised by him at the close of his term in Nepal; and (III) the actual time of completion of the stages.

Stage	(I) Initial	(II) Revised	(III) Actual
1.	Dec. 1969	May 1970	Oct. 1970
2.	Feb. 1970	July 1970	June 1971
3.	Mar. 1970	Oct 1970	Apr. 1972
4.	May 1970	Feb. 1971	–

---

[200] O. Glenn Stahl, Public Personnel Administration, pp. 146-167.

This timetable was for Gazetted posts only. The Non-Gazetted effort never quite got underway! It can be seen from the above that by April 1972 actual progress on the project was running two years behind Danielson's original schedule, and more than a year behind his revised schedule. Then it got stalled. It appears that further progress on the installation of the classification plan was effectively pigeon-holed by the Council of Ministers.

During Danielson's tenure from October 1969 to March 1970 even Stage One, that of job description and analysis, was not completed. A Job Description Questionnaire for Gazetted Posts had been prepared in both Nepali and English, and distribution had begun in December 1969. Some 2,670 Gazetted posts (out of a total of about 3,300) were selected for the questionnaire sample. They were spread out over the Centre (Kathmandu Valley) and twelve carefully selected districts in field. The district sample was about 17 percent of the total sample of posts. By the end of Danielson's term in Nepal in late March 1970 only about 48 percent of the distributed questionnaires had been returned.[201] Danielson had initially hoped that 90 percent of the questionnaires could have been distributed and collected within 90 days![202] It is also interesting to note that returns from the Centre (about 44 percent) seem to have lagged noticeably behind those from the outside districts (about 68 percent)! Danielson gave a very interesting reason for this quite disappointing pace of work:

(A) Unique problem which contributes to the delay in returning forms is the educational system and tradition of the Nepalese people. Very few Nepalese are competent in creative writing. We have asked each Gazetted Officer of His Majesty's Government to fill up the form telling in his own words what his duties and responsibilities are. Often, I have found, this is the first time that many experienced Government officials ever have been called upon to write a creative statement. [203]

There may be some truth in what he says. Anyone who has tried to distribute and collect questionnaires in Nepal (as was also attempted for this work) will understand the sort of frustration that he felt. But his point about the general inability for creative writing must be also seen in the light of a general unwillingness among civil servants to express themselves in a full and frank manner, and especially in written form. The explanation might also lie in the larger socio-political context of Nepal, of which the civil servants are a part.

It is interesting to note that the position classification scheme did not enjoy the support of the very Secretary whose agency, the Administrative Management

---

[201] William F. Danielson, Survey of Classification of Gazetted Posts for His Majesty's Government of Nepal (New Delhi: Ford Foundation, 4 April 1970, pp. 13-14
[202] Ibid.,
[203] Ibid., p. 59

Department, was responsible for its installation. He was dubious of the value and relevance of position classification in the Nepali context, and he felt it was much too sophisticated and costly a system for the Nepal Civil Service. It appears therefore that Danielson had to go over this official's head, and directly to the Chief Secretary, for support and assistance for the Position Classification Project.

There seems to have been widespread unease about the classification concept among Nepali civil servants. It was an alien concept that seemed unfamiliar to their psyche and value system and that threatened some revisions in the sensitive area of personnel administration. No sufficient and sustained efforts appear to have been made to educate them about the unfamiliar system that was being so suddenly thrust upon them. Their disinclination to cooperate with the Position Classification project was therefore not entirely surprising.

The general lack of cooperation appears to have moved the Chief Secretary to contemplate punitive measures against officials who were not returning the questionnaires on time. At a meeting of HMG Secretaries on 26 March 1970, the Chief Secretary declared his intention to arrange for the indefinite salary suspensions of errant officials, pending return of the questionnaires.[204] The following day he sent out a letter to each ministry and department stating that officials who were responsible for returning the questionnaires would be named to "Higher Authority" if they failed to return the questionnaires within seven days of the receipt of his letter.[205] But these threats were also not very effective.

During Danielson's short tenure in Nepal only "Stage One" of the Position Classification Project, that of "Job Description and Analysis" of Gazetted posts, was launched but not completed. But he had trained a team of six classification analysts to continue the work after he left.

He had also presented the Chief Secretary with a report on pay that consisted of outlines for a salary plan, to be instituted with the effective implementation of the classification plan, and with the allocation of Gazetted Class posts to the appropriate levels.[206] The subsequent pay raise for civil servants in July 1973 had nothing to do with Danielson's report or with the Position Classification Project. It had a lot more to do with the seeming effort to keep civil service pay in line with rising prices!

The Ford Foundation in New Delhi seems not to have planned for a full-time advisor to succeed Danielson. Instead it provided the services of Ross Pollock (U.S.) on an intermittent basis. Pollock was an Advisor to the Indian Institute of

---

[204] Ibid. p. 37.
[205] Ibid., pp. 36-37
[206] Danielson, "Salary Change Recommendations for Gazetted Post of His Majesty's Government of Nepal", Memo to Chief Secretary, HMG/Nepal, 7 April 1970.

Public Administration. The Institute agreed to limited loans of Pollock's time, and he visited Nepal on an intermittent basis between1967-70, to advise HMG on personnel administration in the civil service. He rarely stayed longer than 3 to 7 days on any one visit. Pollock also told this writer that he did not consider the time spent by him in Nepal as being adequate for him to do his job!

Pollock appears to have had good qualifications for his job in Nepal. Prior to his Indian assignment he had served in the U.S. Civil Service Commission, where he had rotated gradually upwards in a series of jobs in personnel testing, recruitment, training, and career development. In Nepal he helped to bring "Stage One" of the Position Classification Project to completion, and he also gave the Classification Team useful on-the-job training in job description and analysis. The Classification Team considered Pollock to be competent, pragmatic and flexible, and respected him for it. He did his best to keep the classification effort moving and also to sustain interest in it at the higher levels of Government.

The Position Classification Project received the public support of the late King Mahendra in June 1970. In His Address to the 16th Session of the National Assembly the King emphasized the need to define the functions, duties, and responsibilities of different personnel in order to ensure an efficient administration to cope with growing development needs, and to implement the various development projects. The Classification Project was incorporated in the Fourth Plan (1970-75), where its installation in the Nepal Civil Service was made the basis of a modern and efficient system of public administration, and the prerequisite for a subsequent comprehensive career development scheme.[207]

A year later King Mahendra said in His Address to the 18th Session of the National Assembly, on 28 June 1971, that "My Government will implement a position classification plan in order to bring about necessary reforms in administration." So it would seem that HMG was now unequivocally committed to the installation of a position classification scheme for the Nepal Civil Service. But subsequent events were to show that even the dicta of a powerful sovereign can be frustrated in the labyrinthine maze of bureaucratic politics and inertia. It gives some idea of the extent of opposition to the implementation of the position classification scheme in Nepal!

George Thomson Jackson (Canada) followed Pollock as Ford Foundation Advisor to the Position Classification Project. Jackson's services were provided full-time and, with two extensions of tenure, he was in Nepal from October 1970 to December 1971. His job was to assist the Nepali Classification Team to continue and bring to conclusion the Position Classification Project, and to help

---

[207] National Planning Commission, HMG/Nepal, The Fourth Plan: 1970-75 (Kathmandu, Nepal: National Planning Commission, His Majesty's Government of Nepal, July 1970), p. 271.

to develop a pay plan to go with it. Jackson appears to have been well qualified for the job. He had had some 40 years of public administration service in the Canadian Government, some of which were at senior levels; and he had developed an international reputation regarding classification and pay systems for public service organizations. Prior to the Nepal assignment he had been Regional Director of the Canadian University Service Overseas for Nepal, Ceylon, and India (May 1969 to October 1970).

Like his predecessors Danielson and Pollock, he also felt that the time given to him in Nepal was not adequate for him to complete his job! He thought that at least one more year would have been necessary for this. The fourteen months that he had been given were in themselves the results of two extensions in tenure, rather than an original appreciation of the time required. Jackson felt that his work might have been more productive had he been more certain of his length of stay. He felt that if he had had a longer and a more certain indication of his tenure he would also have tried to learn the language of the country. It seems that he was frustrated by discussions around him in a language he was unfamiliar with. Perhaps a related difficulty was that some of his Nepali counterparts had a maybe less than comfortable mastery of English.

Jackson was also frustrated by the low productivity of the Nepali Classification Team. Not that the Team was entirely at fault. With only four members it was rather understaffed. Repeated requests by Jackson for more members produced no results. The Team itself seems to have had a tentative existence, since not all of its members were permanently assigned to the Administrative Management Department, leave alone to its Position Classification Section. The heavy workload and lack of added help created frustration in the Team, with some negative results on production and motivation. The Team appears to have developed an inbuilt resistance to correction and change. It seems that when fresh information and proper classification justified the allocation of more levels to certain occupations, or the higher classification of certain posts, there was resistance to change because of the added work that would be involved, and the desire to avoid delays and push on regardless.

A problem, which seems to have become more serious with the "Preparation of Class Standards and the Classification Plan" was the resistance of civil servants unhappy with the allocation of levels to their particular Services and positions. The problem was especially serious with the technicians and specialists. This writer was told by some very senior administrators that it was the opposition of these technicians and specialists, and their influence in high places that resulted in the failure to install the classification scheme. The engineers, for instance, were not happy that their group of occupations were to be classified only up to grade 9 – out of a total of 12 grades. Jackson felt they could not be given the topmost grade of 12, which would have put them on a par with the Secretaries to HMG. But the engineers were told they could be given grades 10 and 11 at a later date, as the classification effort developed momentum. This did not satisfy them. The lawyers were also not happy that while the administrative-executive group ranged right up to grade 12, the judicial group of occupations was ranged up to grade 10 only. Unhappy lawyers can be quite a problem! There were other cases too. Jackson warned that if something were not done soon there would be so much resistance to the classification proposal and plan that it might never be implemented. And it was not!

It seems that while the Classification Team worked on the allocation of levels from the perspective of the "job", most civil servants looked upon levels from the perspective of their existing "rank", and the "prestige" of particular occupations and professions. The classification effort seems to have enhanced the differences in perspectives between technicians and generalists. It also highlighted the reservations felt about the Administrative Management Department (AMD) by the other ministries and departments of HMG. The AMD did not have the status, authority or influence to overcome these problems.

The New Promotion Rules

The Position Classification Project was also sidelined by the "New Promotion Rules" of September 1971. These Rules emanated from the *Janch Bujh Kendra* (Investigation and Inquiry Centre) that was closely linked to the Royal Palace Secretariat. These Rules sought to introduce an element of objectivity into the civil service promotion system through a largely mechanical and mathematical approach to the measurement of merit. They were based on the existing system of "rank classification", fragmentation, and closed-service careerism.

For several years, at least since 1969, the civil service promotion system had almost come to a halt because of differences over what constituted merit, and how it was to be measured and made the basis of a viable and objective promotion system. It was felt that any further delay in promotions would cause too much resentment among civil servants. HMG therefore decided to go ahead with the first round of promotions under the New Promotion Rules.

This process took some nine months until well into mid-1972. This was at the cost of emphasis upon, and attention to, the incomplete Position Classification Project, which also clashed conceptually with the New Promotion Rules. It is also because of this de-emphasis that Jackson's tenure in Nepal ended in December 1971. By this time the project on position classification was at "Stage Three" – "Preparation of Class Standards and Classification Plan" (See the timetable of stages above).

The New Promotion Rules of September 1971 appear to have provided a convenient handle with which opponents could delay and frustrate the Position Classification Project. In January 1972 the proponents of the classification effort had lost their two principal supporters. HM King Mahendra passed away in January 1972. The Chief Secretary who had been a vigorous and consistent advocate of the project had also completed his term of office.

It seems that the new Chief Secretary was less than enamoured of the position classification concept. He seems to have seen it as a novel irrelevance and nuisance to the civil service system. Then in April 1972 the Prime Minister (he was also Finance Minister) dropped his General Administration portfolio, and with it his political stewardship of the Position Classification Project. The portfolio went to a Minister, who held it along with several other portfolios. He supported the classification effort, but was preoccupied with other matters, and he had the administration portfolio for one year only.

It seems that in February 1972 the Classification Team had sent to the Council of Ministers a draft Civil Service Amendment Act that contained changes in the New Promotion Rules that would be necessary for implementation of the position classification scheme. In March 1972 the Team had completed work on the "Preparation of the Class Standards and Classification Plan".[208] These were sent to the Council of Ministers. The documents were forwarded to the Royal Palace Secretariat, where it seems the *Janch Bujh Kendra* (Investigation and Inquiry Centre) gave them some consideration. At any rate word came back from the Council of Ministers that the Classification Standards and Plan needed further study and elaboration, including the development of a pay plan and an appeal mechanism. The more precise intention was to pigeon-hole the classification effort; the opposition to it had become problematical, and the Council of Ministers was disinclined to give it decisive support.

In the latter part of 1972 the thinking in the Administrative Management Department turned towards the so-called "Faculty System". This system appears to have been designed to: (1) retain but improve upon the existing "rank classification" system; (2) generate the least possible resistance from civil servants; and (3) not make any undue demands for establishment and for maintenance upon the limited resources likely to be available for improvement of the system of personnel administration. With the proposed "Faculty System" the existing eleven Services were to be retained, but each Service was to be divided into "faculties". For instance, the Engineering Service was to be divided into such faculties as electrical, civil and mechanical engineering, and so on. It was thought that some 50-100 faculties might be identified for the Nepal Civil

---

[208] The Classification scheme outlined in these documents consisted of some 47 occupations and 12 levels (1-5 for the equivalent of the existing Non-Gazetted Classes, and 6-12 for the equivalent of the existing Gazetted Classes).

Service. Promotion was to be within faculties, so as to help overcome the problem of the people being put into jobs for which they were not qualified. There was to be opportunity for transfer between faculties where the types of work were closely related. The intention seems to have been to create a series of career fields and career ladders, and to have a comprehensive job description scheme covering all Gazetted Class posts; presumably extending to Non-Gazetted posts later.

The distinction between Gazetted and Non-Gazetted Class posts was to be retained. The existing grade structure was also to be retained. It was felt that immediate attempts to increase the number of grades from the existing eight would again reopen the questions of whose job was to be classified at higher levels. This was an issue that had aroused a lot of controversy and contributed to the resistance to the position classification effort.

The "Faculty System" approach seems to have been informed by the belief that the Nepal Civil Service was not yet ready for the installation of a fully developed position classification system. The approach sought to learn from some of the more positive features of the position classification system without proposing a wholesale conversion of the existing system of personnel administration. The aim seems to have been to go for an incremental approach that was pragmatic and marked by the spirit of compromise. The approach seems to be largely the product of Nepali initiative and thinking. By late 1974 the proposed "Faculty System" seemed to have got the tentative support of both the Royal Palace and the Public Service Commission. Initial trials were to begin with the five technical Services. Whether the "Faculty System" would become an administration-wide reality remained to be seen.

Perspectives on the Nepali Experience

In the light of the experience above perhaps "position classification" was an alien system that was not suited to the Nepali administrative ecology. It stressed aspects of the personnel process that may have suited a certain type of American psyche but was probably at odds with the general Nepali psyche. The stress seemed to be on organization as a machine rather than as a social grouping. It looked to be a mechanical rather than a human approach to personnel administration. It sought the objectivity of measurement and precision for the personnel process, but it might lose a significant element of human discretion and interest and concern in the process. It seemed to some that the position classification system put too much stress on material rewards and incentives like pay, and too little on social rewards and incentives like status and prestige.

Perhaps position classification was too sophisticated a system for Nepali needs. It tended to compartmentalize the civil service into numerous specialties and sub-specialties. This can make for an unnecessarily specialized civil service system that hinders mobility of personnel and flexibility in their use. It might contribute to fragmented perspectives in the civil service, and the personnel system may then become too rigid in its operation.

Glenn Stahl noted that "Once a classification plan is adopted, it is pointless to do anything less than provide for continuous, painstaking maintenance on a current basis."[209] This can be a demanding and expensive process. Perhaps countries like Nepal need to be wary of new "refinements" like the position classification system. Such gadgets can become a white elephant that demands an increasing amount of the scarce resources of government. It might also add to the protective and narcissistic (and materialistic) orientation of a public bureaucracy that ranks with the socio-economic elites, and that is difficult to control because of the weakness and immaturity of the nominally superior political processes of government.

Perhaps the Position Classification Project was an unnecessary exercise in the pursuit of rather abstract administrative perfection, and informed by alien value systems. The foray may have diverted attention from the intermediate and more immediate needs in Nepal, such as for a strong and effective central personnel agency in HMG; for a more open civil service system; for a more flexible grade structure; and for comprehensive schemes of job description and career development. It ought to be possible to attend to the pursuit and realization of these needs, without going in for a full-scale position classification scheme.

In the context of the Nepal Civil Service perhaps the position classification system was an alien gadget whose sophistication may attract, but whose complexities could make too many demands upon limited resources. Perhaps His Majesty's Government was not then in a position to fully understand the implications of the position classification system for Nepal. In itself it was no panacea for the ills of the personnel process, or of the system of administration in the country. The social costs of instituting a position classification system can be high, since the values upon which it is based may clash with local values. Why incur such costs if it is far from clear that a position classification system is indeed a necessity for the personnel process or for administrative development in the country? It ought to be realized and accepted that in public administration there is no one and universal best way of doing things!

---

[209] Stahl, Public Personnel Administrative, p. 162.

CHAPTER 14

PERSPECTIVES ON THE FOREIGN ADVISORY EFFORTS [210]

The Indian Government undertook the first foreign advisory efforts to improve the public administration system in Nepal. In these efforts one can see some of the more serious defects that a critic might expect to find in attempts at transnational inducement of administrative development. Like some other foreign advisory efforts, that of the Indians was also too concerned with the perspective of the donor as opposed to that of the recipient. The Indian interest in Nepal was primarily political – perhaps too much so. India was interested in keeping Nepal within its own political and strategic sphere of influence.

The Indian Government tried to safeguard its special interests in Nepal by inducing the growth of political and administration systems based upon Indian models and looking to India for advice and assistance. The basic idea was that India was both necessary and sufficient for Nepal, with the presumption being that what was good for India was good for Nepal, and that future development ought to follow the Indian example. It seems that the Indians would have preferred to maintain a donor monopoly in what they saw as the sensitive area of public administration. All this tended to give their technical assistance an unduly political flavor. It made for a style and content of technical assistance that may not have been suitable to Nepali needs and realities; and it seemed to side-step or to ignore the more desirable and in the longer term the more sustainable process of evolution through continuity and innovation.

The Indian advisors seem not to have really understood the Nepali system of administration. Nor is it at all clear that they seriously attempted to do so. Rather they tried to model the Nepali administrative system upon the Indian frame of reference that they did understand, and that they had inherited from British India. They appear to have done this in a somewhat pro-consular manner that was closer to inducement and imposition rather than to consultation and cooperation. Their style may have reflected their basic convictions about the superiority and transferability of their own British-induced system of administration.

---

[210] See Appendix 3 for a list of foreign advisors in public administration from Feb 1951 to June 1975.

The Nepali administrative system that resulted was a confusing amalgam of what was inherited by default, and what was imitated by inducement and imposition. The best of the Rana system of administration was discarded, while it's more negative aspects appear to have been fortified by some defects of the Indian system. One result was a closed-career system that was too protective in its orientation. There was a tendency to abstract administrative perfection, and an inclination to see public administration as an end in itself, rather than as an instrument of public service. Some foreign advisors had noted a tendency to entertain primarily those recommendations that might enhance the image of "integrity" of a closed-career system, as well as to reduce the amount of discretion allowed to officials or agencies.

This rather protectionist and negative perspective seems to have motivated, to a large degree, the interest in such initiatives as the Public Service Commission, the Civil Service Act and Rules, and some other efforts at "reform" or "development" of the system.

The Indians did succeed in giving Nepali administration a generally Indianized system and form. They tended to do so by ignoring the inherited and the indigenous while seeking a comprehensive restructuring of Nepali administration along Indian lines. There were some regrettable social costs. There was a tendency towards local confusion and sense of inadequacy, as well as an unnecessary sense of rupture and dichotomy with the past.

Modernity tended to be thought to be synonymous with a sweeping rejection of Nepali systems, and with a comprehensive and not very imaginative imitation of what was non-Nepali. This can lead to the emasculation of the local confidence, intellect and initiative that must be the basis for sufficient and sustained national (and administrative) development. The Indian efforts might be said to have contributed to an increasing sense of dependence upon foreign technical assistance efforts to develop the public administration system in Nepal. This then contributed to the parallel disinclination on the Nepali side to undertake sufficient and sustained efforts and initiatives towards such development.

Foreign technical assistance efforts tended to be a crutch that Nepalis were unwilling to do without. Some Nepalis may have had a sort of visceral resentment to the foreign advisor, who seemed to them to be proof of native emasculation and inadequacy, and who they may have seen as a symbol of their own developmental inferiority. Such complexes, to which the Indian advisory effort contributed initially and perhaps in large measure, cannot have been healthy for the foreign advisory efforts, or for the national development towards which they were directed.

The Nepali side never quite seemed to develop the requisite degree of ability to coordinate and consolidate the foreign technical assistance efforts in public administration, and to give them a coherent central design and purpose. This was also due to the limited administrative resources available. It may also have been a question of a very dependent aid recipient feeling unable to exercise due control over the many donor agencies, each with its own interests and perspectives. The donors seem to have been unable or unwilling to cooperate meaningfully amongst themselves. There was perhaps a tendency to dominate or to monopolize an area of assistance, or to fragment it into exclusive divisions, or to get out.

The Indians were predominant in the earlier years of technical assistance in public administration. They quit this field when the United Nations Technical Assistance Program (UNTA) entered it in a relatively big way from about 1957. The UNTA effort itself seemed to wind down from about 1966, some three years after technical assistance from the United States via the U.S. AID Program (AID/Nepal) came into this field. In these entries and exits the Nepalis themselves appear not to have had much say.

The AID/Nepal effort in public administration gives some indication of this. The formal beginning of U.S. assistance to Nepal began with the signing of the bilateral Technical Cooperation Agreement on 23 January 1951. The U.S. Technical Cooperation Mission opened its office in Kathmandu a year later. But the Nepal Government kept the Americans out of the public administration area, which it felt was too sensitive to permit the entry of a major cold war power. This was perhaps also a quite faithful reflection of Indian thinking.

But from about 1960 the U.S. pressure to get in became much too strong. As a scholar on foreign aid and politics in Nepal has noted, the Americans felt that inadequacies in public administration constituted a major stumbling block to progress, and "Further American aid, the mission made it clear, was contingent upon the acceptance of an American-supported program of administrative reform."[211] The Government of Nepal accepted this. It was a time when, for internal political reasons, and pressures from India, the Government was feeling insecure and isolated. But Nepal was also at the time quite heavily dependent upon U.S. aid for its development programs. India had itself been receiving significant U.S. food and other aid.

The American entry into public administration development in Nepal was perhaps somewhat disruptive of the ongoing UN efforts. The Nepali side did not seem to have the ability to simultaneously coordinate the efforts of both these donors. The UN effort was maybe capable of representing a broader field of interests than those of any single donor country. It had in Nepal a Senior Public

---

[211] Eugene Bramer Mihaly, Foreign Aid and Politics in Nepal (London: Oxford University Press, 1965), p. 135.

Administration Advisor who might have been able to give the needed coordination to the various technical assistance efforts in public administration. But the Americans appear not to have been interested in coordination under a multilateral umbrella. They wished to be on their own, and UNTA quit the field.

By late 1974 the Americans themselves appear to have decided to abandon the public administration field in Nepal. It appears that US/AID (United States Agency for International Development) in Washington DC had begun to be reluctant to work frontally on public administration in Asia, which it saw as too vague an area, too bottomless, never-ending, politically sensitive, and so on. It seems that at most US/ AID was willing to consider some limited technical assistance to "vertical" projects that addressed the administrative problems relevant to each particular project. But it wished to keep away from "horizontal" projects that tackled public administration subjects per se – personnel administration, O&M, in-service training, and so on.

It is true that "horizontal" progress can be glacially slow. But can the "vertical" approach really succeed in a sea of "horizontal" inadequacies? It is also interesting to note that the Americans appear to have had a penchant for the "horizontal" in the early 1960s, when HMG was reluctant to engage in any position with them in public administration. But, when in the early 1970s HMG was more willing to entertain the "horizontal" with them, it was the Americans who wanted only limited "vertical" engagement or nothing! This sort of shift in perspectives and preferences for engagement in the horizontal or vertical positions can be challenging for the most committed of partners!

The Nepali side appears not to have had any major say in these changes in preferences and positions; or programs and priorities. The decisions seemed quite often to have been made by the donor. Logically, a country program developed with local counterparts would be a better way to develop perspectives on country needs and priorities. As it is, the Americans had perhaps an unrealistic perspective of the possibilities and of the pace of change in Nepal.

The picture was hardly better with the Ford Foundation, which supervised its Nepal efforts from New Delhi – a questionable practice in itself. The Foundation leadership in New Delhi appears to have had a decidedly economist bias which led it to concentrate its Nepali efforts in what seemed to be the broad area of economic development and business management. By the time of its support to the position classification effort (1969-71) the Foundation had become rather rigid in its preferences, and it would appear that it never did acquire an adequate perspective and appreciation of the public administration needs in Nepal.

It seems that it became a constant struggle to get the Ford Foundation to maintain an adequate input into public administration development efforts in Nepal. The Foundation leadership in New Delhi appears to have developed the convenient belief that HMG was not willing to accept help in the rather sensitive area of public administration. But the reluctance was on the other side! By the late 1960s there were significant elements in HMG who did want the Foundation to switch its assistance from economic planning and business management to public administration. The Foundation in New Delhi preferred to ignore this.

The donor perspective could sometimes operate rather arbitrarily and decisively in deciding the fate of projects. The efforts to establish an Institute of Public Administration were dealt a deathblow when AID/Nepal, until then the major aid donor, withdrew rather unilaterally and inexplicably from this project in late 1964. The Nepali side was left stunned and bitter at this seemingly erratic behavior. In March 1970 the Administrative Management Department proposed that the Administrative Staff College be established to help meet the substantial training needs of the Nepal Civil Service. The proposal was basically a product of Nepali initiatives, and it appears to have had some potential for enhancing the administrative training capability within the country. But AID/Nepal thought that the proposal was not exciting enough and declined to support it.

The Ford Foundation leadership in New Delhi appears to have seen the proposed Administrative Staff College (ASC) as a potential rival to the Centre for Economic Development and Administration (CEDA) that it had helped to establish a year earlier. It worked successfully to stop the ASC initiative and to have some of its proposed in-service training functions given to CEDA, where it seems they were not very successfully done. Ironically, this may have contributed in some measure to CEDA's own existential problems!

Observations and Conclusions

The technical assistance efforts in public administration in Nepal have tended to lack a sustained long-run approach with sufficient flexibility to adapt to the underlying needs of the country. In general there appears to have been: (1) a failure to provide sufficient and sustained assistance for administrative development; (2) a failure to sustain an advisor in the field for a sufficient length of time to see a project through to completion; and (3) a failure to provide continuity between one advisor and another without undue time-lag and loss of momentum in effort.

The donors may also have had a too unrealistic perception of the possibilities and pace of change in Nepal. Such deficient perspectives and an inadequate and uncertain tenure can be serious constraints to the work of the foreign advisor.

It takes time to understand the administrative system of a country and the socio-political ecology in which it operates; to build relationships with the Nepalis; and to persuade officials to accept change and reform. In many cases the tenure of advisors was too short for them to be really effective in their job.

The quality of advisors may in some instances have left something to be desired. Perhaps greater care could have been given to the selection of advisors and matching them to the requirements, and indeed the challenges, of the job to be done. Some appear to have had competence in one area but were utilized in another. Some had expertise in part of an area but were asked to produce over the whole. Some, with impressive résumés and skills, would have done well in their own system and environment, but could not adjust to that of Nepal. The Nepali situation was perhaps simpler but more difficult, demanding maybe less sophistication but more creativity.

There was also the problem of orientation. Many advisors tended to know very little about Nepal prior to their assignment. There appears to have been no formal orientation program arranged for them by either the donor or recipient agencies in the host country. The advisors were left largely to their own devices and they tended to depend heavily on books and reports. But most of these tend to be written by foreigners and hence they may sometimes constitute a reinforcement of misconceptions and misinformation about local needs and realities. The problem of orientation was not helped by the fact that many advisors tended to concentrate their movement in Nepal primarily to the capital city and its environment. Visits to the field might also sometimes be too few and too short, and also too pre-programmed and too formal.

Within Kathmandu the advisors appear in many cases to have led a privileged and cloistered existence. Their salaries and allowance can range from ten to twenty times that of their Nepali counterparts. Their children would usually go to special schools for foreigners. The advisors and their families would naturally tend to mix with other expatriates in the foreign aid and diplomatic communities. The Nepalis whom they met socially would be at the upper levels of government and society. This can present problems of orientation and perspective, and sometimes generate local resentment of their more privileged lifestyle.

It is not easy for the advisors to maintain genuine patterns of collaboration with their local counterparts. There may be big differences in lifestyles and value systems and perspectives. It is also not easy to escape the superior-inferior relationship in the technical assistance process. It seems that in the Nepali case the foreign advisory efforts have tended to be less collaborative than might be expected. Local counterparts have tended to be used as aides for purposes of communication and information gathering. They have not usually participated as equals in the work of identifying administrative development needs, and of suggesting and shaping the change and reform necessary to meet these needs.

This is a pity, because genuine collaboration can educate both the advisor and the recipient. It can help to establish a valuable degree of complementarity between the two and to make communications a two-way process. It can help to minimize the feeling of emasculation and inadequacy that foreign advisory efforts can quite unintentionally generate.

Genuine collaboration would also benefit from an administrative development capability on the recipient side. Such a capability has not yet been sufficiently developed, indigenized and institutionalized in Nepal. There must be this capability within the country to absorb and to coordinate technical assistance and to give it central design, coherence and purpose.

Too much of the technical assistance efforts in public administration have been based at least implicitly on the assumption that there is one best way of doing things. Confusion is added when advisors from different systems recommended their own version of the one best way! Some advisors appear not to have had the imagination and creativity, and the sense of restraint, to adapt their expertise and native experience to recipient system needs and realities.

Quite often the advice given was producer-oriented rather than consumer oriented. It was based upon what the advisor could produce rather than upon what the recipient system might need, or was likely to be able to adopt, adapt and implement. In a sense the advisors might be looked upon as salesmen who tried to sell the country the gadgets they possessed, rather than those that it might need. They might have been persuasive, but this can get Nepal into areas whose pros and cons are not understood, and whose relevance is questionable.

The efforts of the advisors were not always informed by a sense of continuity! Advisors tended quite often to take a different line from that of their predecessors, and sometimes from their contemporaries.

Walter Fischer (1957-58), Wilson Hart (1965), and Sir Eric Franklin (1964-66) came up with three different locations and emphases for a central personnel agency. Hartvig Nissen (1957-60), Merrill Goodall (1962-63), and Frank O'Neill (1963-64) centered much of their efforts on proposals for an Institute of Public Administration. But S.T. Divers (1959-62), Alfred Linsell (1962-63) and Sir Eric Franklin (1964-66) chose not to support this push. Louis Kroeger (1962) even dismissed the proposed Institute project as unnecessary! And AID/Nepal first agreed to be the major aid donor for the Institute of Public Administration, and then abruptly backed away in late 1964. This sort of thing cannot do much good for the effectiveness of the foreign advisory efforts. It can also make for a very bemused, quite perplexed and rather passive recipient system.

In many cases it might be that the most important part of the advisor's efforts was the final report, which in too many cases may have been largely ignored. This is a sad waste of resources. It can also result in an element of lack of responsibility, since the advisors do not then have to stay behind to justify their recommendations, or to witness the strength or error of their output during the process of implementation. Some advisors might then be tempted to be somewhat superficial, and imitative of their native frames of reference, and their reports and recommendations might tend to be too theoretical, and to lack an adequate perspective of recipient system needs and realities. Foreign advisory efforts should ideally go beyond writing reports and making recommendations, and put much more stress on actual implementation in the field.

This work has attempted to survey and analyze the foreign advisory efforts that in the years from 1951 to 1974 sought to enhance the administrative development capability of His Majesty's Government of Nepal. It has been the contention that such a capability was the key to suitable and sufficient and sustained development of the system of public administration of the country.

The foreign advisory efforts appear not to have succeeded to the commensurate and significant extent in enhancing such a capability. Among some problems were the lack of central design and institutional perspective; and the lack of coherence, coordination and consistency. The efforts seem to have been overly influenced by the perspectives of the foreign advisors and donor nations and agencies, and not to have been adequately informed by recipient system realities and perspectives.

The foreign advisory efforts have fallen short on the fundamental need to develop an indigenous and institutional capability for administrative development in Nepal. This in turn curtailed the ability of the recipient system to use such assistance to telling effect, and it also resulted in the advisory efforts seeming to be too foreign, as they did not manage to relate to the local ecology of government and administration in the country.

Ideally, technical assistance efforts are about the two-way transmission of information and ideas between the donors and the recipients. But in the Nepal case there appears not to have developed the necessary degree of complementarity between the originators and recipients of the advisory efforts. In some cases it is doubtful whether there was local comprehension of the nature and implications of the administrative improvements that were proposed, and sometimes acted upon. It was not ideal two-way cooperation and collaboration.

A senior Nepali official made some interesting observations on the foreign assistance efforts in developing countries:

Recently one has witnessed an increasing sense of resentment in developing countries towards a somewhat paternalistic attitude on the part of the expatriates who take it on themselves to define the problems of the Third World. I do not advocate a hands-off policy, but at the same time I feel strongly that there is no such thing as a panacea to our problems worked out by expatriates from a foreign land. [212]

---

[212] Bhekh Bahadur Thapa, "The Way Between," Address to the Third Meeting of the Canadian Science Writers' Association, Toronto, Ontario, Canada, February 1973, p.9.

He noted that at the receiving end there was not only "advice-fatigue" but utter frustration from the studies and rhetoric that seemed to be the main product of international cooperation.[213] He added that such cooperation must be geared to enhancing the capacity of each recipient nation to take the difficult task of development into its own hands.[214]

These observations also have relevance to the foreign advisory efforts in public administration that are the objects of this survey and study. It may be said that for public administration development in Nepal the sort of foreign advisory assistance of the past is no longer very cost-effective or relevant vis-à-vis local needs and realities. The efforts appear to have been characterized by a fragmentary transfer of information from an uncoordinated series of transient foreign advisors to a passive and perplexed recipient system (which also had high turnover at the top political levels and at the senior working levels of administration). Not enough attention was given to the institutionalization of the ideas and values that were sought to be transferred. The donor agencies were perhaps not too clear and coherent and consistent in their approach to public administration technical assistance. They were sometimes ambivalent about involvement in this area.

It would perhaps not be unfair to suggest of the donor agencies that they: (1) did not sufficiently comprehend the relevance of the administrative system to the process of government and development in Nepal; (2) did not take their advisory efforts seriously enough; and (3) had a general lack of faith in the desire and/or ability of the Nepalis to institute change and reform. There cannot be any place for some of the vague, haphazard and paternalistic foreign advisory efforts of the past.

There is certainly place for technical assistance in public administration. But the efforts must be more fully directed and coordinated by Nepali perspectives and agencies. The initiative, imagination and energy must come first from the Nepalis. Technical assistance should be a purposeful supplement to administrative development in Nepal and concentrate on the provision of assistance for the development of a Nepali administrative development capability. This means giving greater stress to institution-building in Nepal, supplemented by participant training overseas. The emphasis must be on helping Nepalis to develop a capability to: (1) decide what they need for administrative development; and (2) generate the requisite local expertise to do the necessary about it. The stress must be on indigenization and institutionalization. The technical assistance efforts must be based on respect for Nepalis and on faith in their ability to develop their own system of public administration.

---

[213] Ibid. p. 9.
[214] Ibid; p.10

Public administration deficiencies constitute a major obstacle to development in the country, and the problem is likely to become more serious with time. There is still some way to go in developing a meaningful capability to do something about this – after some twenty-five years of technical assistance in public administration. It is a somber thought. It is urgent that much more be done about the development of public administration in Nepal, and about the development of an indigenous capability for the same. The initiative must come from Government, which in the past has tended to be much too passive and perplexed.

Immediate and urgent efforts must be directed to the development of an indigenous and institutional capability for administrative development in Nepal. There can be no short-cuts to this primary need. The foreign advisory efforts cannot be a substitute for such an indigenized and institutionalized capability in Nepal.

It is for Government to indicate whether it understands the problem, and values the need sufficiently enough, to allocate enough of its own relatively scarce resources for the development and sustenance of such a capability. The country's leadership must have the political will that is necessary for sustained, deliberate and purposeful activity for administrative development. It seems that such a will has been sometimes present but almost never sufficient or sustained. Responsibility for the development of public administration in Nepal must lie with the Nepalis. The foreign advisors can go only so far as the Nepalis will!

Appendix 1

OBSERVATIONS OF A SENIOR CIVIL SERVANT

(Excerpt from the unpublished manuscripts of a former civil servant of the Government of Nepal. It refers to the technical assistance in public administration provided by the Government of India in the early 1950s.)

The (Indian) advisors were mostly high-ranking I.C.S. (Indian Civil Service) men. They were all seasoned veterans, mostly British trained. They were near perfect as far as their own job was concerned, which meant they were *pucca* (thorough) bureaucrats, religiously believing in their own British pattern. In their eyes no other pattern was feasible or possible.

The gentlemen simply could not believe that Nepal, never ruled by a foreign conqueror, never administered according to a foreign pattern, ever working in strict compliance with its own genius, ever preserving its own best and assimilating others' best, was something entirely different from India. Nor did they care to think whether an absolutely foreign system would work or not.

Trained all their life only to rule (as members of the elitist I.C.S.) or to be ruled (as subjects of British India), their job in Nepal was absolutely new to them for which they were least fitted, but they would never acknowledge this since it would be detrimental to their prestige. In their predicament they had no other alternative except to prescribe a reproduction of New Delhi, with adaptations here and there. When some high-ranking Nepali officials suggested to them that such a pattern may not suit Nepal's genius, or Nepal's resources, they were given a firm but stereotyped reply: "It is a policy question", meaning thereby that discussion on the matter was taboo.

Appendix 2

OBSERVATIONS OF A SENIOR ARMY OFFICER

(Excerpt from the diary of a former senior officer of the Royal Nepal Army. It refers to the Indian Military Mission that came to Nepal in April 1952.)

Originally the Indian Military Mission was to stay in Nepal for a year only. They are here for nearly two years now and there is no sign of their leaving yet. Personally I think their mission is more political than military and they are here to stay. As such they have since the very beginning been moving about like Lords and Barons, all the time deliberately hurting the sentiment and feelings of the (Nepali) officer class. Those of us who do not like to be treated as mere nincompoops and say so frankly are being watched.

Indianization is fast taking place and nobody seems intent or able to stop it. It is a disgrace to be downtrodden by a nation who were dependents till the other day, or for that matter by anybody. There is no sense in pretending to be an honorable member of His Majesty's Armed Forces while all the time being booted and tossed around by them.

Rules and regulations have been the worst casualties in the so-called reorganization. Consequently there is nothing but disorder in the army. Seniority of service has been dubbed as the sole criterion for promotion.

(Note: The Indian Military Mission was involved in the radical restructuring of the Nepal Army; and it seems later in the sub rosa establishment of several checkposts manned by Indian military personnel along the Nepal-China border. It seems that these checkposts, and presumably the Mission, were formally closed in April 1969; but a military post established in 1962 at Kalapani on the north-western Nepal-India border, close to China, was not.)

Appendix 3

LIST OF FOREIGN ADVISORS

NAME	COUNTRY	DONOR	TENURE	CONCENTRATION
1. Govind Narain	India	India	Feb 1951-April 1954	General Administration
2. J.M. Srinagesh	India	India	April 1951-Apr 1952	General Administration
3. N.M. Buch	India	India	May 1952-June 1952	Admin Reorganization
4. K.P. Mathrani	India	India	May 1952-June 1952	Admin Reorganization
5. S.K. Anand	India	India	May 1952-June 1952	Admin Reorganization
6. B.G. Murdeswar	India	India	May 1954-May 1961	Law and Administration
7. Hartvig Nissen	Norway	UNTA	Jan 1957-Jan 1960	General Administration
8. Walter Fischer	Austria	UNTA	Dec 1957-Sep 1958	Personnel Admin
9. S.T. Divers	UK	UNTA	Sep 1959-Feb 1962	General Administration
10. H.A. McK. Billings	UK	UNTA	March 1960-Feb 1961	In-Service Training
11. Merrill R. Goodall	USA	UNTA	March 1962-Aug 1963	General Administration
12. Alfred Linsell	UK	UNTA	March 1962-June 1963	In-Service Training
13. Sir Eric Franklin	UK	UNTA	May 1964-Dec 1966	General Administration
14. Wilson Hart	USA	UNTA	Feb 1965-Dec 1965	Personnel Admin
15. Edward McCrensky	USA	UNTA	Nov 1968-Nov 1968	Personnel Admin
16. Louis J. Kroeger	USA	US/AID	Jan 1962-Feb 1962	General Administration
17. Harold L Smock	USA	US/AID	June 1963-June 1965	O&M
18. George A. Melanson	USA	US/AID	July 1963-July 1965	In-Service Training
19. Frank G. O'Neill	USA	US/AID	Dec 1963-Sept 1964	General Administration
20. Howard L Grigsby	USA	US/AID	Sept 1966-Sept 1968	In-Service Training
21. John H. Hettler	USA	US/AID	Oct 1966-Feb 1969	O&M
22. Robert W. Ferrell	USA	US/AID	Dec 1966-Feb 1969	O&M
23. Lee D. Bomberger	USA	US/AID	Aug 1970-Sept 1974	O&M
24. O. Glen Stahl	USA	Ford	March 1969-June 1969	Personnel Admin
25. William Danielson	USA	Ford	Oct 1969-March 1970	Position Classification
26. Ross Pollock	USA	Ford	(1967-1970)	Position Classification
27. George Jackson	Canada	Ford	Oct 1970-Dec 1971	Position Classification
28. John A. Dettman	USA	Ford	Jan 1969-Aug 1971	CEDA
29. Jose Abueva	Philippines	Ford	May 1973-June 1975	CEDA

Note: S.K. Anand (India) stayed on for a year as Police Advisor after the other members of the Buch Committee had returned to India; Merrill R. Goodall had come to Nepal before as a Consultant in Public Administration (April-May 1952) to then Prime Minister M.P. Koirala when he was a Fulbright Research Scholar and Visiting Professor at Delhi University, and later again in 1979-80 when he was the Fulbright Visiting Professor in Public Administration (at Tribhuvan University in Kathmandu); Ross Pollock was based in New Delhi and worked and visited from there. Note on donors: India (the Government of India); UNTA (the United Nations Technical Assistance Program); US/AID Nepal (the United States Agency for International Development); and Ford (the Ford Foundation).

Bibliography

Books and Articles

Agarwal, H.N. "The Administrative System of Nepal: 1901-60". D. Litt. thesis, Patna University, India, 1969.

Almond, Gabriel and Coleman, James S., eds. The Politics of Developing Areas. Princeton, N.J.: Princeton University Press, 1960.

Almond Gabriel and Powel, G. Bingham. Comparative Politics: A Developmental Approach. Boston: Little, Brown and Co., 1966.

Appleby, P.H. Public Administration in India: Report of a Survey. New Delhi: Government of India. (1953)

Appleby, P.H. Re-examination of India's Administrative System. New Delhi: Government of India. (1956)

Blau, Peter M. Bureaucracy in Modern Society. New York: Random House, 1954.

Braibanti, R.J., ed. Asian Bureaucratic Systems Emergent from the British Imperial Tradition. Durham. N.C. Duke University Press, 1966.

Braibanti, R.J. "Transnational Inducement of Administrative Reform". In Approaches to Development: Politics, Administration, and Change, pp. 133-85. Edited by John D. Montgomery and William J. Siffin. New York: McGraw Hill Inc., 1966.

Caiden, Gerald E. Administrative Reform. Chicago: Aldine Publishing Company, 1969.

Candidio, Norma De. "Further Thoughts on the Failure of Technical Assistance in Public Administration Abroad: A Rejoinder to Garth Jones". Journal of Comparative Administration 2 (February 1971): 379-94.

Easton. Joseph W., ed. Institution Building and Development. Beverly Hills, California: Sage Publication, 1972.

Etzioni, Amitai. Modern Organizations. Englewood Cliffs, New Jersey: Prentice-Hall, Inc., 1964.

Gerth, H.H. and Mills, C. Wright. From Max Weber: Essays in Sociology. New York: Oxford University Press, 1958.

Gongal, Sushila Devi. Survey of the Reports of Foreign Experts in the Administration of Nepal. Kathmandu, Nepal: Centre for Economic Development and Administration, 1973.

Goodall, Betsy A. "Tanka Prasad Acharya: A Political Biography". Ph. D. dissertation, Claremont Graduate School, California, 1974

Goodall, Merrill R. "Administrative Change in Nepal". In Asian Bureaucratic Systems Emergent from the British Imperial Tradition, pp. 605643. Ed. Ralph J. Braibanti. Durham, N.C.: Duke University Press. 1966.

Goodall, Merrill R. "Bureaucracy and Bureaucrats: Some Themes Drawn From The Nepal Experience". Asian Survey 15 (October 1975): 892-95.

Gupta, Anirudha. Politics in Nepal. Bombay: Allied Publishers Pvt. Ltd., 1964.

Heady, Ferrell. Public Administration: A Comparative Perspective. Englewood Cliffs, N.J. Prentice Hall, 1966.

Heady, Ferrell and Stokes, Sybil L., eds. Papers in Comparative Public Administration. Ann Arbor, Michigan: Institute of Public Administration, University of Michigan, 1962.

Hsuch, S.S., ed. Public Administration in South and Southeast Asia. Brussels: International Institute of Administration, 1962.

IIchman, Warren F. "Rising Expectations and the Revolution in Development Administration". Public Administration Review 25 (December 1965): 314-28.

Jones, Garth N. "Failure of Technical Assistance in Public Administration Abroad". Journal of Comparative Administration. 2 (May 1970): 3-38.

Joshi, Bhuwan Lall and Rose, Leo E. Democratic Innovations in Nepal. Berkeley: University of California Press, 1966.

Joshi, Nanda Lall. Evolution of Public Administration in Nepal. Kathmandu, Nepal: Centre for Economic Development and Administration. 1973.

Khanal, B.P. "Personnel Management in the Nepal Public Service - Some Suggestions". *Prashasan* (The Nepali Journal of Public Administration). Year 5, No.1, February 1974.

Khatri, Bhubaneshwar. "Disbursement of His Majesty's Government Fund and Accountability". Kathmandu, Nepal, 1968 (Typewritten).

Landon, Percival. Nepal. 2 vols. London: Constable, 1982.

Lepawsky, Albert. Administration. New York: Alfred A. Knopf, 1952.

Levi, Werner. "Government and Politics in Nepal: I." Far Eastern Survey 21 (17 December 1952) 185-191.

Levi, Werner. "Government and Politics in Nepal: II." Far Eastern Survey 22 (14 January 1953) 5-10.

Levi, Werner. "Political Rivalries in Nepal". Far Eastern Survey 23 (July 1954) 102-107.

Levi, Werner. "Politics in Nepal". Eastern World, November 1954, pp. 1012.

Levi, Werner. "Politics in Nepal". Far Eastern Survey 25 (March 1956): 3946.

Levi, Werner. "Nepal's New Era". Far Eastern Survey 28 (October 1959): 150-56.

Malla, K.P. and Rana, Pasupati S. Nepal in Perspective. Kathmandu, Nepal: Centre for Economic Development and Administration, 1973.

Mihaly, Eugene B. Foreign Aid and Politics in Nepal. London: Oxford University Press, 1965.

Mills, C. Wright. The Power Elite. New York: Oxford University Press, 1956.

Montgomery, John D. Foreign Aid in International Politics. Englewood Cliffs, N.J. Prentice Hall Inc., 1967.

Montgomery, John D. and Siffin, William J. Approaches to Development: Politics, Administration and Change. New York: McGraw Hill, Inc., 1966.

Mosher, Frederick C. "The Public Service in the Temporary Society". Public Administration Review 31 (January-February 1971): 41-62.

Mosher, William E.; Kingsley, John D.; and Stahl, O. Glenn. Public Personnel Administration. New York: Harper and Brothers, 3rd ed.

Nair, Kusum. Blossoms in the Dust. New York: Fredrick A. Praeger, 1962.

Narayan, Shriman. India and Nepal: An Exercise in Diplomacy. Hind Pocket Books Pvt. Ltd., 1971.

Neupane, P. The Constitution and Constitutions of Nepal. Kathmandu, Nepal: Ratna Pustak Bhandar, 1969.

Nigro, Felix A. Public Administration: Readings and Documents. New York: Rinehart and Co, Inc., 1951.

Nye, J.S. "Corruption and Political Development: A Cost Benefit Analysis". American Political Science Review 61 (June 1967): 417-27.

Pandey, Devendra Raj. "Nepal's Central Planning Organisation: An Analysis of Its Effectiveness in an Inter-Organisational Environment ". Ph.D. dissertation, University of Pittsburgh, 1969.

Pradhan, Prachanda. ed. Aspects of Development Administration. Kathmandu, Nepal: Centre for Economic Development and Administration, 1971.

Pradhan, Prachanda. "Bureaucracy and Development in Nepal". Ph. D. dissertation, Claremont Graduate School, California, 1969.

Presthus, Robert. The Organizational Society. New York: Alfred A. Knopf, 1962.

Regmi, D.R. A Century of Family Autocracy in Nepal. Banaras: Commercial Printing Works, 1950.

Regmi, D.R. Modern Nepal: Rise and Growth in the Eighteenth Century. Calcutta: K.L. Mukhopadhaya, 1961.

Riggs, Fred. Administration in Developing Countries. Boston: Houghton Mifflin Company, 1964.

Riggs, Fred W. ed. Frontiers of Development Administration. Durham, North Carolina: Duke University Press, 1970.

Rose, Leo E. and Fisher, Margaret W. The Politics of Nepal: Persistence and Change in an Asian Monarchy. Ithaca: Cornell University Press, 1970.

Rudolph, Lloyd and Susanne. The Modernity of Tradition. University of Chicago Press, 1967.

Selznick, Phillip. TVA and the Grass Roots. Berkeley: University of California Press, 1949.

Shah, Rishikesh. "Nepal and India - Friends and Strangers". Nepal Council of World Affairs, 12 July 1968.

Shah, Rishikesh. "The Political Development and Modernisation of Nepal: An Evolution of the Prospect for Nation-Building". Kathmandu, Nepal, 1974 (Unpublished MSS).

Shrestha, Mangal K. A Handbook of Public Administration in Nepal. Kathmandu, Nepal: His Majesty's Government of Nepal, Department of Publicity, Ministry of Panchayat Affairs, 1965.

Shresta, Mangal K. "Development of Senior Administrators in Nepal". Paper presented at the Seminar on the Development of Senior Administrators, Bangkok, Thailand, December 8-15, 1969

Shrestha, Mangal K. Trends in Public Administration in Nepal. Kathmandu, Nepal: His Majesty's Government of Nepal. Department of Information, Ministry of Information and Broadcasting, 1969.

Shrestha, Nutan R. "Need for Position Classification in HMG Civil Service". Prashasan (Nepali Journal of Public Administration), Year 3, No.2, 1972.

Simon, Herbert A. Administrative Behavior. 2nd ed. New York: MacMillan and Company, 1957.

Simon, Herbert A.; Smithburg, Donald W. and Thompson, Victor A. Public Administration. New York: Alfred A. Knopf, 1970.

Stahl, O. Glenn. Public Personnel Administration. Calcutta: Oxford and International Book House Publishing Company, 1962.

Stein, Harold. ed. Public Administration and Policy Development. New York: Harcourt, Brace and Company, 1952.

Swerdlow, Irving. ed. Development Administration: Concepts and Problems. Syracuse: University of Syracuse Press, 1963.

Thapa, Bhekh Bahadur. "Planning for Development in Nepal". Ph. D. dissertation, Claremont Graduate School, California, 1966.

Thapa, Bhekh Bahadur. "The Way Between". Address to the Third Meeting of the Canadian Science Writers' Association, Toronto, Ontario, Canada, 23 February 1973.

United Nations, Department of Economic and Social Affairs. A Handbook of Public Administration. New York: United Nations, 1961.

Upadhyaya, Shyam Prasad. *Nepalko Prashasanik Vyavasta* (Administrative System of Nepal). Kathmandu, Nepal. Sajha Publications, 1964.

Weidner, E.W. ed. Development Administration in Asia. Durham, N.C.: Duke University Press, 1970.

Weidner, E.W. Technical Assistance in Public Administration Overseas: The Case for Development Administration. Chicago: Public Administration Service, 1964.

White, Leonard D. Introduction to the Study of Public Administration. New York: Macmillan and Company, 1942.

Wilson, Woodrow. "Essay on the Study of Administration". Political Science Quarterly 2 (June 1987): 197-222

Reports and Documents

Administrative Management Department, HMG/Nepal. Civil Service Administration Manual. Kathmandu, Nepal, 1968.

Administrative Management Department, HMG / Nepal. Management Survey of the Administrative Management Department of His Majesty's Government of Nepal (Draft Report). Kathmandu, Nepal, September 1974.

Administrative Reform Commission. Report. Kathmandu, Nepal, September 1968.

Agreement of Cooperation between His Majesty's Government of Nepal, Tribhuvan University, and the Ford Foundation for the Establishment of the Centre for Economic Development and Administration. Kathmandu, Nepal 15 May 1969.

Bomberger, Lee D. "A Positive Approach to Personnel Management." Paper presented at the Top Management Seminar, Centre for Economic Development and Administration, Kathmandu, Nepal 4 December 1973.

Bomberger, Lee D. Administrative Management Services to His Majesty's Government of Nepal: Final Report. Kathmandu, Nepal: Development and Resources Corporation. (15 September 1974).

Bomberger, Lee D. "Manpower Development Training Project". *Prashasan* (The Nepali Journal of Public Administration), No 10, June 1974.

Bomberger, Lee D. "Proposed Work Plan". Memo presented to Chief Secretary, HMG/Nepal, 11September 1970.

Bomberger, Lee D. "The Need for Civil Service Reform in Nepal". *Prashasan* (The Nepali Journal of Public Administration), Year 4, No.2, July 1973.

Bomberger, Lee D. Organising for Improved Personnel Management in His Majesty's Government of Nepal. Kathmandu, Nepal, (December 1970).

Bomberger, Lee D. Proposed Organisation of the Administrative Management Department. Kathmandu, Nepal. (4 November 1971).

Bomberger, Lee D. The O&M Function in HMG: Past, Present and Future: Draft Report. Kathmandu, Nepal (15 January 1974).

Centre for Economic Development and Administration. A New and Permanent Status for CEDA: To Enhance its Contribution for National Development. Kathmandu, Nepal, September 1974.

Centre for Economic Development and Administration. "Administration for National Development: A CEDA Residential Administrative Development Program for Second Class Gazetted Officers of HMG/Nepal - A Working Draft". Kathmandu, Nepal, 11 July 1974.

Centre for Economic Development and Administration. Progress Report for the First Eighteen Months of Operation: July 1969 to January 1971. Kathmandu, Nepal, 1971.

Centre for Economic Development and Administration. Progress Report: February 1971 to July 1972. Kathmandu, Nepal, 1972.

Centre for Economic Development and Administration. Progress Report: July 1969 to July 1973. Kathmandu, Nepal, 1973.

Centre for Economic Development and Administration. Reorganising for the New Development Role of Tribhuvan University. Kathmandu, Nepal, 8 March 1974.

Centre for Economic Development and Administration. Conference on Institution Building and Development: June 26 to 30, 1971. Kathmandu, Nepal, 1971.

Chatterjee, R.N. Report on the Accounting System of Nepal. Kathmandu, Nepal. (May 1967).

Danielson, William F. Interim Report on Survey Classification of Posts for His Majesty's Government of Nepal. Kathmandu, Nepal. (19 March 1970).

Danielson, William F. "Salary Change Recommendations for Gazetted Posts to His Majesty's Government of Nepal". Memo presented to Chief Secretary, HMG/Nepal, April 1970.

Danielson, William F. Survey of Classification of Gazetted Posts for His Majesty's Government of Nepal. New Delhi: Ford Foundation, (4 April 1970).

Fischer Walter. Personnel Administration in Nepal: Final Report. Kathmandu, Nepal. (October 1958).

Franklin, Sir Eric. Development of Public Administration in Nepal. Kathmandu, Nepal. (1966).

Franklin, Sir Eric. Report on the Administrative Machinery of National Trading Ltd. Kathmandu, Nepal. (1966).

Franklin, Sir Eric. Report on the Administrative Machinery of the Royal Nepal Airlines Corporation. Kathmandu, Nepal. (March 1966).

Franklin, Sir Eric. Report on the Development of the Public Administration Department. Kathmandu, Nepal. (September 1964).

Franklin, Sir Eric. Report on the Organisation of the Nepal Electricity Corporation. Kathmandu, Nepal. (1966).

Franklin, Sir Eric. Report on the Relationship between His Majesty's Government and Public Enterprises in Nepal. Kathmandu, Nepal. (1966).

Franklin, Sir Eric. Special Report on the Nepal Transport Organisation. Kathmandu, Nepal. (1966).

Goodall, Merrill R. Development of Public Administration in Nepal. Kathmandu, Nepal. (August 1963).

Hagen, Toni. Observations on Certain Aspects of Economic and Social Development Problems in Nepal. New York: United Nations, Department of Economic and Social Affairs. (10 July 1959).

Hart, Wilson. Draft Final Report. Kathmandu, Nepal. (13 January 1966).

Hart, Wilson. Second Progress Report. Kathmandu, Nepal. (1 August 1965).

Himsworth, Eric. Report on the Fiscal System of Nepal. Kathmandu, Nepal. (1959). Revised ed. The Fiscal System of Nepal. Kathmandu, Nepal (1964).

His Majesty's Government of Nepal, Committee on Administration. Report. Kathmandu, Nepal, July 1962.

Janch Bujh Kendra (Royal Investigation and Inquiry Centre). Plan for Strengthening the Public Service Commission. Kathmandu, Nepal, 1974.

Kroeger, Louis J. A Public Administration Program for His Majesty's Government of Nepal. San Francisco: Griffenhagen-Kroeger Inc. (March 1962).

Linsell, Alfred. In-Service Training in Nepal: March 1962 to February 1963. Kathmandu, Nepal. (February 1963).

Linsell, Alfred. Report on Secretarial Management. Kathmandu, Nepal. (1962).

Malla, Tej Prakash and Bomberger, Lee D. A Plan for Expanding the O&M Function in His Majesty's Government of Nepal. Kathmandu, Nepal. (13 March 1972).

McCrensky, Edward. Proposal for a Unified Civil Service for His Majesty's Government of Nepal. New York: United Nation. (10 June 1969).

Melanson, George A. and Joshi, Nanda Lall. Scientific Organisation of Work. Kathmandu, Nepal: Public Administration Department, His Majesty's Government of Nepal.

National Planning Commission, HMG/Nepal. The Fourth Plan: 1970-75. Kathmandu, Nepal: National Planning Commission, His Majesty's Government of Nepal, July 1970.

Nepal Administrative Reorganisation Committee (Buch Committee). Report. Ministry of External Affairs, Government of India, 1952.

Nepalese-American Cooperation: A Summary of American Aid to Nepal, 1951-72.Kathmandu:UnitedStatesAgency for International Development/Nepal, 1972.

O'Neill, Frank G. Draft Report on Proposed Public Administration Institute, Nepal. Kathmandu, Nepal. (3 March 1964).

O&M Section, Administrative Reform Division, Secretariat of the Council of Ministers, HMG/ Nepal. (With assistance of the Public Administration Service). A Survey Report on Internal Administration and General Office Practices. Kathmandu, Nepal, February 1968.

O&M Section, Administrative Reform Division, Administrative Management Department, HMG/ Nepal. (With assistance of the Public Administration Service). Manual of Internal Administration and General Office Practices. Kathmandu, Nepal, July 1968.

O&M Section, Administrative Reform Division, Administrative Management Department, HMG/ Nepal. (With assistance of the Public Administration Service). Memorandum Report on Organisation and Administration of the Civil Personnel Records Centre. Kathmandu, Nepal, July 1968.

Organisation of His Majesty's Government of Nepal. Kathmandu, Nepal: Department of Publicity, Ministry of Panchayat Affairs, HMG/Nepal, April 1963.

Participants Directory, HMG- U.S. AID. Kathmandu, Nepal: United States Agency for International Development/Nepal, 8 March 1974.

Pradhan, Gorakshya Bahadur and Melanson, George A. Training and Inspiring the Worker. Kathmandu, Nepal: Public Administration Department, His Majesty's Government of Nepal. (1964)

Price, Harry B., ed. Economic Survey of Nepal. Report No. TAO/NEP/3. New York: United Nations. (1961).

Public Administration Department, HMG/Nepal. A Survey of Field Administration of His Majesty's Government of Nepal. Kathmandu, Nepal. August 1964.

Public Administration Service. Project for Improving Government Organization and Methods and Management Training, Government of Nepal: Final Report. Chicago: Public Administration Service. (May 1969).

Stahl, O. Glenn. A Strong Civil Service for Nepal. Kathmandu, Nepal. (June 1969). Reprinted in *Prashasan* (The Nepali Journal of Public Administration), Year 2, No. 1, April 1970.

Tersman, Rune. Supervision of Public Enterprises in Nepal. Kathmandu, Nepal: United Nations. (June 1963).

Sources and Note

Nepal ko Rajpatra (Nepal Gazette). Kathmandu, Nepal: His Majesty's Government of Nepal.

Nepal Law and Translation Series. Kathmandu, Nepal: Mahesh C. Regmi, Nepal Press Digest (Pvt.) Ltd.

Nepal Press Digest (Weekly). Kathmandu, Nepal: Mahesh C. Regmi, Nepal Press Digest Pvt. Ltd.

Prashasan (Nepali Journal of Public Administration). Kathmandu, Nepal: Administrative Management Department, His Majesty's Government of Nepal.

Nizamati Kitab Khana (Civil Personnel Records Centre), Kathmandu, Nepal.

Administrative Management Department Library, Kathmandu, Nepal.

Ford Foundation Library, New Delhi, India.

Tribhuvan University Library, Kathmandu, Nepal.

United Nations Development Program Library, Kathmandu, Nepal.

U.S. Agency for International Development, Kathmandu, Nepal.

Note: Some 30 former foreign advisors and aid agency personnel as well as some 52 Nepalis (former Prime Ministers and Ministers; Secretaries, Joint Secretaries and Under Secretaries of the Civil Service; and staff of CEDA, the Centre for Economic Development and Administration) responded to two detailed questionnaires, and/or gave their insights and provided supplementary information via separate personal interviews, or through personal correspondence with the writer.